MURTY CLASSICAL
LIBRARY OF INDIA

Sheldon Pollock, General Editor

BHARAVI
ARJUNA AND THE HUNTER

MCLI 9

BHARAVI

भारवि

ARJUNA
AND THE HUNTER

Edited and translated by
INDIRA VISWANATHAN PETERSON

MURTY CLASSICAL LIBRARY OF INDIA
HARVARD UNIVERSITY PRESS
Cambridge, Massachusetts
London, England
2016

SERIES DESIGN BY M9DESIGN

Library of Congress Cataloging-in-Publication Data

Bharavi.
[Kiratarjuniya. English]
Arjuna and the hunter / Bharavi ;
edited and translated by Indira Viswanathan Peterson.
pages cm. — (Murty Classical Library of India; 9)
Includes bibliographical references and index.
ISBN 978-0-674-50496-7 (cloth : alk. paper)
I. Peterson, Indira Viswanathan, 1950– editor, translator.
II. Title.
PK3791.B252K5813 2016
891'.21—dc23   2015016324

To Appa
For lighting the way of knowledge

CONTENTS

INTRODUCTION

The Worlds of a Sanskrit Classic

Arjuna and the Hunter (*Kirātārjunīya*), the only known work of Bharavi, is a Sanskrit court epic poem in eighteen chapters and 1,040 verses. The poem's theme is the narrative of the hero Arjuna's combat with the god Shiva in the guise of a hunter, an important episode in the *Āraṇyakaparvan* (Forest Book) of the *Mahābhārata,* the epic of the great war of the Kuru clans.[1] *Arjuna* is celebrated as one of the five masterpieces of the court epic (*mahākāvya*) genre, the most prestigious genre of classical Sanskrit poetry (*kāvya*).[2]

As is the case with many early Sanskrit authors, very little is known about Bharavi. The poet appears to have flourished in south India, some time after the celebrated Kalidasa (fourth–fifth centuries C.E.) and earlier than the seventh century. Ravikirti, a panegyrist of the Chalukya king Pulakeshin II, named Bharavi and Kalidasa as famous poets in an inscription of 634 C.E.[3] Dandin, a generation after Ravikirti and author of *The Mirror for Poetry,* a pioneering work on poetics, associated Bharavi with the Pallavas and other south Indian kings.[4]

In the *Mahābhārata* episode on which Bharavi based his poem, the Pandava hero Arjuna performs ascetic self-mortification (*tapas*) in a Himalayan forest in order to win Shiva's favor and obtain the boon of a supernatural weapon from him. The Pashupata weapon will help the five Pandava brothers to overcome their cousins, the Kauravas, in their just war and regain the kingdom that the Kauravas had taken from them in a rigged dicing match. The drama of the episode turns on the trial Shiva sets for the hero. Disguised as a *kirāta,* a hunter from a mountain tribe, Shiva picks a quarrel with Arjuna over the shooting of a boar and tests his courage in combat, ultimately revealing himself and granting him the desired weapon. The epic narrative illuminates heroic action, sacred duty, and cosmo-moral order (dharma), self-restraint and austerity, devotion (bhakti) and divine benevolence, core values in the culture of ancient India's Brahman and warrior elites and enduring themes in the Hindu tradition.

Bharavi was the first poet to write a court epic on a *Mahābhārata* episode. *Arjuna* is also the first full-fledged literary treatment of the narrative of the hero and the hunter, which became a popular theme in south Indian literature and art after the seventh century. Early Tamil poets alluded to it in their hymns of devotion to Shiva.[5] Arjuna's austerities and Shiva's boon to the hero are strikingly portrayed in a great monolithic relief sculpture commissioned by the Pallava king Narasimhavarman II at the seashore temple complex in Mamallapuram.[6] In later centuries the hunter narrative was frequently treated in literary and religious texts produced in Sanskrit and Kannada, and was depicted in sculpture in the region's Shiva temples.[7] Bharavi's poem stands apart from most other renderings of the episode by virtue of its primarily aesthetic preoccupations. Written in the *kāvya* belletristic style, the poem was aimed at an audience of connoisseurs who were expected to respond to it according to aesthetic criteria. By all accounts *Arjuna* quickly became the model for the Sanskrit court epic. While Bharavi worked within a literary tradition that prized norm and convention, his poem bears the stamp of his distinctive voice and many innovations in form and style. The innovations themselves became the norm. The early critic Dandin appears to have based his influential description of the court epic genre on Bharavi's practice.[8] Later poets modeled their *mahākāvyas* on *Arjuna;* Magha wrote *The Slaying of Shishupala* expressly to surpass Bharavi,[9] and no fewer than thirty-five commentaries from various regions of India were written on his poem. It should come as no surprise that *Arjuna* had become a seminal text in the Sanskrit literary canon almost from its origins, and remains so to this day.[10]

Kāvya, that is, fine literature, composed in verse or prose (or both together), was cultivated in Sanskrit and allied languages at courts and other elite milieux in India from the beginning of the first millennium.[11] Conventional, idealized portrayals of character and incident are the staple of *kāvya* works, written in the main to glorify elite patrons and court culture itself.[12] The typical hero is a king, warrior, or courtier, and works in the principal genres—court epic, drama, and lyric—delineated the themes of pleasure and success, cherished as the aims of life appropriate to the man engaged in worldly action.[13] But success and pleasure—political and economic gain, erotic pleasure, the enjoyment of beauty— are framed in *kāvya* by the overarching value of cosmo-moral order and sacred duty (dharma). The persona of the warrior king is also imbued with a measure of the ascetic self-control necessary for upholding moral order. Embedded in Hindu, Buddhist, and Jain religious presuppositions about the cosmos, the natural, human, and divine worlds of Sanskrit court poetry exist in a relation of permeable boundaries, lifting court poems from the specifics of court culture to universals of human experience. Indian wisdom traditions likewise inform *kāvya* poetry, broadening its vision. *Kāvya's* principal preoccupation, however, is with aesthetic value, measured in terms of beauty, virtuosity, and elegance of form and expression, undergirded by erudition. Vividly embodied in the concepts of figures of speech and aesthetic emotion, these are the ideals that concern the Sanskrit literary theorists and guide reader response to poems such as *Arjuna*.[14]

Introducing the first complete English translation of *Arjuna* to a new readership requires, first, illuminating the contexts of Sanskrit literary culture and the courtly world of early medieval India in which the poem was produced and received. Yet since literary works find serendipitous "afterlives" in translation,[15] this introduction also aims to serve as an aid for the twenty-first-century reader encountering the poem as both a work of art and a human document speaking to aesthetic and moral concerns in our own time.

Bharavi and Sanskrit Court Epic Poetry

The court epic—"extended poem" (*mahākāvya*) or "composition in *sargas*" (*sargabandha*)—is a long work in verse, divided into chapters called *sargas*.[16] Finely crafted poems written for learned readers and treating exalted heroes and elevated themes, Sanskrit *mahākāvyas* have more in common with literary epics such as Virgil's *Aeneid* than with the *Mahābhārata* or the *Iliad*. While court epic poems are not always based on older epic narratives, the typical *mahākāvya* plot traces the exploits of a noble hero, culminating in his victory over enemies or adverse forces.[17] *Mahākāvyas* are also "epic" in their expansive scope. The court epic is distinguished by extended treatment of aspects of political life and courtly culture, myth, legend, and landscape. In his list of topics for description in a *mahākāvya* Dandin names "cities, oceans, mountains, seasons, the rising of the sun and moon, playing in pleasure parks and in water, drinking parties and the delights of lovemaking, the separation of lovers, weddings, the birth of a son, councils of war, spies, military expeditions, battles, and the victory of the hero."[18] Court epics are also required to treat "the fruits of the four aims of life," that is, to embrace the whole range of human aspiration, touching on the moral life, wealth and success, pleasure, and transcendence over karma and mundane existence.[19] Lastly, *mahākāvyas* are expected to evoke an overarching aesthetic emotion (*rasa*), resonating with fundamental, powerful human emotions, most prominently the heroic and the erotic.[20] When the early critic Bhamaha described the court epic as a "great poem, a poem about great things,"[21] he must have had in mind not only the size and elevated subject matter of the *mahākāvya* but also its amplitude of scale and vision.

In one respect Sanskrit court epics differ from both primary heroic epics and other kinds of narrative poems: they are composed of short, tightly structured, grammatically self-contained verses.[22] The formal properties of *kāvya* verse demand ellipsis and compaction of language, achieved through grammatical and syntactical resources such as Sanskrit's facility for compounding. Likewise, *kāvya* verses are notable for the density of imagery and meaning packed into a small space. Made up of (usually) symmetrical quarter units (*pāda*), each brief verse presents a single complex yet coherent thought, image, or idea, delivered in a striking style that fully exploits the formal and semantic richness of the Sanskrit language. Reader response to the *kāvya* verse entails unraveling and reconstituting complex, precisely calibrated imaginative relationships among grammatical structures, images, and meanings within the framework of the verse, in order to savor figures of speech, aspects of aesthetic emotion, or epigrammatical thought. The experience of reading a Sanskrit court epic is thus very different from reading other kinds of long works. The reader's primary and most sustained engagement is with the individual verse. The focus of attention at the next level is the topical sequence, followed by *sarga* chapters and the work as a whole.

Arjuna is esteemed as a profound treatment of a culturally important narrative, but its exalted status in the Sanskrit literary canon is founded above all on Bharavi's contributions to the development of the court epic form. In the estimation of Sanskrit readers and critics *Arjuna* is an exemplary poem because of Bharavi's sustained excellence in writing verses that challenge the reader, elegantly fulfilling the Sanskrit poet's mandate to "deepen [the reader's] apprehension by goading to new life the supine energies of word and grammar."[23] With *Arjuna* Bharavi established court epic as the *kāvya* poet's premier arena for the dazzling displays of virtuosity that were to become the hallmark of poetic craft in Sanskrit. At the level of the verse, he emphasizes and exposes grammatical, metrical, and formal difficulty, the weight of philosophical thought, scientific learning and erudite diction, and complexity in figures of speech and structures of argument. At the level of the work as a whole *Arjuna* is in every respect more elaborate than its predecessors; Bharavi offers a greater variety of meters, longer chapters, and longer speeches and descriptions than earlier poets, all features that became entrenched in the court epic style.[24] Besides favoring polysemy and other kinds of wordplay throughout the poem, the poet also devotes portions of an entire chapter in *Arjuna* to verses forming palindromes and other aural and visual patterns, a practice enthusiastically embraced by later poets.[25]

In sum, Bharavi both actually intensifies the challenges posed by *kāvya* verse and self-consciously draws attention to these challenges. Mallinatha, the late thirteenth-century author of the best known commentary on *Arjuna*, likens the experience of reading Bharavi's verses to that of cracking open the hard shell of a coconut in order to taste its sweet juice.[26] To another commentator, Bharavi's poem is a wild elephant that can be mastered only with the elephant goad of his commentary.[27] Queen Gangadevi, a thirteenth-century south Indian poet and admirer of Bharavi, was perhaps closer to the mark when she wrote, in a court epic of her own, "Bharavi's verse is a garland of *bakula* flowers, releasing fragrance when you crush it—the connoisseur's delight."[28] But Bharavi is no mannerist. If the commentators stress the difficulty of negotiating his poetry, readerly opinion, embodied in a popular stanza, names intellectual weight as its dominant characteristic. The poet is celebrated, the stanza states, for "intellectual heft" (*arthagauravam*), that is, the depth and richness of thought and meaning with which he charges each verse.[29] In fact, the description applies equally to the poem as a whole. Illuminating the elevated moral and human concerns of the epic episode, in *Arjuna* Bharavi has also achieved a tightly constructed poem, a work whose every feature is pressed into the service of a unified architectonics.

The Shape of the Poem

THE NARRATIVE

Arjuna opens with a series of speeches concerning the course of action that the Pandavas need to take in order to counter the continuing machinations of the Kaurava Duryodhana, who had unjustly seized their kingdom as a stake in the gambling match. A spy reports to Yudhishthira, living in exile with his brothers and their common wife Draupadi. Duryodhana is holding on to the Kuru kingdom through false pretenses of just rule, and will not honor his obligation to return it to the Pandavas at the end of their exile. Queen Draupadi, smoldering with anger on account of her public humiliation at the dice match, berates Yudhishthira for his passivity and lack of pride, and urges him to attack his enemy and win back the kingdom. Bhima exhorts his elder brother to act immediately, citing warrior honor and political expediency. Yudhishthira demurs, arguing that precipitate action would be ruinous, for strategic as well as moral reasons. The sage Vyasa, a Kuru elder and author of the *Mahābhārata* epic, arrives and advises Yudhishthira to take immediate action. The king must send Arjuna to the Himalayas to undertake austerities to please Indra, king of gods, and win weapons that will lead the Pandavas to victory in war. At the end of the third chapter, the family priest arms Arjuna, and he sets off for the Himalayas, instructed by the sage and guided by a mountain spirit.

In the three chapters that follow, Bharavi describes Arjuna's journey to the Himalayas, the wonders of the Himalaya mountain, and the warrior prince's ascetic practice in a mountain hermitage. Himalayan ascetics complain to Indra, king of gods and Arjuna's divine father, about the threat they face from an unknown warrior who is amassing great power by performing extreme austerities. Pleased as he is with Arjuna's determination and self-control, Indra wishes to test the hero and dispatches his courtesans, the apsaras nymphs, to seduce him. Chapters 7–9 are devoted to the journey and erotic revels of the apsarases, who travel from Indra's celestial city to the Himalayas in flying chariots, accompanied by an army led by the gandharva demigods, skilled musicians and the nymphs' partners. The women gather flowers in the mountain's forests with their lovers, and enjoy bathing in the river Ganga. Sunset and moonrise are described, and the apsarases and gandharvas have a drinking party and spend the night making love. In the tenth chapter Bharavi describes the nymphs' attempts to seduce Arjuna; the women conjure up all six seasons at once, dance, and flirt with him, but to no avail. Arjuna remains steadfast in his ascetic discipline, and the apsarases return disappointed to Indra and report the failure of their mission.

Delighted though he is with his hero-son's integrity of character, Indra subjects him to yet another test. Arriving at Arjuna's hermitage disguised as an aged Brahman, he questions the appropriateness of a warrior undertaking austerity. Asceticism, Indra argues, should be performed solely by world renouncers, to attain liberation from existence. Arjuna fiercely defends his asceticism, saying that his guru has instructed him to please the warrior god Indra with austerities in order to win weapons for conducting just war. A pleased Indra reveals his identity and directs Arjuna to propitiate the great god Shiva, who alone can grant him what he seeks. When the hero performs more severe forms of austerity, affecting the cosmos with his ascetic power, the mountain dwellers take refuge in Shiva. The god reveals a plan he has devised to test the hero's courage in combat: disguised as a hunter chief, he will pick a quarrel with Arjuna over a boar, a demon in disguise, that will maliciously attack the hero. Shiva will claim the boar as his own trophy, and Arjuna will defend his honor by fighting with the hunter chief and his vast army, consisting of Shiva's spirit attendants who have been magically transformed. The drama unfolds as planned. The boar attacks Arjuna; the hero and the god simultaneously shoot; Shiva sends a hunter to retrieve an arrow from the beast's carcass, claiming it as his master's. Arjuna refuses to give up the arrow, which he believes to be his own, and berates the envoy and his lord for their greed and insolence. Shiva orders his troops to attack Arjuna.

From chapter 14 on, the poem is devoted to descriptions of Arjuna's combat, first with Shiva's troops, and then with the god himself. Although the hero displays supreme heroism in single-handed combat with Shiva's troops, he is unable to defeat them. His attempts to defeat Shiva are equally futile, even after an exchange of supernatural weapons. He is reduced to fighting the god with trees and rocks, and finally with his bare fists. In the last chapter the hero and the god wrestle with each other. Pleased with Arjuna's determination and unparalleled heroism, Shiva reveals his divine identity. The Pandava sings a hymn of praise for the god; Shiva gives him the Pashupata weapon, other gods give him other divine weapons; and Arjuna returns to Yudhishthira with Shiva's blessing.

TRANSFORMATIONS: FROM *MAHĀBHĀRATA* EPISODE TO COURT POEM

Bharavi employs a number of strategies to transform an episode from an older epic into an elegant court epic poem. He reshapes the *Mahābhārata's* ethical thematic and translates it into the courtly idiom and ideals of his time. He turns epic material into *kāvya* by infusing the narrative with topics and themes that enable it to acquire the encyclopedic scope of the court epic poem. At the same time, by repeatedly drawing attention throughout the poem to the hero as a paradoxical figure, a warrior practicing asceticism, he imbues *Arjuna* with a dramatic tension that is nearly unique in the history of court epic. We may now examine the sites of these transformations—the speeches and descriptive sequences that are the court epic's building blocks, and the hero's character and actions—and the compositional strategies they entail.

The choice of the *Mahābhārata's* hunter episode as his poem's theme enables Bharavi to plunge immediately and dramatically into the ethical and political issues that are his concern. The narrative of Shiva's boon of the Pashupata weapon both highlights Arjuna's special status as a warrior-hero and signals the certainty of Pandava victory in the great war. The principal characters—the Pandavas and Queen Draupadi, their enemy Duryodhana, the sage Vyasa—and the humiliation of the heroes and their queen in the ignoble dice game, the central event of the *Mahābhārata,* are vividly evoked in the speeches that mainly constitute the first three chapters in *Arjuna.* Here the meandering discussion of strategy among the older epics' characters is transformed into a carefully structured debate, embodied in elegant speeches. The entire sequence becomes an exemplary treatment of the court epic topics of political intelligence, counsel, and strategy, framed in the spirit and idiom of early medieval treatises on kingship and political theory, in particular Kautilya's *Arthaśāstra,* the classic of the genre.

Bharavi was the first poet to give long speeches a prominent place in the court epic genre, and he set the standard for later poets. Persuasive speeches are a routine backdrop to action in epic literature, but the speeches in *Arjuna* are specimens of courtly eloquence. Drawing on refined tools of logic and rhetoric, and self-consciously invoking the attributes of eloquence, the speakers in the first three chapters deliver powerful, elegant, beautifully structured orations, advancing their own arguments and responding to others'. The same elegance and elevated tone is reprised in the debates featured further in the poem, between Indra and Arjuna, and Arjuna and Shiva's envoy. Indeed, everyone in *Arjuna*, from Queen Draupadi to the spirit who shows Arjuna the way to the Himalayas, is a courtly orator.[30] But court epics also articulate a broader humanism, and Bharavi's speeches are admired in particular for the wisdom embodied in the epigrams in which they abound.[31]

Descriptive sequences on set topics are the definitive feature of the court epic genre and the principal arena for competition among poets. Like the elegant speeches in *Arjuna,* Bharavi made elaborate, extended descriptive sequences fashioned out of complex and striking verses his trademark, influencing later poets and earning the admiration of readers. For example, he devotes an entire chapter of *Arjuna* (chapter 5) to a description of the Himalaya mountain that is nothing short of a tour de force. The sequence is notable for its variety of meters, fantasy, and images evoking brilliant light phenomena. Also embedded in this virtuoso sequence are allusions to the god Shiva, his consort Parvati, Himalaya's daughter, and the wedding of the divine couple on the mountain. The chapter is both an homage to Kalidasa—*The Birth of Kumara* opens with a scintillating description of the natural and supernatural beauties of the Himalayas in fifteen verses, and the poem's central theme is the wedding of Shiva and Parvati—and a virtuosic "improvement" on the older poet's art. Other motives and principles are at work in the descriptions that dominate the poem, of Arjuna's austerities and combat. Bharavi uses each of these descriptions as an occasion for illuminating new aspects of asceticism and combat; practicing more intense austerities than before in order to propitiate Shiva, Arjuna is shown as growing from a hero with ascetic powers into a cosmic force. Running the gamut of battle description, ranging from the hero's feats in single-handedly facing a large army to Shiva and Arjuna's duel with magical missiles and Arjuna's wrestling match with Shiva, the combat sequences enable Bharavi to display virtuosity at its utmost.

Bharavi's descriptions of the aerial journey of the apsarases, Indra's celestial courtesans, and the revels of these voluptuous beauties and their lovers on the banks of the river Ganga, sequences that the *kāvya* poet added to the epic narrative, operate in the worlds of natural beauty and erotic pleasure. In these passages of Bharavi's invention, nymphs and demigods play the part of courtly lovers, and scenes of courtly life are enlivened by the conceits of aerial flight and magical mansions conjured up in Himalayan landscapes.[32] But the sequences also enable Bharavi to introduce at the appropriate juncture in his work the ubiquitous theme of the ascetic's seduction (or attempted seduction) by the courtesan.[33] Counterposed to Arjuna's (literally) elevating ascent of the Himalayas, the apsarases' descent on the mountain is the first step in a campaign to destroy the hero's ascetic endeavor. Testifying to the success of Bharavi's innovation, the theme of Arjuna's attempted seduction by the nymphs became part of many subsequent retellings of the hunter narrative, including temple sculpture, even when they deviate from the court poet in other respects.[34]

The descriptions of Arjuna's austerities, his arguments and confrontations with those who challenge him, and his combat with Shiva and his troops trace the hero's relentless progress toward his goal. The celestial courtesans tempt Arjuna with sexual pleasure, the hunter's envoy with wealth, and Indra with liberation from mundane existence, all worthy pursuits for the householder or the world renouncer, but Arjuna resists these temptations and cleaves to a warrior's sacred duty (dharma), manifesting steadfast determination both in practicing ascetic self-control and in confronting his challengers in active heroic combat.[35] The sequences on ascetic practice, evoking the aesthetic emotion of contemplative peace, provide the contrast required for the full flowering of the work's dominant aesthetic emotion, the heroic (*vīra*), based on the stable emotion of "tireless energy in pursuing an undertaking" (*utsāha*). Yet, in austerity as in combat, the hero manifests determination, vigor, presence of mind, dignity, and other attributes that contribute to the evocation of the heroic emotion.[36] The varied descriptions of asceticism and combat together illuminate Arjuna as a unique yet ideal warrior.

Bharavi's poem highlights the distinctive combination of self-control, heroism, and devotion that characterizes Arjuna and makes him the iconic court epic hero. The perfect warrior must also be the perfect man of discipline (yogi), acting justly in the world, transcending sensual desire and self-interest. Arjuna's austerities render him fit for his encounter with Shiva and ultimately for disciplined action in the war against the Kauravas. As the son of Indra, king of gods, among the five Pandava brothers it is Arjuna who embodies the qualities of the exemplary warrior.[37] But Arjuna is also an exemplary man and devotee. He has a special relationship with Krishna, the incarnation of Vishnu the preserver god, who aids the Pandavas and the cause of just war in the Mahabharata. Arjuna is Nara ("Man"), the human partner of Vishnu's rites of austerity in a former age, and inseparable friend of Krishna in the Mahabharata narrative.[38] It is he who receives Krishna's teaching and self-revelation in the *Bhagavadgītā,* the god's discourse on dharma on the battlefield. In Bharavi's poem the climax of Arjuna's combat with Shiva in disguise is neither a warrior's triumph over an enemy nor a gesture of complete submission, but rather a theophany and boon as reward for the hero's dedication to the heroic code of honorable action. As in the *Bhagavadgītā,* in *Arjuna,* too, the hero responds to the vision of a god with a devotee's hymn of praise.[39] The classical poets often homologized their royal patron to Rama, perfect man and king, and a direct incarnation of Vishnu. But Bharavi's Arjuna, whose humanity enables him to be a devotee as well as a disciplined warrior, was even closer to the courtly ideal. Among the many writers who followed Bharavi's lead was Mpu Kanwa, an eleventh-century poet who made Arjuna's heroic feats, including his encounter with Shiva, the theme of his Old Javanese court poem, written in praise of his patron-king Airlangga of East Java.[40]

Bharavi's treatment of Arjuna's asceticism and combat with Shiva is distinguished by an intensity that sets the poem apart from other renderings of the narrative. In the seemingly incongruous figure of Arjuna as an armed ascetic, in the frequent use of figures of speech and formal arrangements highlighting tension and paradox, and in the poem's many debates over the ethics of a warrior's practice of austerity for worldly ends, Bharavi presents the warrior-ascetic as a conundrum to be confronted and resolved. How can a warrior harness the peaceful means of self-discipline to achieve violent ends? How can a man be an active hero and a self-controlled yogi at the same time? The poem ends with a vision of Arjuna "towering over all the worlds with the innate courage of a warrior, and blazing with the fire of austerity" (*Arjuna* 18.47), harmoniously uniting qualities that merely appeared to be contradictory.[41]

Reading Arjuna: The Pleasures of the Text in Translation
No modern translation of a Sanskrit court poem can aspire to convey the pleasures of the *kāvya* poet's art that are inextricably embedded in features of language and versification. There is a palpable distance between modern English prose and a *kāvya* idiom couched in an inflected classical language deeply enmeshed in early medieval Indian culture. It is, however, entirely possible to convey in translation the shape and heft of figuration and thought in Bharavi's verse, and the processes by which image and idea are illumined. Let us look at some aspects of the pleasures of the text that can be sustained in a well-crafted translation, first within the microcosm of the verse, and then in Arjuna's celebrated descriptive sequences.

VERSE AND IMAGE
Comparison, drawing attention to similitude between two objects, is the Sanskrit poet's key strategy for the presentation of ideas and images within the microcosm of the verse, for

expanding the universe of the stanza, so to speak. Beginning with simile (*upamā*), metaphor (*rūpaka*), and "poetic fancy" (*utprekṣā*), a figure that is particularly prized in Sanskrit poetry, poets use a number of subtly differentiated figures of speech to posit and elaborate a relationship between the object that is being described and a standard of comparison that is applied to it.[42] The standard employed in a figure of speech such as the simile in *kāvya* poetry is often drawn from a sphere of experience quite unrelated to the object being described, conducing to the desired effect, the expansion of the verse's ambit. *Kāvya* figures of speech, often beginning with a stock comparison such as that of a woman's face with a lotus flower, illumine intimate, organic relationships between seemingly unrelated objects, and among human, natural, and mythic worlds. Each verse in *Arjuna* focuses on particular aspects of objects and the connections it makes between them; most often the poem's imagery, in a manner characteristic of court poetry, is intensely visual. In *Arjuna*, as in the best *kāvya* poetry, idea and image are illumined by the complex, virtuosic unfolding of imaginative connections, accessible even in translation. A look at a few verses from Bharavi will enable us to discern some of the strategies and principles at work in this process of illumination.

In some verses Bharavi focuses intensely on particular nuances and details of the stock images of *kāvya* poetry. Warriors are like a blazing fire; a woman's face is like a lotus flower. Here are two instances of the poet's variations on these standard comparisons:

17.2   Delighted to fight against a mighty warrior, yet
        downcast at the enemy's success, he looked like
        a fire on a mountain, its brilliance dimmed by
        billowing smoke.[43]

8.25   (The women's) faces with half-closed eyes, studded
        with perspiration, looked as lovely as lotuses with
        half-open petals covered with dewdrops.

Elsewhere an image stands out on account of its felicitous
appropriateness to the context. Here is Arjuna taking leave
of Draupadi before he sets out on his journey:

3.37   As his eager eyes met the woman's captivating gaze,
        sweet with the flow of true love, Arjuna's joyful
        heart served as palms cupped in courtesy, to
        welcome a loving gift of delicious provision for
        the journey.

In another verse the comparison of a row of bees to a chain
pivots on the specific aspect of the action being described,
of an elephant in the gandharva army hastily getting up from
his bed.

7.31   A king elephant, waking from the sleep of exhaustion,
        rose from his bed, leaving it wet with sweet ichor,
        and the row of bees for a moment alighting looked
        like his chain falling as he hastily got up.

But as in other aspects of poetic art, Bharavi's investment in striking expression extends to the poem's range of imagery as well. In the following verses the comparisons stand out precisely because they boldly link objects and ideas that are not usually paired.

17.36 Arjuna confidently put his hand inside the mouth of his empty quiver, like a thirsty elephant inserting its trunk into a rock cleft on a mountain that other elephants have drunk dry.

16.38 The glittering row of snakes, coils curved like the trunks of cosmic elephants and shimmering blue like rare dark sapphires, swelled like a line of waves in the ocean that was the sky.

Attending to the reasoning that underlies the linkages made in similes and other figures of speech that are characteristic of poetic speech forms an important part of reader response to Sanskrit *kāvya* verse. Bharavi favors a number of figures in which the armature of logic and reasoning is intrinsically foregrounded. In the examples that follow the poet employs, in order, the figures "doubt," "corroboration," and "garland of causes," all of which highlight aspects of reasoning.[44]

8.53 As the women swam in the river close to their lovers, their curved eyes—usually restless—were closed, their limbs quivered, and their breasts heaved with sighs. Were they overcome by the weariness of exercise, or by desire?

5.16   The servant of Kubera, god of wealth, spoke
        affectionately and sweetly to Arjuna as he stood
        filled with wonder at the sight of the mountain.
        Eloquence excels when it is timely.

2.14   Misfortune overcomes the man who fails to act; one
        beset by misfortune has no future prospects;
        he who has no hope for the future is fated to be
        insignificant; a man of little importance can never
        be the abode of royal fortune.

Descriptive Sequences: Imagery and Movement
Counterbalancing the seeming autonomy of the individual
verse, structural aspects of persuasive argument afford an
intrinsic frame around which the great speeches in *Arjuna*
are built. In contrast, the poem's descriptive sequences are
organized around a variety of principles and frameworks
that endow the sequences with a dynamism that cuts across
the isolation of verse and image. Foremost among these
frameworks are representations of movement through space
and time. In chapters 4 and 5 we follow along as Arjuna walks
through autumn fields and climbs the Himalaya mountain,
and in chapters 7 through 11 we trace the topographies of the
flight of the apsarases and gandharvas and their descent on
the mountain, followed by their walk in the woodlands and
play in the waters of the river Ganga. Time and the changes
wrought by time dominate yet other passages, most nota-
bly the requisite descriptions of sunset and moonrise that
precede the delineation of the erotic revels of the apsarases

and their lovers. Describing the progression of sunset and nightfall, the poet invites us to view subtle yet swift changes that transform the appearance of the sky, articulated, of course, in spectacular visual imagery. At the beginning of chapter 9 the sky puts on the fleeting beauty of the evening "like a swaying strand of pearls, with the sun suspended on one side, shining like a great pendant gem with its gleaming rays" (9.2). A few verses further down, "Suffused with the evening twilight spreading over massed clouds," the western sky looks "beautiful, like the ocean colored by the glow of coral hidden beneath the waves" (9.9). When the moon has risen, its "snow-white rays ... , streaming from behind the mountain," shine "against a sky the color of a blue lotus, like the waters of the Ganga merging with the ocean" (9.19).

Bharavi makes subtle use of imagery to draw the reader's attention to shifts in the progression of narrative or the shape of a descriptive sequence. There are, for example, occasions on which he deliberately breaks the even rhythm of autonomous verses by interposing a short sequence of grammatically connected verses, marked by clusters of images. Standing in strong contrast to individual verses, with their focus on single images, such sequences may mark, among other things, a major shift in the narrative or a moment of emotional or dramatic intensity.[45] A case in point is a sequence of eight connected verses (14.35–42) describing Arjuna as seen by Shiva's troops, when, commanded by Shiva to attack the hero they converge on him "like water-laden clouds converging on a mountain at the end of summer." In the above sequence Bharavi elevates his hero to mythic and cosmic stature through a superabundance of comparisons with awe-inspiring phenomena in nature (mountains, bulls, fire), as well as with the great gods—Shiva as Pashupati, lord of the beasts, and Vishnu, both in his primal form as Purusha, the highest Person, and in his incarnation as the primeval boar Varaha, who lifted the earth sphere out of the cosmic ocean in which a demon had hidden it. Impressively piled up on one another, these images are also particularly resonant with the concrete scene of Arjuna standing over the boar that he has just shot.

Bharavi is equally adept at employing images to signal transitions and closure in sequences of verses and chapters. In the following example, the clustering of similes in a single verse marks a juncture in the narrative.

12.17　Then, like virtues in need of cultivation, like policies
　　　　in need of discriminating intelligence, the nemesis
　　　　of bad strategy, like contracts in need of proper
　　　　observance, the helpless sages sought refuge in
　　　　Shiva.

Elsewhere, a shift in the content of imagery foreshadows topics that are to follow.

8.57　Stained by mixing with sandalwood cream and flecked
　　　　by the sparkling gems spilled from broken jewelry,
　　　　the undulating river, once the women had finished
　　　　playing and left, looked like a rumpled bed after a
　　　　night of lovemaking.

Appearing at the end of a chapter and of a long sequence describing the nymphs and their lovers bathing in the Ganga, the verse signals the transition to the themes of the drinking party and lovemaking that will be described in the following chapter.[46]

Economy of imagery is perhaps the most impressive among Bharavi's artistic strategies for shaping descriptive sequences. Variations on a small number of themes bind together verses placed at varying intervals in a descriptive passage, as in the sequence on the apsarases playing in the water.

8.25   Faces with half-closed eyes, studded with
         perspiration, looked as lovely as lotuses with half-
         open petals covered with dewdrops.

8.44   Her water graced by the reflection of the nymphs'
         smiling faces, whose glowing beauty put its
         lotuses to shame, the river Ganga reaped the
         benefit of her clarity.

8.47   Half hidden by long, spreading curls disheveled from
         swimming, the nymphs' faces in the water looked
         like lotuses covered by swarms of black bees.

In the three verses cited above, the poet not only varies the face-lotus theme to advantage, but also exploits with considerable flair the unique appropriateness of the comparison to the riverine setting of the nymphs' activities.

Arjuna's descriptive sequences remind one of the miniature painting albums of early modern Indian royal courts, in which each individual painting treats a particular vignette or aspect of a larger theme in courtly life, such as play in pleasure parks, harem life, or lovers in seasonal settings. A more direct comparison may be made between Bharavi's dynamic descriptions and techniques of performance in Indian classical music, especially the improvised, fluid, nonlinear elaboration of raga scales through variations on a theme.[47] If Sanskrit poetry's traditional stock of images and *Arjuna's* affinities with miniature painting and the ragas, or melodic patterns, of Indian music seem to place Bharavi's poem squarely in the world of premodern Indian courts, it is equally possible to approach the poem's riches through the counter-realistic lenses of global modern aesthetic and visual regimes, particularly in film. The fantasy and synesthesia of the flight of the apsarases and elephants have much in common with the animated visual sequences coordinated with Beethoven's Symphony No. 6 (*Pastoral*) in *Fantasia,* the 1940 animation film in which Walt Disney experimented with representing and blending classical music with colors and animated images.[48] *Arjuna's* cosmic and magical imagery are completely compatible with the sensibility of modern science fiction and fantasy. An exciting portal to the worlds of India's classical literature and thought, Bharavi's beautifully crafted poem has much to offer to the modern reader by way of aesthetic pleasure as well as the weighty intellectual and human issues it addresses.

Acknowledgments

I am grateful to the MCLI Editorial Board and Harvard University Press for inviting me to publish a translation of Bharavi's *Kirātārjunīya* in what promises to be an illustrious series on the Indian classics. It seems especially appropriate to publish Bharavi with Harvard University Press just a little over a hundred years after the first complete translation of the *Kirātārjunīya* in a European language (Carl Cappeller's 1912 German translation) appeared in the Harvard Oriental Series. Working with my editor, Sheldon Pollock, has been sheer pleasure. The translation has benefited in innumerable ways from his careful reading, vast knowledge, friendly and constructive suggestions for improvement, and his unerring taste. I have enjoyed our conversations about translating Bharavi. My debts to Harunaga Isaacson are great. I am deeply grateful to him: for preparing and sharing the Göttingen digital text of the *Kirātārjunīya;* for sending me text editions with various commentaries, including the Munich manuscript of Prakashavarsha's commentary; for alternative readings and new insights into the poem's difficult wordplay chapter; above all, for his friendship and generosity. I thank Dániel Balogh for preparing in record time an accurate *devanāgarī* text for this translation, based on my edition of the text. I am also grateful to Ivy Tillman, Caro Pinto, and Aime De-Grenier of the Mount Holyoke College Library's Research and Technology Support team for helping me prepare the manuscript for submission. Thanks as always to Mark and Maya for their unfailing support. And thanks, too, to all the friends and colleagues who have urged me over

the years to undertake a complete translation of Bharavi.
Here it is, at last!

NOTES

1   *Mahābhārata*, Critical Edition, 3.31.24–42 (*Kairātaparvan*).
2   On Sanskrit *kāvya* poetry, see Ingalls 1968: 1–31. For a detailed study of Bharavi's *Kirātārjunīya*, see Peterson 2003. For a brief discussion, see Warder 1977: 198–233.
3   Kielhorn 1900.
4   Peterson 2003: 23–24.
5   Peterson 2003: 25, and Peterson 1989: 35, 129, 137, 139, 174, 254–255, and 288.
6   Rabe 1997; Peterson 2003: 24–25; Narasimhavarman ruled from 630–668 C.E.
7   Rao 1979; Peterson 2003: 161–184.
8   Dandin, *Kāvyādarśa (KĀ)* 1.14–19.
9   *The Slaying of Shishupala: Śiśupālavadha* of Magha (8th century C.E.).
10 The commentaries (published and unpublished) are listed in Raghavan 1968: 161–165.
11 Pollock (2006) shows how, by the second millennium, while court poetry's prestige continued to be associated with the Sanskrit language as the language of power, the *kāvya* style itself functioned as a portable marker of courtly cosmopolitanism, becoming instrumental in the development of literary cultures in diverse languages in India and beyond.
12 Ingalls 1968: 23–28; Smith 1985: 55–102.
13 Love (*kāma*) and success (*artha*) are two of four aims of life enjoined upon the Hindu man (the other two are dharma [religion, sacred duty, law] and *mokṣa* [transcendence of worldly life]). *Kāma* and *artha* are particularly appropriate for the householder stage in the list of four life stages—student, householder, forest dweller, and renouncer.
14 Figures of speech: *alaṃkāra*, literally, "ornament"; aesthetic emotion: *rasa*, the aesthetic emotion or emotions produced in and by a literary text. See Ingalls 1968: 9–18.
15 Benjamin 1968: 71.

16 For definitions and descriptions of the Sanskrit court epic, see Peterson 2003: 7–20, and Smith 1985: 1–102; on the major *mahākāvyas*, see Lienhard 1984: 159–196.

17 The critic Dandin says that court epics may be based on legend, history, and myth (*KĀ* 1.14). The martial metaphor dominates even poems that are not directly about conflict.

18 Dandin, *KĀ* 1.16–17. For a translation of the complete text of Dandin's definition (*KĀ* 1.14–20), see Peterson 2003: 8–9.

19 Dandin, *KĀ* 1.15.

20 Dandin, *KĀ* 1.18. On *rasa*, see Bharata's *Nāṭyaśāstra*, chapters 6 and 7.

21 Bhamaha (c. seventh century C.E.), *Kāvyālaṃkāra* (Ornament of Poetry) 1.19.

22 Court epic verses are closely allied to the independent or "detached" poem, consisting of a single verse, that constitutes a signature genre in Sanskrit poetry (Lienhard 1984: 67–75; Ingalls 1968: 37–42). Sanskrit lyric meters range in length from *śloka*, with eight syllables per quarter, to *sragdharā*, with twenty-three syllables per quarter verse.

23 Steiner 1978: 40.

24 Court epic chapters are composed in a variety of meters, with a single meter usually deployed throughout a chapter. The choice of meter is often governed by the topic or mood of the particular chapter.

25 *Kir.* chapter 15.

26 "Bharavi's verse is split open in a moment like a coconut; may connoisseurs savor its core brimming with juice/aesthetic delight (*rasa*)." Mallinatha, *Ghaṇṭāpatha* commentary on the *Kirātārjunīya*, Introduction, verse 7, in *Kirātārjunīya* 1933: 1.

27 "Who in the world can subdue *Arjuna and the Hunter,* that wild, rebellious elephant, without the help of this powerful elephant goad, Vidyamadhava's commentary?" Vidyamadhava, commentary on the *Kirātārjunīya*, Introduction, verse 8, in *Kirātārjunīya* 1934: 3.

28 *Madhurāvijaya* (The Conquest of Madhura), 1.9.

29 *Bhāraver arthagauravam:* "Bhāravi's verse is characterized by intellectual heft." The adjective *guru*, "weighty, heavy" (from which the noun "*gauravam*" is derived) carries the connotations of "dense, rich, complex, elevated, great, dignified." Among the meanings of "*artha*" are "meaning" and "substance."

30 Bharavi's characters compliment one another on their oratorical skills: e.g., Yudhishthira's remarks to Bhima (*Kir.* 2.26–28), or Arjuna's to the hunter chief's envoy (14.3–6).

31 It is for these reasons the first three chapters of *Arjuna* have garnered the greatest number of commentaries and are most intensively studied in the classical curriculum.

32 Kalidasa treats the trope of the aerial journey several times, in his dramas as well as well as in his lyric and court epic poems; examples include the floating cloud in *Meghadūta* (The Messenger Cloud), Rama and Sita's flight in *Raghuvaṃśa* (The Lineage of Raghu), chapter 13; and the aerial journey of the seven sages in *Kumārasaṃbhava* (The Birth of Kumara), chapter 6.

33 On this theme, see Doniger 1973: 40–52.

34 The eleventh-century Kannada poem *Vikramārjunavijaya* of Pampa (Rao 1979: 5–6) and sculptural panels of the hunter narrative at the Hoysalesvara temple in Halebid (ibid., 33–34, and Plate XIV b), as well as the eleventh-century Old Javanese poem *Arjunawiwāha* include a temptation sequence.

35 Through these sequences Bharavi portrays the hero's response to each of the aims of life included in the traditional scheme of four aims.

36 According to the Sanskrit theorists, aesthetic emotion is brought about by transitory emotional states (e.g., Arjuna's anger when provoked by the hunter) and conditional elements, such as the hunter's challenge (for the heroic emotion). See *Nāṭyaśāstra* of Bharata, 6.46–62; and 7.1–92 (*NŚ* pp. 56–75).

37 All five Pandava brothers are sons of gods. On Arjuna as the exemplary warrior, see Peterson 2003: 28–30.

38 Bharavi refers to Arjuna's partnership with Vishnu-Krishna as the sage Nara, and their austerities in the Badari hermitage, in *Arjuna* 6.19, 12.33, and 15.45. See the discussion in Peterson 2003: 147–148.

39 In writing a poem of eighteen chapters, Bharavi appears to be alluding to the eighteen books of the *Mahābhārata*, as well as the *Bhagavadgītā's* eighteen chapters. There are further resonances in chapter 11 of *Arjuna*.

40 See Robson 2008 for a complete translation of *Arjunawiwāha*. Peterson 2003: 161–162 and 173–183 discusses the poem's relationship to Bharavi's *Arjuna*.

41 Bharavi's preoccupation with these themes, and his polemical style of presenting them in his poem, no doubt stem from the south Indian historical context of his poem. In the first millennium the Deccan region of south India was the site of major contestations between Brahmanical Hinduism and the so-called heterodox religions, Buddhism and Jainism, which advocated stringent nonviolence and foregrounded monastic practices and ideals.

42 For a list of figures of speech, with definitions, see the *Sāhityadarpaṇa* (Mirror for Literature) of Vishvanatha, 1965, edited by P. V. Kane, *pariccheda* 10, pp. 88–331; also see Gerow 1971.

43 This verse is part of a grammatically connected sequence of six verses (17.1–6). However, each verse in the sequence focuses on a particular image and relations among words within the verse.

44 Doubt: *saṃdeha,* a figure in which the point of the verse is the doubt aroused by the similarity of two objects as to their true identities. Corroboration: *arthāntaranyāsa,* a figure favored by the court epic poets, in which a general statement corroborates, or illuminates, the universal validity of the idea presented in a verse. Garland of causes: *kāraṇamālā,* a figure that illumines the relations presented within a verse among several objects or ideas in the form of a chain of cause and effect.

45 In the translation, verses in the poem that are connected through syntax or similar means have been grouped together to form a paragraph.

46 In *Kir.* 8 the change from *vaṃśastha,* the chapter's main meter, to *vasantatilakā* in vv. 55, 56, and 57 marks the transition to a new topic and, in this case, a new chapter.

47 Peterson 2003: 104–107.

48 A sequence depicting centaurs, cupids, fauns, and other figures from classical mythology frolicking in a pastoral setting is the film's visual correlative to Beethoven's music. Zeus disrupts a bacchanalian revel by creating a storm and hurling lightning bolts at the revelers.

NOTE ON THE TEXT
AND TRANSLATION

Note on the Text

The *editio princeps* of Bharavi's *Kirātārjunīya* (*Kir.*) was published in Kidderpore (near Calcutta) in 1814, along with the *Ghaṇṭāpatha* (Bell Road) of Mallinatha (c. 1400), the most influential commentary on the work.[1] Several editions were produced in Calcutta throughout the nineteenth century. In 1885 the Nirnaya Sagar Press in Bombay published an important edition of the *Kirātārjunīya* with Mallinatha's commentary and variant readings. Pandit Durgaprasad and Kashinath Pandurang Parab published revised versions of this edition from 1889 to 1904, providing improved readings. The Nirnaya Sagar Press (NSP) edition was reprinted several times, with slight revisions.[2] Partial editions of Bharavi have been published, especially for the first three chapters of the text, and with commentaries by other commentators.

The edited text I have produced for the Murty Classical Library of India (MCLI) is based primarily on the 1933 reprint of the NSP edition (N), and on Mallinatha's commentary.[3] In preparing the MCLI text, I have consulted several editions, including ones providing commentaries other than the *Ghaṇṭāpatha*. I have compared the N text with the University of Göttingen digitized text of the *Kirātārjunīya*, in roman script, itself based on an older NSP edition,[4] but incorporating variant readings from commentators other than Mallinatha.[5] I have also consulted the complete Calcutta edition of 1913, with Mallinatha's commentary,[6] and the partial

xxxix

text editions published with the commentaries of Chitrabhanu,[7] Devarajyajvan, Vidyamadhava,[8] Jonaraja, Nrisimha, and Prakashavarsha.[9] The *Laghuṭīkā* commentary on the entire text of the *Kirātārjunīya* by Prakashavarsha (c. 900), the oldest known commentator on Bharavi's work, digitally accessed in a manuscript housed at the Bayerische Staatsbibliothek in Munich,[10] was eminently useful, both in checking the poem's text and in finding concise, sensible, and insightful interpretations of Bharavi's challenging verses. For the MCLI text edition I have adopted variant readings (departures from N) only in a very few instances. In crafting the first complete English translation of this difficult poem I have been for the most part guided by Mallinatha's commentary, but there are instances where I have preferred the interpretations of Prakashavarsha and Chitrabhanu.

Note on the Translation

Bharavi's poem has never been translated into English in its entirety. Carl Cappeller's 1912 German prose rendering is the only complete translation to date of the *Kirātārjunīya* in a European language.[11] While this is an excellent scholarly translation, it is dated, and limited to readers with knowledge of German. Of the three English translations of substantial portions of the *Kirātārjunīya* that have appeared in the last one hundred and twenty years, only two are readily accessible.[12] The earlier of these, R. C. Dutt's "The Hunter and the Hero" (1894),[13] is a dated verse rendering in the archaic diction and style of English ballads and translations of bardic poetry, modeled on Tennyson and other High

Victorian English poets. K. P. Kaisher Bahadur's 1970 verse translation of chapters 1–12 of the poem is beset by numerous problems, including inaccuracy, ungrammatical English, and doggerel versification, but above all by the peculiar interpretations adopted by the translator in his determination to prove that Bharavi was a Nepali poet and his work, a poem about Nepal.[14] Clearly, it is time for a reliable—and readable—modern English translation of Bharavi's poem. In the spirit of the MCLI series, in crafting this translation I have aimed at producing an accurate rendering based on meticulous scholarship, but one that will be readily accessible to nonspecialist readers.

The MCLI translation of Bharavi is cast in elevated poetic prose in the modern English idiom. However, keeping the verses separate, as in the original, has enabled me to engage with the *kāvya* stanza as the central compositional unit in the Sanskrit court epic; it also enables the reader, it is hoped, to respond to the individual verse as the court epic's quintessential aesthetic microcosm. That microcosm is characterized above all by formal complexity, and the density that arises from diverse sorts of poetic material—images, compounds, words with multiple meanings, and so on—coming together in the verse.

No attempt has been made here to image in English the complexities of Sanskrit grammar and syntax in Bharavi's verse, or to try to find counterparts to their formal and aural aspects; it is inevitable that these will be lost in translation. In the case of the figure of speech *śleṣa*, "polysemy," I have incorporated into the translation as far as possible the multiple meanings of the Sanskrit originals, without mimicking the formal aspects of the figure of speech. Perhaps most difficult to render into English, and contributing greatly to the density of form and meaning in Bharavi's verse, is the compound. A compound (*samāsa*) is a grammatical entity treated as constituting a single word, although it is composed of multiple components whose relationships to one another must be decoded to yield the "word's" exact meaning. My English renderings of Bharavi's word-packed verses, by contrast, are characterized by the analytic syntax and relatively short words of modern English speech.

We know that Bharavi's verses are imbued with other kinds of heft, those of images and ideas, inhabiting the microcosm of the verse in complex relationships to one another. In my translation I have made every effort to map within each verse or cluster of verses in the *Kirātārjunīya* the dynamic and development of argument, thought, and figures of speech (*alaṃkāra*) that I have argued are central to the poetics of court epic. Analyzing a verse culled from the sequence in chapter 8, describing the apsarases playing in the water, will demonstrate how artfully Bharavi deploys Sanskrit *kāvya's* rich resources in language and imagery, to achieve verses with a quintessentially *kāvya* sensibility and appeal:

8.42 The timid nymphs could not excel the waves in
   beauty: their faces were radiant, their strands of
   pearls swayed, their complexions were superbly
   fair, but the waves had lotuses, and surging foam,
   and the saffron washed away from their bodies.

In the Sanskrit original of the above verse, Bharavi exploits the free word order of the Sanskrit language and its facility for compounding words, in combination with the *kāvya* mandate for using a wide variety of figures of speech, to create an elegantly complex structure within the individual verse.[15]

śubhānanāḥ (a) *sāmburuheṣu* (b) *bhīravo* (a)
(The nymphs) with -radiant-faces, (a) (in/among the waves) with-lotuses, (b) the timid ones (a)
vilolahārāś (a) *calaphenapaṅktiṣu* (b)
(the women) with-swaying-strands of pearls, (a)
(among the waves) with-surging-foam, (b)
nitāntagauryo (a) *hṛtakuṅkumeṣv* (b) *alaṃ* (c)
The superbly fair (women) (a), (among the waves) that-had-washed-away-the-saffron, (b) sufficient (c)
na lebhire tāḥ (a) *parabhāgam* (c) *ūrmiṣu* (b)
(the women) could not gain (a) advantageous contrast/ superiority/excellence (c) among the waves. (b)

The verse is dense with compounds describing the women, their actions, and the water in which they are playing. The words in category "a," applicable to the nymphs, who are the agents of the verbal action, are placed next to and alternate with words applicable to the waves (category "b") among which the women are playing, and with the words that establish the relationship of absence of contrast and excellence (category "c") between the women and the waves.[16] The verse linguistically, figuratively, and visually embodies the juxtaposition of the two, and mimics their contest for superiority over each other. Furthermore, in this verse, as is often the case with the use of epithets and descriptive phrases in *kāvya* poetry, epithets and compound phrases, by describing an object, serve the function of naming the object. Thus *śubhānanāḥ* ([females] "possessing radiant faces") names the women, and *calaphenapaṅktiṣu* ("among the ones that possess surging foam"; b), the waves. Both phrases are compound words, requiring the reader to work out the relationships that obtain among the component elements of the compound, moving from the end of the word to its beginning. Finally, critics and connoisseurs discern in this verse not one but two figures of speech: *sāmānya* (identity, absence of distinction) and *yathāsaṃkhya* (relative order).[17]

I have shown in the introduction that Bharavi is a consummate artist in composing descriptive and rhetorical sequences with verses that connect and resonate with one another in various ways. I hope that my translation captures something of the flow and dynamism of Bharavi's sequences. Lexical variation is one of the many strategies that the court poet deploys both to set each verse in relief against its neighbors and to weave the verses together in a variegated tapestry of words and meanings that offsets the repetitive rhythm of verses set in the same meter. Bharavi puts Sanskrit's vast and perennially productive vocabulary to effective use in varying images and words that both link the verses in a sequence and endow each new sequence with a unique flavor. For instance, in a sequence of thirty verses in chapter 8, describing the apsarases playing in the river Ganga,[18] he uses more than thirteen words to refer to "women" or "nymphs." Some of these, like *vadhū*, are generic terms denoting "young woman," while others, such as *mānīnī* (the angry one), or *natabhrū* (woman with arched eyebrows) serve as epithets and descriptions that depict particular aspects of the women's appearance or state of mind, and enable readers to view them from changing perspectives.[19] Bharavi's characterizations of Shiva and Arjuna are among the most productive areas for lexical variation in the *Kirātārjunīya*. The poet uses multiple epithets and names for both god and hero. "Son of Pritha" (*pārtha*), "Indra's son" (*indrasūnu*), "Winner of wealth" (*dhanaṃjaya*), and "hero with the monkey banner" (*kapidhvaja*) are only a few of the titles by which Arjuna is named in the poem, while "Bestower of blessings" (*śambhu*), "Moon-crowned god" (*śaśadharamauli*) and "Seizer" (*hara*) are among Shiva's many names. I have not systematically translated these names at every instance, using "Arjuna" or "Shiva" instead. Elsewhere, as in chapter 17.1–64, I have tried to match Bharavi's rich vocabulary for heroism and heroic deeds with a varied palette of English words.

NOTES

1   Bell road: royal highway. On Mallinatha's commentary, see Roodbergen 1984.

2   The last edition of Durgaprasad and Parab noted by Raghavan 1968 is dated 1902. Editions up to 1933 may be found listed in the OCLC-WorldCat online database. The many partial and complete editions of the *Kirātārjunīya* text, published mainly in various Sanskrit series in Benares, along with modern Sanskrit and Hindi commentaries and other aids, all follow the Nirnaya Sagar Press editions of the text.

3   "N." *Kir.* 1933. In preparing the MCLI text I have corrected

typographical and other errors found in the base edition, and emended some readings.

4 "N1." *Kir.* 1889.

5 "G." *Kir.* n.d. (2). Göttingen digitized text of the *Kirātārjunīya* of Bharavi in roman script.

6 "C." *Kir.* 1913.

7 "Ci." *Kir.* 1918.

8 "C1." *Kir.* 1934.

9 "J." *Kir.* 2008. This is a partial edition, covering only chapters 1–3, with the commentaries of Jonaraja, Nrisimha, and Prakashavarsha.

10 "P." *Kir.* n.d. (1).

11 Cappeller 1912.

12 I have not been able to locate a copy of Pangarker 1902.

13 Dutt 1894.

14 Bahadur 1972 and 1974.

15 I have not represented the words in their original or "base" forms, prior to changes made by inflection and euphonic combination (sandhi), but simply as they appear in the verse. For a close discussion of the properties of the Sanskrit language and their effect on writing and reading *kāvya* poetry, see Nathan 1976: 6–9.

16 In the representation of this verse with interlinear glosses, words in parentheses indicate implied ideas or words.

17 Figures of speech are identified in endnotes.

18 *Kir.* 8.27–57.

19 On the typology of young women in Sanskrit poetry, see Ingalls 1968; and Ingalls 1962.

CHAPTER 1

Queen Draupadi Calls for Action

१ श्रियः कुरूणामधिपस्य पालनीं प्रजासु वृत्तिं यमयुङ्क्त वेदितुम् ।
स वर्णिलिङ्गी विदितः समाययौ युधिष्ठिरं द्वैतवने वनेचरः ॥

२ कृतप्रणामस्य महीं महीभुजे जितां सपत्नेन निवेदयिष्यतः ।
न विव्यथे तस्य मनो न हि प्रियं प्रवक्तुमिच्छन्ति मृषा हितैषिणः ॥

३ द्विषां विघाताय विधातुमिच्छतो रहस्यनुज्ञामधिगम्य भूभृतः ।
स सौष्ठवौदार्यविशेषशालिनीं विनिश्चितार्थामिति वाचमाददे ॥

४ क्रियासु युक्तैर्नृप चारचक्षुषो न वञ्चनीयाः प्रभवोऽनुजीविभिः ।
अतोऽर्हसि क्षन्तुमसाधु साधु वा हितं मनोहारि च दुर्लभं वचः ॥

५ स किंसखा साधु न शास्ति योऽधिपं हितान्न यः संशृणुते स
किंप्रभुः ।
सदानुकूलेषु हि कुर्वते रतिं नृपेष्वमात्येषु च सर्वसंपदः ॥

६ निसर्गदुर्बोधमबोधविक्लवाः क्व भूपतीनां चरितं क्व जन्तवः ।
तवानुभावोऽयमवेदि यन्मया निगूढतत्त्वं नयवर्त्म विद्विषाम् ॥

Yudhishthira had sent a forest dweller to learn how the   1
king of the Kurus,[1] anxious to safeguard his sovereign
rule, was behaving toward his subjects. Once he had
gathered intelligence disguised as a religious student
he returned to the Dvaita forest hermitage.[2]

As he bowed to Yudhishthira, preparing to tell him that   2
Duryodhana, his rival, had conquered the earth, he
did not hesitate. Well-intentioned servants do not
speak pleasant falsehoods.[3]

Gaining a private audience with the king, who was eager   3
to act and destroy his enemies, he spoke, delivering
a well-founded speech dignified by carefully chosen
words, rich in meaning.

"King, servants entrusted with missions ought not to   4
deceive rulers, whose spies serve as their eyes. So
kindly bear with my words, whether pleasant or
unpleasant. A speech both charming and beneficent at
once is a rare thing.

He who fails to give his king good advice is a bad   5
counselor. He who fails to listen to good counsel is a
bad king. Prosperity favors only kings and ministers
who work together in perfect harmony.

The conduct of kings is by nature difficult to comprehend;   6
men like me are fettered by ignorance. It is through
your power alone that I was able to fathom the
enemy's statecraft, whose workings are impossible
to penetrate.

७ विशङ्कमानो भवतः पराभवं नृपासनस्थो ऽपि वनाधिवासिनः ।
दुरोदरच्छद्मजितां समीहते नयेन जेतुं जगतीं सुयोधनः ॥

८ तथापि जिह्मः स भवज्जिगीषया तनोति शुभ्रं गुणसंपदा यशः ।
समुन्नयन्भूतिमनार्यसंगमादूरं विरोधो ऽपि समं महात्मभिः ॥

९ कृतारिषड्वर्गजयेन मानवीमगम्यरूपां पदवीं प्रपित्सुना ।
विभज्य नक्तंदिवमस्ततन्द्रिणा वितन्यते तेन नयेन पौरुषम् ॥

१० सखीनिव प्रीतियुजो ऽनुजीविनः समानमानान्सुहृदश्च बन्धुभिः ।
स संततं दर्शयते गतस्मयः कृताधिपत्यामिव साधु बन्धुताम् ॥

११ असक्तमाराधयतो यथायथं विभज्य भक्त्या समपक्षपातया ।
गुणानुरागादिव सख्यमीयिवान्न बाधते ऽस्य त्रिगणः परस्परम् ॥

Afraid you will defeat him in battle, even though you live   7
in forest exile while he sits on the throne, Suyodhana*
is trying to win through policy the world he had won
by the dice game ruse.

Crook though he is, he is anxious to surpass you in   8
every respect and so wins spotless fame through an
impressive display of virtue. Even enmity with the
great, since it elevates a man, surpasses friendship
with ignoble men.

Aspiring to join the ranks of rulers who practice the   9
precepts of King Manu, a goal difficult to attain, he
subdues the six passions, enemies of self-mastery. He
diligently performs manly action by means of right
conduct, through tasks apportioned to proper times
of day and night.⁴

Setting aside pride, he shows off his courtesy, which is   10
quite sincere. He treats his servants like dear friends,
accords to his friends the honor due to kinsmen, and
honors his kinsmen as if they were kings.

Since he serves each of them in turn, appropriately, and   11
paying equal attention to each, with devotion and
without care for personal benefit, it seems that the
three aims of life—religion, wealth, and love—no
longer clash with one another, having become friends
through mutual love of his virtues.⁵

―――

* Another name of Duryodhana.

१२ निरत्ययं साम न दानवर्जितं न भूरि दानं विरहय्य सत्क्रियाम् ।
प्रवर्तते तस्य विशेषशालिनी गुणानुरोधेन विना न सत्क्रिया ॥

१३ वसूनि वाञ्छन्न वशी न मन्युना स्वधर्म इत्येव निवृत्तकारणः ।
गुरूपदिष्टेन रिपौ सुते ऽपि वा निहन्ति दण्डेन स धर्मविप्लवम् ॥

१४ विधाय रक्षान्परितः परेतरानशङ्किताकारमुपैति शङ्कितः ।
क्रियापवर्गेष्वनुजीविसात्कृताः कृतज्ञतामस्य वदन्ति संपदः ॥

१५ अनारतं तेन पदेषु लम्भिता विभज्य सम्यग्विनियोगसत्क्रियाः ।
फलन्त्युपायाः परिबृंहितायतीरुपेत्य संघर्षमिवार्थसंपदः ॥

१६ अनेकराजन्यरथाश्वसंकुलं तदीयमास्थाननिकेतनाजिरम् ।
नयत्ययुग्मच्छदगन्धिरार्द्रतां भृशं नृपोपायनदन्तिनां मदः ॥

१७ सुखेन लभ्या दधतः कृषीवलैरकृष्टपच्या इव सस्यसंपदः ।
वितन्वति क्षेममदेवमातृकाश्रिराय तस्मिन्कुरवश्चकासति ॥

His tactics of conciliation are effective, since they are   12
always accompanied by gifts; his generous gifts
are always given with courtesy; and his courtesy,
conferring distinction, always favors merit.[6]

Not from desire for wealth nor out of anger but with   13
perfect self-control, acting only from a sense of kingly
duty and not from any selfish motive, and guided by
the judges' instructions, he punishes equally a son or
an enemy for their crimes.

Acutely suspicious of treachery, he has surrounded   14
himself with trusted guards and spies, yet pretends to
be utterly trusting. The gifts with which he rewards
his men at the successful completion of their tasks
proclaim his gratitude.

Directed toward the right targets with careful   15
discernment, the four means of policy—conciliation,
gifts, division, and war—feel honored to be employed
by him, and seem to compete with one another to
constantly increase his prosperity for the long term.

Streams of ichor, fragrant like the seven-leaf flower,[7]   16
flowing from elephants gifted by kings, muddy
the courtyard of his assembly hall, crowded with
feudatory princes and their horses and chariots.

Under his nurturing rule, the well-irrigated land of the   17
Kurus prospers, no longer dependent on rainfall, and
yielding abundant grain, harvested with ease as if it
had never been cultivated by farmers.

१८ उदारकीर्तेरुदयं दयावतः प्रशान्तबाधं दिशतो ऽभिरक्षया ।
स्वयं प्रदुग्धे ऽस्य गुणैरुपसुता वसूपमानस्य वसूनि मेदिनी ॥

१९ महौजसो मानधना धनार्चिता धनुभृतः संयति लब्धकीर्तयः ।
न संहतास्तस्य न भिन्नवृत्तयः प्रियाणि वाञ्छन्त्यसुभिः समी-
हितुम् ॥

२० महीभृतां सञ्चरितैश्चरैः क्रियाः स वेद निःशेषमशेषितक्रियः ।
महोदयैस्तस्य हितानुबन्धिभिः प्रतीयते धातुरिवेहितं फलैः ॥

२१ न तेन सज्यं क्वचिदुद्धतं धनुः कृतं न वा कोपविजिह्ममाननम् ।
गुणानुरागेण शिरोभिरुह्यते नराधिपैर्माल्यमिवास्य शासनम् ॥

२२ स यौवराज्ये नवयौवनोद्धतं निधाय दुःशासनमिद्धशासनः ।
मखेष्वखिन्नो ऽनुमतः पुरोधसा धिनोति हव्येन हिरण्यरेतसम् ॥

२३ प्रलीनभूपालमपि स्थिरायति प्रशासदावारिधि मण्डलं भुवः ।
स चिन्तयत्येव भियस्त्वदेष्यतीरहो दुरन्ता बलवद्विरोधिता ॥

Moved by the virtues of that illustrious and munificent   18
    king who rivals Kubera, god of wealth, a
    compassionate warrior whose protection has relieved
    distress and secured her flourishing, the earth of her
    own accord flows with riches for him.

Formidable archers, warriors who treasure personal   19
    honor, famed in battle and well rewarded by the king,
    stand united in loyalty, ready to give their own lives to
    serve him.

Sparing no effort in the pursuit of policy, he gathers   20
    complete intelligence on the activities of all kings
    through his trusted spies; but his own plans, like those
    of the ordainer of the world,* reveal themselves only
    in their beneficent and prosperous outcomes.

He never raises his bow to shoot arrows at enemies; his   21
    face is never contorted in anger. Out of love for his
    virtues, kings bear his command like a garland on
    their heads.

The monarch, unopposed, has installed Duhshasana, an   22
    impetuous young man, as heir apparent. Instructed
    by the family priest, he himself diligently performs
    sacrifices, propitiating the god of fire with offerings.

Unchallenged by any rival, he commands enduring rule   23
    over the entire circle of the earth, to the oceans'
    shores—and yet he is obsessed with fear of you.
    Enmity with powerful men always ends in disaster.

---

* Brahma, the creator in the Hindu triad.

२४ कथाप्रसङ्गेन जनैरुदाह्नतादनुस्मृताखण्डलसूनुविक्रमः ।
तवाभिधानाद्व्यथते नताननः स दुःसहान्मन्त्रपदादिवोरगः ॥

२५ तदाशु कर्तुं त्वयि जिह्ममुद्यते विधीयतां तत्र विधेयमुत्तरम् ।
परप्रणीतानि वचांसि चिन्वतां प्रवृत्तिसाराः खलु मादृशां
धियः१ ॥

२६ इतीरयित्वा गिरमात्तसक्रिये गते ऽथ पत्यौ वनसंनिवासिनाम् ।
प्रविश्य कृष्णासदनं महीभुजा तदाचचक्षे ऽनुजसंनिधौ वचः ॥

२७ निशम्य सिद्धिं द्विषतामपाकृतीस्ततस्ततस्त्या विनियन्तुमक्षमा ।
नृपस्य मन्युव्यवसायदीपिनीरुदाजहार द्रुपदात्मजा गिरः ॥

२८ भवादृशेषु प्रमदाजनोदितं भवत्यधिक्षेप इवानुशासनम् ।
तथापि वक्तुं व्यवसाययन्ति मां निरस्तनारीसमया दुराधयः ॥

२९ अखण्डमाखण्डलतुल्यधामभिश्चिरं धृता भूपतिभिः स्ववंशजैः ।
त्वयात्महस्तेन मही मदच्युता मतङ्गजेन स्रगिवापवर्जिता ॥

He cannot bear to hear people mentioning your name in 24
conversation. Reminded at once of the heroic deeds of
Arjuna, son of Indra, he hangs down his head in terror,
like a snake, hood sunken, recoiling in pain from a
physician's unbearably powerful incantation.[8]
Therefore, you must quickly take action against this man, 25
who is plotting you harm. But to be sure, men like
myself, who merely garner the words of others, have
minds fit only to convey information."
When the chief of foresters had finished his report, 26
received his reward, and left, the king entered
Krishna* Draupadi's apartment and told her the news
in the presence of his brothers.
When Drupada's daughter heard that their enemies 27
were flourishing, she could no longer hold back the
resentment they had provoked. She spoke words
designed to arouse the king's anger, to stir him to
action.
"For a woman to advise men like you is almost an insult. 28
And yet, my anguish compels me to overstep the
limits of womanly conduct and makes me speak up.
The kings of your line, brave as Indra, have ruled the 29
earth for a long time, without a break. But now with
your own hand you have thrown it away, like a rutting
elephant tearing off his garland with his trunk.[9]

---

* "Krishna (*kṛṣṇā*), 'dark woman,'" a second name of Draupadi.

11

३० व्रजन्ति ते मूढधियः पराभवं भवन्ति मायाविषु ये न मायिनः ।
प्रविश्य हि घ्नन्ति शठास्तथाविधानसंवृताङ्गान्निशिता इवेषवः ॥

३१ गुणानुरक्तामनुरक्तसाधनः कुलाभिमानी कुलजां नराधिपः ।
परैस्त्वदन्यः क इवापहारयेन्मनोरमामात्मवधूमिव श्रियम् ॥

३२ भवन्तमेतर्हि मनस्विगर्हिते विवर्तमानं नरदेव वर्त्मनि ।
कथं न मन्युर्ज्वलयत्युदीरितः शमीतरुं शुष्कमिवाग्निरुच्छिखः ॥

३३ अवन्ध्यकोपस्य विहन्तुरापदां भवन्ति वश्याः स्वयमेव देहिनः ।
अमर्षशून्येन जनस्य जन्तुना न जातहार्देन न विद्विषादरः ॥

३४ परिभ्रमँल्लोहितचन्दनोचितः पदातिरन्तर्गिरि रेणुरूषितः ।
महारथः सत्यधनस्य मानसं दुनोति नो कच्चिदयं वृकोदरः ॥

३५ विजित्य यः प्राज्यमयच्छदुत्तरान्कुरूनकुप्यं वसु वासवोपमः ।
स वल्कवासांसि तवाधुनाहरन्करोति मन्युं न कथं धनंजयः ॥

Fools who do not use craft against the crafty are destined   30
for defeat. Deceivers will penetrate their secrets and
destroy them, like sharp arrows that pierce and kill
the warrior who has no armor to protect him.

What other king, proud of his birth and assured of loyal   31
friends, would let enemies steal the fortune of his
royal house, which is attached to him because of his
skillful use of policy, like a lovely highborn wife in love
with her husband's virtues?[10]

King, as you walk a path scorned by self-respecting men,   32
how can anger not inflame you, as a kindled fire blazes
up and engulfs a withered *śamī* tree?[11]

Men willingly submit to the warrior who makes effective   33
use of anger to redress his wrongs. But people have no
respect for anyone, friend or foe, lacking indignation.

You who treasure truth, does your heart not ache to see   34
Bhima, who used to anoint himself with the finest
fragrant sandalwood cream, now covered with dust,
who once rode in a great chariot, now wandering the
mountains on foot?

Arjuna, winner of wealth, warrior who rivals Indra, who   35
once conquered the Northern Kuru land and brought
you fabled treasure of silver and gold, now fetches you
the bark you wear. Why are you not stirred to anger?[12]

३६ वनान्तशय्याकठिनीकृताकृती कचाचितौ विष्वगिवागजौ गजौ ।
कथं त्वमेतौ धृतिसंयमौ यमौ विलोकयन्नुत्सहसे न बाधितुम् ॥

३७ इमामहं वेद न तावकीं धियं विचित्ररूपाः खलु चित्तवृत्तयः ।
विचिन्तयन्त्या भवदापदं परां रुजन्ति चेतः प्रसभं ममाधयः ॥

३८ पुराधिरूढः शयनं महाधनं विबोध्यसे यः स्तुतिगीतिमङ्गलैः ।
अदभ्रदर्भामधिशाय्य स स्थलीं जहासि निद्रामशिवैः शिवारुतैः ॥

३९ पुरोपनीतं नृप रामणीयकं द्विजातिशेषेण यदेतदन्धसा ।
तदद्य ते वन्यफलाशिनः परं परैति कार्श्यं यशसा समं वपुः ॥

४० अनारतं यौ मणिपीठशायिनावरञ्जयद्राजशिरःस्रजां रजः ।
निषीदतस्तौ चरणौ वनेषु ते मृगद्विजालूनशिखेषु बर्हिषाम् ॥

४१ द्विषन्निमित्ता यदियं दशा ततः समूलमुन्मूलयतीव मे मनः ।
परैरपर्यासितवीर्यसंपदां पराभवो ऽप्युत्सव एव मानिनाम् ॥

Look at these twins,* bodies hardened from sleeping on   36
the forest floor and hair unkempt, looking like wild
elephants from the mountains! How can you still
remain calm and content?

I do not understand your attitude—but then, men's minds   37
work in such different ways! When I think of your
utter misfortune, the pain simply breaks my heart.

You, who once slept on a luxurious bed and woke up to   38
the auspicious songs and eulogies of bards, now lie on
ground overgrown with rough *kuśa* grass and awaken
to the ominous howls of jackals.

King, your body was once sleek, nourished by the rich food   39
you dined on after giving Brahmans their share. Now
you live on wild berries, and your body, along with
your fame, grows painfully lean.

Your feet always rested on a bejeweled footstool, and were   40
gilded by pollen from the floral chaplets on the heads
of kings. Now they tread on clumps of sharp *kuśa*
grass cropped by deer and clipped by Brahmans for
their rites.

It wrenches my heart to think that the enemy is the cause   41
of your plight. A man of self-respect may rejoice even
in defeat, so long as his enemies have not broken his
courage.

---

* Nakula and Sahadeva, sons of Madri and Pandu, are the youngest
of the Pandava brothers.

४२ विहाय शान्तिं नृप धाम तत्पुनः प्रसीद संधेहि वधाय विद्विषाम् ।
व्रजन्ति शत्रूनवधूय निःस्पृहाः शमेन सिद्धिं मुनयो न भूभृतः ॥

४३ पुरःसरा धामवतां यशोधनाः सुदुःसहं प्राप्य निकारमीदृशम् ।
भवादृशाश्चेदधिकुर्वते रतिं² निराश्रया हन्त हता मनस्विता ॥

४४ अथ क्षमामेव निरस्तविक्रमश्चिराय पर्येषि सुखस्य साधनम् ।
विहाय लक्ष्मीपतिलक्ष्म कार्मुकं जटाधरः सज्जुहुधीह पावकम् ॥

४५ न समयपरिरक्षणं क्षमं ते निकृतिपरेषु परेषु भूरिधाम्नः ।
अरिषु हि विजयार्थिनः क्षितीशा विदधति सोपधि संधिदूषणानि ॥

४६ विधिसमयनियोगाद्दीप्तिसंहारजिह्मं
शिथिलबलमगाधे³ मग्नमापत्पयोधौ ।
रिपुतिमिरमुदस्योदीयमानं दिनादौ
दिनकृतमिव लक्ष्मीस्त्वां समभ्येतु भूयः ॥

16

Oh my lord, give up peace! I beg you, assume your fighting   42
spirit once more, so that you may kill the enemy! It is
only detached ascetics, not kings, who conquer their
enemies, the passions, and achieve perfection through
peace.

If men like you, foremost among warriors who value their   43
fame above all else, quietly accept such insult from the
enemy, alas, self-respect is dead, for it has lost its only
home!

If you choose to reject manly action, and see forbearance   44
as the road to future happiness, then throw away
your bow, symbol of royalty, wear your hair matted
in knots, stay here in this grove of ascetics, and make
offerings in the sacred fire!

Since your enemies are bent on destroying you through   45
deceit, it is not proper for a powerful warrior like you
to hold to your promise. Kings who want to conquer
can always find ways to break treaties made with
enemies.

You are like the sun grown dim from the withdrawal of   46
light by the decree of fate and time, with feeble rays,
sunken in the fathomless ocean: your splendor dulled
from the loss of fighting spirit imposed by the fateful
decree of your promise, you are weak, and sunk deep
in misfortune. May fortune's radiance return to you
when you rise to overcome your enemies, even as it
returns to the sun at daybreak when he rises to dispel
darkness!"[13]

CHAPTER 2

Yudhishthira and Bhima Debate Policy

१ विहितां प्रियया मनःप्रियामथ निश्चित्य गिरं गरीयसीम् ।
उपपत्तिमदूर्जिताश्रयं नृपमूचे वचनं वृकोदरः ॥

२ यदवोचत वीक्ष्य मानिनी परितः स्नेहमयेन चक्षुषा ।
अपि वागधिपस्य दुर्वचं वचनं तद्विदधीत विस्मयम् ॥

३ विषमो ऽपि विगाह्यते नयः कृततीर्थः पयसामिवाशयः ।
स तु तत्र विशेषदुर्लभः सदुपन्यस्यति कृत्यवर्त्म यः ॥

४ परिणामसुखे गरीयसि व्यथके ऽस्मिन्वचसि क्षतौजसाम् ।
अतिवीर्यवतीव भेषजे बहुरल्पीयसि दृश्यते गुणः ॥

५ इयमिष्टगुणाय रोचतां रुचिरार्था भवते ऽपि भारती ।
ननु वक्तृविशेषनिःस्पृहा गुणगृह्या वचने विपश्चितः ॥

६ चतसृष्वपि ते विवेकिनी नृप विद्यासु निरूढिमागता ।
कथमेत्य मतिर्विपर्ययं करिणी पङ्कमिवावसीदति ॥

Then Bhima, who found his beloved wife's words both   1
pleasing and profound, addressed the king in a
powerful speech full of strong arguments.

"Considering the matter from every angle, out of   2
affection for us, the proud woman has delivered an
accomplished oration, a speech to astonish Brihaspati,
lord of speech, himself.

Though statecraft is difficult to fathom, one may master   3
it through careful study of the authorities, just as one
can enter an impassable lake once a passageway has
been built. But in both cases, a person who can set
forth the true and proper path for others to follow is
hard to find.

In this trenchant speech that promises beneficial results,   4
although it is distasteful to those who have lost their
strength, I see great efficacy in small compass, as in a
potent drug.

This pleasing speech should please you too, since you   5
prize virtue. And surely any wise man who values
virtue judges a speech by its merit and not by who has
spoken it!

King, how can your discriminating intellect that has   6
mastered the four knowledge systems—critical
reasoning, study of the Vedas, economics, and
government—now behave in this contrary fashion,
like an elephant sinking in mire?[1]

७ विधुरं किमतः परं पररैवगीतां गमिते दशामिमाम् ।
अवसीदति यत्सुरैरपि त्वयि संभावितवृत्ति पौरुषम् ॥

८ द्विषतामुदयः सुमेधसा गुरुरस्वन्ततरः सुमर्षणः ।
न महानपि भूतिमिच्छता फलसंपत्प्रवणः परिक्षयः ॥

९ अचिरेण परस्य भूयसीं विपरीतां विगणय्य चात्मनः ।
क्षययुक्तिमुपेक्षते कृती कुरुते तत्प्रतिकारमन्यथा ॥

१० अनुपालयतामुदेष्यतीं प्रभुशक्तिं द्विषतामनीहया ।
अपयान्त्यचिरान्महीभुजां जननिर्वादभयादिव श्रियः ॥

११ क्षययुक्तमपि स्वभावजं दधतं धाम शिवं समृद्धये ।
प्रणमन्त्यनपायमुत्थितं प्रतिपच्चन्द्रमिव प्रजा नृपम् ॥

१२ प्रभवः खलु कोशदण्डयोः कृतपञ्चाङ्गविनिर्णयो नयः ।
स विधेयपदेषु दक्षतां नियतिं लोक इवानुरुध्यते ॥

What could be more painful than this, that your 7
reputation for manly action, honored by the gods
themselves, has perished, now that your enemies have
reduced you to this shameful state?

A wise man wishing to prosper can easily put up with the 8
growing ascendancy of his enemies, if it will end badly
for them, but not with their decline, however great, if
it will eventually lead to their success.[2]

A clever man bides his time if he judges that the enemy 9
will soon meet with downfall, whereas the chances
of his own decline are less. When the situation is
the reverse—with the enemy rising quickly while he
himself is headed for a fall—he takes measures to
counter the course of events.

If kings remain passive and pay no heed as their enemies 10
amass wealth and military resources, all their royal
fortune will soon desert them, as though fearing a
public scandal.[3]

A king's resources for power may be weakened, yet his 11
subjects will bow to him if he steadily applies himself
to building them up, with his innate and beneficial
energy unharmed, just as men worship the new
moon, rising and continuing to grow with its natural,
auspicious light.[4]

Policy firmly formulated after carefully considering the 12
five points of deliberation is the foundation of a king's
treasury and army. But policy depends on the ability
to act quickly and efficiently, just as surely as common
men depend on fate for success.[5]

१३ अभिमानवतो मनस्विनः प्रियमुच्चैः पदमारुरुक्षतः ।
विनिपातनिवर्तनक्षमं मतमालम्बनमात्मपौरुषम् ॥

१४ विपदो ऽभिभवन्त्यविक्रमं रहयत्यापदुपेतमायितिः ।
नियता लघुता निरायतेरगरीयान्न पदं नृपश्रियः ॥

१५ तदलं प्रतिपक्षमुन्नतेरवलम्ब्य व्यवसायवन्ध्यताम् ।
निवसन्ति पराक्रमाश्रया न विषादेन समं समृद्धयः ॥

१६ अथ चेदवधिः प्रतीक्ष्यते कथमाविष्कृतजिह्मवृत्तिना ।
धृतराष्ट्रसुतेन सुत्यजाश्चिरमास्वाद्य नरेन्द्रसंपदः ॥

१७ द्विषता विहितं त्वयाथवा यदि लब्धा पुनरात्मनः पदम् ।
जननाथ तवानुजन्मनां कृतमाविष्कृतपौरुषैर्भुजैः ॥

१८ मदसिक्तमुखैर्मृगाधिपः करिभिर्वर्तयते स्वयं हतैः ।
लघयन्खलु तेजसा जगन्न महानिच्छति भूतिमन्यतः ॥

When a high-minded and self-respecting man aspires to   13
attain a coveted and worthy position, he must depend
on his own effort as the only resource for averting
failure.

Misfortune overcomes the man who fails to act; one beset   14
by misfortune has no future prospects; he who has no
hope for the future is fated to be insignificant; a man
of little importance can never be the abode of royal
fortune.[6]

Therefore, put an end to your lack of resolution, that   15
enemy of advancement! Success arises from bold
action, and does not keep company with despondency.

If you are waiting out the stipulated time of exile, how can   16
you hope that Dhritarashtra's son,* who has shown
himself to be a cheat, will readily give up the privileges
of royalty that he has so long enjoyed?

If, on the other hand, you expect to receive back your   17
kingdom when your enemy returns it, my king, what
use are your brothers' arms, that have performed so
many heroic deeds?

The lion, king of beasts, lives on rutting elephants that he   18
has killed himself. The great man who towers over the
whole world with his might does not depend on others
for increasing his power.

---

* Duryodhana.

१९ अभिमानधनस्य गत्वैररसुभिः स्थासु यशश्चिचीषतः ।
अचिरांशुविलासचञ्चला ननु लक्ष्मीः फलमानुषङ्गिकम् ॥

२० ज्वलितं न हिरण्यरेतसं चयमास्कन्दति भस्मनां जनः ।
अभिभूतिभयादसूनतः सुखमुज्झन्ति न धाम मानिनः ॥

२१ किमपेक्ष्य फलं पयोधरान्श्वनतः प्रार्थयते मृगाधिपः ।
प्रकृतिः खलु सा महीयसः सहते नान्यसमुन्नतिं यया ॥

२२ कुरु तन्मतिमेव विक्रमे नृप निर्धूय तमः प्रमादजम् ।
ध्रुवमेतदवेहि विद्विषां त्वदनुत्साहहता विपत्तयः ॥

२३ द्विरदानिव दिग्विभावितांश्चतुरस्तोयनिधीनिवायतः ।
प्रसहेत रणे तवानुजान्द्विषतां कः शतमन्युतेजसः ॥

२४ ज्वलतस्तव जातवेदसः सततं वैरिकृतस्य चेतसि ।
विदधातु शमं शिवेतरा रिपुनारीनयनाम्बुसंततिः ॥

२५ इति दर्शितविक्रियं सुतं मरुतः कोपपरीतमानसम् ।
उपसान्त्वयितुं महीपतिर्द्विरदं दुष्टमिवोपचक्रमे ॥

२६ अपवर्जितविप्लवे शुचौ हृदयग्राहिणि मङ्गलास्पदे ।
विमला तव विस्तरे गिरां मतिरादर्श इवाभिदृश्यते ॥

To a man who values self-respect above all, to one who   19
would give up transient life to gain lasting fame,
wealth is fickle as a flash of lightning and surely no
more than an incidental gain!

People will tread on a heap of ashes, but not on a blazing   20
fire. So men of self-respect, for fear of disgrace, are
ready to give up their lives, but not their fierce pride.

What does the king of beasts expect to gain when he   21
springs at thundering clouds? It is, after all, the nature
of the great man not to tolerate the rise of his enemies.

Therefore, king, shake off the delusion caused by   22
misjudgment. Set your mind on bold action.
Understand that your enemies' downfall has been
delayed solely by your indecision.

Who among your enemies is capable of withstanding   23
your illustrious brothers, warriors endowed with
the fighting spirit of Indra, as they charge forward in
battle, like those elephants celebrated to the horizons,
or the four great oceans?[7]

May the fire that steadily burns in your heart, kindled by   24
our enemies, be quenched by the unending tears of
their grieving women!"

When Bhima, overcome by anger, had thus expressed his   25
agitation, the king began to pacify him like a trainer
calming an elephant run amok.

"Your flawless intellect is reflected in your speech, which   26
is free of logical fallacies and grammatical errors, as in
a clear, polished mirror, pleasing and propitious.[8]

२७ स्फुटता न पदैरपाकृता न च न स्वीकृतमर्थगौरवम् ।
रचिता पृथगर्थता गिरां न च सामर्थ्यमपोहितं क्वचित् ॥

२८ उपपत्तिरुदाहृता बलादनुमानेन न चागमः क्षतः ।
इदमीदृगनीदृगाशयः प्रसभं वक्तुमुपक्रमेत कः ॥

२९ अवितृप्ततया तथापि मे हृदयं निर्णयमेव धावति ।
अवसाययितुं क्षमाः सुखं न विधेयेषु विशेषसंपदः ॥

३० सहसा विदधीत न क्रियामविवेकः परमापदां पदम् ।
वृणते हि विमृश्यकारिणं गुणलुब्धाः स्वयमेव संपदः ॥

३१ अभिवर्षति यो ऽनुपालयन्विधिबीजानि विवेकवारिणा ।
स सदा फलशालिनीं क्रियां शरदं लोक इवाधितिष्ठति ॥

३२ शुचि भूषयति श्रुतं वपुः प्रशमस्तस्य भवत्यलंक्रिया ।
प्रशमाभरणं पराक्रमः स नयापादितसिद्धिभूषणः ॥

Your words are absolutely clear, yet richly charged with   27
meaning. Each utterance carries its own sense, yet
nowhere is the contextual force obscured.

You have presented your case forcefully, with supporting   28
arguments, yet your reasoning does not contradict
the authoritative texts. Could a man who lacked your
conviction have spoken as convincingly as you have,
and on the spur of the moment?

Even so, my heart is not satisfied, and continues to look   29
for the right decision. In undertakings that demand
action it is not easy to sift through the complex
gradations of strategy.

A man should not act in haste; lack of discrimination is   30
the prime source of misfortune. Prosperity loves the
virtues, and will of its own accord choose the man who
thinks before he acts.[9]

He who nurtures the seed of his plans for the future and   31
waters it with judicious deliberation is sure to harvest
the rich fruit of action like the prudent farmer who
gathers a bountiful harvest in autumn.

Pure knowledge adorns a man's body, acquired by the   32
study of the sacred texts; a calm spirit is the ornament
of learning; decisive action adorns the calm spirit;
success achieved through policy based on right
conduct is action's ornament.[10]

३३ मतिभेदतमस्तिरोहिते गहने कृत्यविधौ विवेकिनाम् ।
सुकृतः परिशुद्ध आगमः कुरुते दीप इवार्थदर्शनम् ॥

३४ स्पृहणीयगुणैर्महात्मभिश्चरिते वर्त्मनि यच्छतां मनः ।
विधिहेतुरहेतुरागसां विनिपातो ऽपि समः समुन्नतेः ॥

३५ शिवमौपयिकं गरीयसीं फलनिष्पत्तिमदूषितायतिम् ।
विगणय्य नयन्ति पौरुषं विजितक्रोधरया जिगीषवः ॥

३६ अपनेयमुदेतुमिच्छता तिमिरं रोषमयं धिया पुरः ।
अविभिद्य निशाकृतं तमः प्रभया नांशुमताप्युदीयते ॥

३७ बलवानपि कोपजन्मनस्तमसो नाभिभवं रुणद्धि यः ।
क्षयपक्ष इवैन्दवीः कलाः सकला हन्ति स शक्तिसंपदः ॥

३८ समवृत्तिरुपैति मार्दवं समये यश्च तनोति तिग्मताम् ।
अधितिष्ठति लोकमोजसा स विवस्वानिव मेदिनीपतिः ॥

When the darkness of disagreement obscures   33
and complicates the course of action, science
carefully studied and comprehended helps men of
discrimination perceive the right solution, as a bright
lamp, well placed and burning steadily, illumines
objects in the dark.[11]

When men are determined to emulate the conduct of   34
great men of excellent character, even failure equals
success, for it is blameless, caused merely by the
vagaries of fortune.

Would-be conquerors must first conquer the   35
overpowering force of anger; then, making sure that
the accomplishment of their goal will yield beneficial
and substantial results, they should direct their manly
efforts toward determining favorable means.[12]

A king who aspires to eminence must first dispel the   36
obscuring darkness of anger with the light of a
discriminating intellect. Even the sun does not rise
until it has dispelled the darkness of night with its
light.

Even a strong ruler ruins all his means to power when   37
he fails to resist the assault of delusion arising from
anger, just as the dark fortnight destroys all the digits
of the moon.

The flexible, even-handed monarch, who is gentle or fierce   38
as occasion demands, rules over the earth with his
powerful brilliance, like the sun.

३९ क्व चिराय परिग्रहः श्रियां क्व च दुष्टेन्द्रियवाजिवश्यता ।
शरदभ्रचलाश्चलेन्द्रियैरसुरक्षा हि बहुच्छलाः श्रियः ॥

४० किमसामयिकं वितन्वता मनसः क्षोभमुपात्तरंहसः ।
क्रियते पतिरुच्चकैरपां भवता धीरतयाधरीकृतः ॥

४१ श्रुतमप्यधिगम्य ये रिपून्विनयन्ते न शरीरजन्मनः ।
जनयन्त्यचिराय संपदामयशस्ते खलु चापलाश्रयम् ॥

४२ अतिपातितकालसाधना स्वशरीरेन्द्रियवर्गतापनी ।
जनवन्न भवन्तमक्षमा नयसिद्धेरपनेतुमर्हति ॥

४३ उपकारकमायतेर्भृशं प्रसवः कर्मफलस्य भूरिणः ।
अनपायि निबर्हणं द्विषां न तितिक्षासममस्ति साधनम् ॥

४४ प्रणतिप्रवणान्विहाय नः सहजस्नेहनिबद्धचेतसः ।
प्रणमन्ति सदा सुयोधनं प्रथमे मानभृतां न वृष्णयः ॥

४५ सुहृदः सहजास्तथेतरे मतमेषां न विलङ्घयन्ति ये ।
विनयादिव यापयन्ति ते धृतराष्ट्रात्मजमात्मसिद्धये ॥

४६ अभियोग इमान्महीभुजो भवता तस्य ततः कृतावधेः ।
प्रविघाटयिता समुत्पतन्हरिदश्वः कमलाकरानिव ॥

How can a man hold onto royal fortune for long when he 39
is himself in the hold of those wild horses, the organs
of sense? Treacherous fortune, fleeting as an autumn
cloud, quickly slips away from men whose senses are
fickle.

Why betray the untimely agitation of an excited mind? 40
Why raise the status of the ocean, which you once
surpassed on account of your composure?

Men who have studied science, yet fail to discipline the 41
passions, enemies born of a man's own body, soon
taint royal fortune with the stigma of infidelity.[13]

A quick temper makes a man neglect the right opportunity 42
and means of action, hurts his body and senses. Do
not let anger deprive you of the success gained from
sound policy, as if you were some common man.

Nothing equals patience as the sure means for the 43
destruction of one's enemies, a means that leads to
good outcomes in the future and produces all kinds of
success in one's actions.

The warriors of the Vrishni clan, first among men of self- 44
respect, hearts bound to us by natural affection,[14]
will not abandon us, who have always held them in
respect, nor will they ever bow to Duryodhana.

In addition to the Vrishnis, our friends by ties of kinship[15] 45
and others in harmony with their views will restrain or
stall Dhritarashtra's son.

He has set a time for the end of your exile. If you attack 46
him now, you will split these kings apart, as the rising
sun breaks open the petals of lotuses.

४७ उपजापसहान्विलङ्घयन्स विधाता नृपतीन्मदोद्धतः ।
सहते न जनो ऽप्यधःक्रियां किमु लोकाधिकधाम राजकम् ॥

४८ असमापितकृत्यसंपदां हतवेगं विनयेन तावता ।
प्रभवन्त्यभिमानशालिनां मदमुत्तम्भयितुं विभूतयः ॥

४९ मदमानसमुद्धतं नृपं न वियुङ्क्ते नियमेन मूढता ।
अतिमूढ उदस्यते नयान्नयहीनादपरज्यते जनः ॥

५० अपरागसमीरणेरितः क्रमशीर्णाकुलमूलसंततिः ।
सुकरस्तरुवत्सहिष्णुना रिपुरुन्मूलयितुं महानपि ॥

५१ अणुरप्युपहन्ति विग्रहः प्रभुमन्तःप्रकृतिप्रकोपजः ।
अखिलं हि हिनस्ति भूधरं तरुशाखान्तनिघर्षजो ऽनलः ॥

५२ मतिमान्विनयप्रमाथिनः समुपेक्षेत समुन्नतिं द्विषः ।
सुजयः खलु तादृगन्तरे विपदन्ता ह्यविनीतसंपदः ॥

५३ लघुवृत्तितया भिदां गतं बहिरन्तश्च नृपस्य मण्डलम् ।
अभिभूय हरत्यनन्तरः शिथिलं कूलमिवापगारयः ॥

Drunk with pride, he will surely insult the kings and make   47
them vulnerable to our offers. Even a common man
does not tolerate insult; how much less do kings,
whose honor is superior to that of other men?

When arrogant men have failed to achieve their goals,   48
power and wealth will stiffen the pride that had been
restrained only by false civility.

A king who is swollen with pride invariably falls prey to   49-50
folly; a fool is deserted by right policy; a king who fails
to rule according to right policy alienates his subjects.
A patient person can easily uproot even a great enemy
rocked by the winds of unpopularity, and his ministers
and officers are estranged from him—a tree shaken by
the wind, with its roots gradually cut and loosened.[16]

Even a small quarrel arising from anger among a king's   51
officers is enough to ruin him. A fire born from the
friction of twigs can burn an entire mountain.

A shrewd man patiently endures the ascent of a wayward   52
enemy. A chance will come to easily defeat him,
since the good fortune of the wayward always ends in
misfortune.

A neighboring king will overcome another's domain, both   53
his intimates and the people at large, if his offensive
conduct has disaffected them from him.[17] And then he
will carry off all, as the current sweeps away an eroded
riverbank."

५४ अनुशासतमित्यनाकुलं नयवर्माकुलमर्जुनाग्रजम् ।
स्वयमर्थ इवाभिवाञ्छितस्तमभीयाय पराशरात्मजः ॥

५५ मधुरैरवशानि लम्भयन्नपि तिर्यञ्जि शमं निरीक्षितैः ।
परितः पटु बिभ्रदेनसां दहनं धाम विलोकनक्षमम् ॥

५६ सहसोपगतः सविस्मयं तपसां सूतिरसूतिरापदाम् ४ ।
दद्दशे जगतीभुजा मुनिः स वपुष्मानिव पुण्यसंचयः ॥

५७ अथोच्चकैरासनतः पराध्यदुद्यन्स धूतारुणवल्कलाग्रः ।
रराज कीर्णाकपिशांशुजालः शृङ्गात्सुमेरोरिव तिग्मरश्मिः ॥

५८ अवहितहृदयो विधाय सो ऽर्हा-
मृषिवट्टषिप्रवरे गुरूपदिष्टाम् ।
तदनुमतमलंचकार पश्चा-
त्प्रशम इव श्रुतमासनं नरेन्द्रः ॥

५९ व्यक्तोदितस्मितमयूखविभासितोष्ठ-
स्तिष्ठन्मुनेरभिमुखं स विकीर्णधाम्नः ।
तन्वन्तमिद्धमभितो गुरुमंशुजालं
लक्ष्मीमुवाह सकलस्य शशाङ्कमूर्तेः ॥

While Yudhishthira was lucidly explaining the way of   54
politics to Arjuna's agitated elder brother, Vyasa, son
of Parashara, arrived before him, like the very object
that he longed for.

. Arriving suddenly the sage—with a gentle gaze that could   55-56
calm even wild beasts, encircled by a dazzling halo
capable of burning evil, yet lovely to behold, fount
of austerity and nemesis of misfortune—appeared
before the king like the store of meritorious deeds
incarnate.

Rising from his rich and lofty throne, the ends of his tawny   57
bark cloth[18] swaying, the king shone like the sun rising
from the crest of Mount Sumeru, streaming rosy rays
of light.

His mind focused on courteous attention, the king   58
welcomed the foremost of sages with the customary
reception worthy of the sage. Then at his bidding he
adorned his throne once more, as tranquility graces
knowledge of the scriptures.

Seated facing the sage who was encircled with a ring of   59
blazing light, Yudhishthira, his lips glowing brightly
with a blossoming smile, had the radiant beauty of the
full moon facing the planet Jupiter.*

---

* "Jupiter," Brihaspati, is also the name of the preceptor of the
gods (*devas*).

37

CHAPTER 3

Vyasa's Counsel

१ ततः शरच्चन्द्रकराभिरामैरुत्सर्पिभिः प्रांशुमिवांशुजालैः ।
बिभ्राणमानीलरुचं पिशङ्गीर्जटास्तडित्वन्तमिवाम्बुवाहम् ॥

२ प्रसादलक्ष्मीं दधतं समग्रां वपुःप्रकर्षेण जनातिगेन ।
प्रसह्य चेतःसु समासजन्तमसंस्तुतानामपि भावमार्द्रम् ॥

३ अनुद्धताकारतया विविक्तां तन्वन्तमन्तःकरणस्य वृत्तिम् ।
माधुर्यविस्रम्भविशेषभाजा कृतोपसंभाषमिवेक्षितेन ॥

४ धर्मात्मजो धर्मनिबन्धिनीनां प्रसूतिमेनःप्रणुदां श्रुतीनाम् ।
हेतुं तदभ्यागमने परीप्सुः सुखोपविष्टं मुनिमाबभाषे ॥

५ अनाप्तपुण्योपचयैर्दुरापा फलस्य निर्धूतरजाः सवित्री ।
तुल्या भवद्दर्शनसंपदेषा वृष्टेर्दिवो वीतबलाहकायाः ॥

६ अद्य क्रियाः कामदुघाः क्रतूनां सत्याशिषः संप्रति भूमिदेवाः ।
आ संसृतेरस्मि जगत्सु जातस्त्वय्यागते यद्बहुमानपात्रम् ॥

७ श्रियं विकर्षत्यपहन्त्यघानि श्रेयः परिस्रौति तनोति कीर्तिम् ।
संदर्शनं लोकगुरोरमोघं तवात्मयोनेरिव किं न धत्ते ॥

With a gleaming dark body and tawny matted hair,   1–4
the sage Vyasa shone like a black cloud laced
with lightning, his tall figure elevated by the light
streaming from him, soft as the rays of the autumn
moon. He embodied perfect peace, and his compelling
appearance, with its superhuman beauty, kindled
affection even in strangers' hearts. His gentle
expression proclaimed the purity of his heart, and
he seemed to converse with men with a kindly gaze
inspiring trust. When the sage was comfortably
seated, Yudhishthira, Dharma's son, addressed him,
keen to know the reason for his visit—him the very
source of the scriptures that establish dharma and
destroy guilt.[1]
"Your visit is like a shower of rain from a cloudless sky,   5
which settles the dust of passion and fulfills all
wishes—a blessing impossible for men to gain without
a store of religious merit.[2]
Today, with your arrival, all my rites of sacrifice have   6
borne fruit, the blessings of Brahmans have come
true, and my praises will be sung in all the worlds till
the end of time.
It attracts good fortune, repels evil, yields the highest   7
good, grants fame—the sight of you, guru of the
world, is unfailing, like the sight of Brahma the self-
created. Is there anything it cannot provide?

८ श्रोतन्मयूखे ऽपि हिमद्युतौ मे ननिर्वृतं निर्वृतिमेति चक्षुः ।
समुज्झितज्ञातिवियोगखेदं त्वत्संनिधावुच्छ्वसतीव चेतः ॥

९ निरास्पदं प्रश्नकुतूहलित्वमस्मास्वधीनं किमु निःस्पृहाणाम् ।
तथापि कल्याणकरीं गिरं ते मां श्रोतुमिच्छा मुखरीकरोति ॥

१० इत्युक्तवानुक्तिविशेषरम्यं मनः समाधाय जयोपपत्तौ ।
उदारचेता गिरमित्युदारां द्वैपायनेनाभिदधे नरेन्द्रः ॥

११ चिचीषतां जन्मवतामलघ्वीं यशोवतंसामुभयत्र भूतिम् ।
अभ्यर्हिता बन्धुषु तुल्यरूपा वृत्तिर्विशेषेण तपोधनानाम् ॥

१२ तथापि निघ्नं नृप तावकीनैः प्रह्लीकृतं मे हृदयं गुणौघैः ।
वीतस्पृहाणामपि मुक्तिभाजां भवन्ति भव्येषु हि पक्षपाताः ॥

१३ सुता न यूयं किमु तस्य राज्ञः सुयोधनं वा न गुणैरतीताः ।
यस्त्यक्तवान्वः स वृथा बलाद्वा मोहं विधत्ते विषयाभिलाषः ॥

१४ जहातु नैनं कथमर्थसिद्धिः संशय्य कर्णादिषु तिष्ठते यः ।
असाधुयोगा हि जयान्तरायाः प्रमाथिनीनां विपदां पदानि ॥

My vision, whose thirst even the moon's ambrosial rays   8
cannot quench, finds perfect repose in your presence.
My heart breathes again, freed at last from the sorrow
of parting from loved ones.

It is surely meaningless to ask why you have come. What,   9
after all, could one who is beyond desire wish to obtain
from the likes of me? And yet, the desire to hear you
utter words of blessing moves me to speak."

When the noble king had delivered this artfully worded   10
speech, Vyasa Dvaipayana, his mind focused on
achieving victory, spoke these noble words:

"Men who seek supreme power, crowned by fame, in both   11–12
this world and the other, must treat all their friends
equally; the rule applies even more strictly to ascetics.
And yet, king, won over by your array of virtues, my
heart is bound to you by devotion. Even those freed
from desire and seeking liberation become attached to
good men.

Are you and your brothers also not the sons of   13
Dhritarashtra, the old Kuru king? Do you not surpass
Duryodhana in virtue? Did Dhritarashtra abandon
you arbitrarily, or was he forced to do so? Greed can
drive men mad.

Success will surely desert him, since he depends on Karna   14
and his ilk for political counsel. Alliance with the
wicked is the sure nemesis of victory, and the source
of catastrophic calamity.[3]

१५ पथश्च्युतायां समितौ रिपूणां धर्म्यां दधानेन धुरं चिराय ।
त्वया विपत्स्वप्यविपत्तिरम्यमाविष्कृतं प्रेम परं गुणेषु ॥

१६ विधाय विध्वंसनमात्मनीनं शमैकवृत्तेर्भवतश्छलेन ।
प्रकाशितत्वन्मतिशीलसाराः कृतोपकारा इव विद्विषस्ते ॥

१७ लभ्या धरित्री तव विक्रमेण ज्यायांश्च वीर्यास्त्रबलैर्विपक्षः ।
अतः प्रकर्षाय विधिर्विधेयः प्रकर्षतन्त्रा हि रणे जयश्रीः ॥

१८ त्रिःसप्तकृत्वो जगतीपतीनां हन्ता गुरुर्यस्य स जामदग्न्यः ।
वीर्यावधूतः स्म तदा विवेद प्रकर्षमाधारवशं गुणानाम् ॥

१९ यस्मिन्ननैश्वर्यकृतव्यलीकः पराभवं प्राप्त इवान्तको ऽपि ।
धुन्वन्धनुः कस्य रणे न कुर्यान्मनो भयैकप्रवणं स भीष्मः ॥

२० सृजन्तमाजाविषुसंहतीर्वः सहेत कोपज्ज्वलितं गुरुं कः ।
परिस्फुरल्लोलशिखाग्रजिह्वं जगज्जिघत्सन्तमिवान्तवह्निम् ॥

When your enemies violated the law in the assembly   15
hall, you persisted in upholding the yoke of dharma.
You did well to passionately cleave to virtue even in
misfortune.

In bringing about your downfall through deceit, even   16
though you practice peace, your enemies have brought
harm upon themselves. By illuminating your good
conduct and strength of mind, they have, in fact, done
you a favor.

The earth can be won back only through bold military   17
action, but the enemy is stronger in martial spirit,
arms, and troops. We must therefore devise a plan to
gain superiority, for victory in battle is obtained only
through superior military strength.

The sage Jamadagni's son Parashurama, instructor of   18
the science of weapons, annihilated the kings of this
earth twenty-one times over. Only when overcome in
combat by the prowess of his pupil Bhishma did he
understand that excellence of attributes depends on
the person who possesses them.[4]

Whose heart does not quake with fear when he hears   19
Bhishma twanging his bow in battle, the hero who
has defeated death itself, for it has been rendered
powerless and cannot touch him?

Who among you can withstand your teacher Drona, when,   20
blazing with anger, he shoots a volley of arrows in
battle, like the fire of the end of time come to swallow
the universe, its dazzling tongues of flame flickering?

२१ निरीक्ष्य संरम्भनिरस्तधैर्यं राधेयमाराधितजामदग्न्यम् ।
असंस्तुतेषु प्रसभं भयेषु जायेत मृत्योरपि पक्षपातः ॥

२२ यया समासादितसाधनेन सुदुश्वरामाचरता तपस्याम् ।
एते दुरापं समवाप्य वीर्यमुन्मूलितारः कपिकेतनेन ॥

२३ महत्त्वयोगाय महामहिम्नामाराधनीं तां नृप देवतानाम् ।
दातुं प्रदानोचित भूरिधाम्नीमुपागतः सिद्धिमिवास्मि विद्याम् ॥

२४ इत्युक्तवन्तं व्रज साधयेति प्रमाणयन्वाक्यमजातशत्रोः ।
प्रसेदिवांसं तमुपाससाद वसन्निवान्ते विनयेन जिष्णुः ॥

२५ निर्याय विद्याथ दिनादिरम्याद्विम्बादिवार्कस्य मुखान्महर्षेः ।
पार्थाननं वह्निकणावदाता दीप्तिः स्फुरत्पद्ममिवाभिपेदे ॥

२६ योगं च तं योग्यतमाय तस्मै तपःप्रभावाद्वितितार सद्यः ।
येनास्य तत्त्वेषु कृते ऽवभासे समुन्मिमीलेव चिराय चक्षुः ॥

46

At the sight of Radha's son, the warrior Karna, who   21
    learned the science of arms by serving Parashurama
    and whose battle fury throws his enemies into abject
    confusion, death itself will make the acquaintance of
    fear.[5]

King, to help you gain superior military power, I have   22-23
    come to give you, who are worthy of such a gift, secret
    knowledge, a mantra of great efficacy, the means for
    propitiating extremely powerful gods, in effect, the
    very embodiment of the achievement of your goal.[6]
    Employing this knowledge, Arjuna, hero with the
    monkey banner,[7] will perform severe austerities to
    obtain the means to your end. Acquiring invincible
    martial power, he will annihilate these men."

When the sage had spoken, Yudhishthira, peerless in   24
    battle, said to Arjuna the brave, "Go, and receive
    the sage's teaching!" and Vyasa was pleased. At his
    brother's command, Arjuna humbly approached
    the sage like a pupil approaching his teacher for
    instruction in sacred knowledge.

Then, as a beam emerges at daybreak from the glowing   25
    orb of the sun and enters a blossoming lotus, the
    secret mantra, bright as a spark of fire, issued from the
    sage's mouth and entered Arjuna's.

At once, through his ascetic power the sage imparted   26
    that yogic knowledge to the hero, who was perfectly
    qualified to receive it, and Arjuna's eyes were opened
    with abiding insight to directly perceive the very
    component elements of the cosmos.[8]

२७ आकारमाशंसितभूरिलाभं दधानमन्तःकरणानुरूपम् ।
नियोजयिष्यन्विजयोदये तं तपःसमाधौ मुनिरित्युवाच ॥

२८ अनेन योगेन विवृद्धतेजा निजां परस्मै पदवीमयच्छन् ।
समाचराचारमुपात्तशस्त्रो जपोपवासाभिषवैर्मुनीनाम् ॥

२९ करिष्यसे यत्र सुदुश्चराणि प्रसत्तये गोत्रभिदस्तपांसि ।
शिलोच्चयं चारुशिलोच्चयं तमेष क्षणान्नेष्यति गुह्यकस्त्वाम् ॥

३० इति ब्रुवाणेन महेन्द्रसूनुं महर्षिणा तेन तिरोबभूवे ।
तं राजराजानुचरो ऽस्य साक्षात्प्रदेशमादेश^र् इवाधितस्थौ ॥

३१ कृतानतिर्व्याहृतसान्त्ववादे जातस्पृहः पुण्यजनः स जिष्णौ ।
इयाय सख्याविव संप्रसादं विश्वासयत्याशु सतां हि योगः ॥

३२ अथोष्णभासेव सुमेरुकुञ्जान्विहीयमानानुदयाय तेन ।
बृहद्द्युतीन्दुःखकृतात्मलाभं तमः शनैः पाण्डुसुतान्प्रपेदे ॥

The sage spoke to him whose handsome figure, like his   27
    spirit, promised unqualified success, instructing
    him in the observance of ascetic practice that would
    ultimately lead to victory in war.

"With your brilliant heroic energy increased by this yogic   28
    knowledge, practice the ascetic's way of life, with rites
    of chanting, fasting, and bathing. Bear weapons, and
    never yield your place to anyone!

In an instant, this *guhyaka** mountain spirit will lead you   29
    to a mountain with beautiful peaks, where you will
    practice severe austerities to please the god Indra,
    breaker of mountains!"[9]

Having spoken thus to Indra's son, the eminent sage   30
    vanished, and in his place there appeared before
    Arjuna a *guhyaka,* servant of Kubera, god of wealth, as
    if he were the sage's instruction incarnate.[10]

The mountain spirit bowed, and, on hearing the friendly   31
    greeting of Arjuna the conqueror, was drawn to him
    as if to a trusted friend. The company of good men
    quickly inspires confidence.

Then, as he prepared to leave them, setting out on   32
    his mission for victory, like the rising sun leaving
    Mount Sumeru, grief, struggling to take shape,
    slowly descended on the brilliant sons of Pandu, like
    darkness falling slowly on the mountain peaks.

---

* A Himalayan mountain spirit, a guardian of treasure.

३३ असंशयालोचितकार्यनुन्नः प्रेम्णा समानीय विभज्यमानः ।
तुल्याद्विभागादिव तन्मनोभिर्दुःखातिभारो ऽपि लघुः स मेने ॥

३४ धैर्येण विश्वास्यतया महर्षेस्तीव्रादरातिप्रभवाच्च मन्योः ।
वीर्यं च विद्वत्सु सुते मघोनः स तेषु न स्थानमवाप शोकः ॥

३५ तान्भूरिधाम्नश्वतुरो ऽपि दूरं विहाय यामानिव वासरस्य ।
एकौघभूतं तदशर्म कृष्णां विभावरीं ध्वान्तमिव प्रपेदे ॥

३६ तुषारलेखाकुलितोत्पलाभे पर्यश्रुणी मङ्गलभङ्गभीरुः ।
अगूढभावापि विलोकने सा न लोचने मीलयितुं विषेहे ॥

३७ अकृत्रिमप्रेमरसाभिरामं रामार्पितं दृष्टिविलोभि दृष्टम् ।
मनःप्रसादाञ्जलिना निकामं जग्राह पाथेयमिवेन्द्रसूनुः ॥

३८ धैर्यावसादेन हृतप्रसादा वन्यद्विपेनेव निदाघसिन्धुः ।
निरुद्धबाष्पोदयसन्नकण्ठमुवाच कृच्छ्रादिति राजपुत्री ॥

50

Although they dismissed it at first, with a firm   33
  commitment to the task before them, when it came
  back to them, it was as though the heavy burden of
  grief, shared equally among them in brotherly love,
  became lighter in their hearts.

Because they were strong of mind, with faith in the sage,   34
  intense anger toward the enemy, and knowledge of
  the prowess of Indra's son—because of all this, grief
  could not gain a foothold in the brothers.

Leaving the four shining warriors far behind, like the four   35
  bright watches of the day, grief gathered into a mass
  and overpowered Krishna Draupadi, the dark queen,
  as total darkness engulfs the night in the dark half of
  the month.

Although she could not hide her emotion as she gazed at   36
  Arjuna, for fear of manifesting a bad omen she dared
  not close her eyes, which were brimming with tears,
  like lotuses lined with frost.

As his eager eyes met the woman's captivating gaze, sweet   37
  with the flow of true love, Arjuna's joyful heart served
  as palms cupped in courtesy, to welcome a loving gift
  of delicious provision for the journey.[11]

Her composure destroyed by loss of self-control, like a   38
  summer stream muddied by a wild elephant, and in a
  voice choked by sobs, the princess spoke these words
  but barely:

३९ मग्नां द्विषच्छद्मनि पङ्कभूते संभावनां भूतिमिवोद्धरिष्यन् ।
आधिद्विषामा तपसां प्रसिद्धेरस्मद्विना मा भृशमुन्मनीभूः ॥

४० यशो ऽधिगन्तुं सुखलिप्सया वा मनुष्यसंख्यामतिवर्तितुं वा ।
निरुत्सुकानामभियोगभाजां समुत्सुकेवाङ्कमुपैति सिद्धिः ॥

४१ लोकं विधात्रा विहितस्य गोप्तुं क्षत्रस्य मुष्णन्वसु जैत्रमोजः ।
तेजस्विताया विजयैकवृत्तेर्निघ्नन्निियं प्राणमिवाभिमानम् ॥

४२ व्रीडानतैराप्तजनोपनीतः संशय्य कृच्छ्रेण नृपैः प्रपन्नः ।
वितानभूतं विततं पृथिव्यां यशः समूहन्निव दिग्विकीर्णम् ॥

४३ वीर्यावदानेषु कृतावमर्षस्तन्वन्नभूतामिव संप्रतीतिम् ।
कुर्वन्प्रयामक्षयमायतीनामर्कत्विषामह्र इवावशेषः ॥

४४ प्रसह्य यो ऽस्मासु परैः प्रयुक्तः स्मर्तुं न शक्यः किमुताधिकर्तुम् ।
नवीकरिष्यत्युपशुष्यदार्द्रः स त्वद्विना मे हृदयं निकारः ॥

"You have set out to restore, like our prosperity, our   39
honor, which lies sunken in the mire of our enemy's
plots. Until you accomplish the goal of austerities that
destroy all evil, may you not be overcome by grief at
our absence!

When a man applies himself without regret, to attain   40
fame, or wealth, or supremacy over men, success will
embrace him of its own accord, like a loving wife.

The humiliation we have endured robbed the whole   41–44
warrior class, created by Brahma to rule and guard
the world, the majesty that lives by conquest alone—
robbed it of the invincible power that is its wealth,
and destroyed the pride that is its very life. The news
was brought to kings by shamefaced friends, and
yet it was doubted. They could hardly believe it, for
that humiliation shrank to nothing a fame that had
pervaded the regions of space and canopied the earth.
The shame wiped out all memory of your famous
heroic deeds, as if they had never existed, and cut
short your future, like the evening ending the sun's
rays for the night. What our enemies forced us to
endure cannot be borne in memory—how did we
endure it in fact? Yet, though my heart might wither
in your absence, that humiliation will keep its wound
still fresh.

४५ प्राप्तो ऽभिमानव्यसनादसह्नं दन्तीव दन्तव्यसनाद्द्विकारम् ।
द्विषत्प्रतापान्तरितोरुतेजाः शरद्घनाकीर्ण इवादिरह्नः ॥

४६ सव्रीडमन्दैरिव निष्क्रियत्वान्नात्यर्थमस्त्रैरवभासमानः ।
यशःक्षयक्षीणजलार्णवाभस्त्वमन्यमाकारमिवाभिपन्नः ॥

४७ दुःशासनामर्षरजोविकीर्णैरिभिर्विनाथैरिव भाग्यनाथैः ।
केशैः कदर्थीकृतवीर्यसारः कच्चित्स एवासि धनंजयस्त्वम् ॥

४८ स क्षत्रियस्त्राणसहः सतां यस्तत्कार्मुकं कर्मसु यस्य शक्तिः ।
वहन्द्वयीं यद्घफले ऽर्थजाते करोत्यसंस्कारहतामिवोक्तिम् ॥

४९ वीतौजसः संनिधिमात्रशेषा भवत्कृतां भूतिमपेक्षमाणाः ।
समानदुःखा इव नस्त्वदीयाः सरूपतां पार्थ गुणा भजन्ते ॥

Your pride broken, you look disfigured, like an elephant 45-47
with broken tusks. Your brilliant heroism eclipsed by
the dominance of the enemies, you are like daybreak
overcast with autumn clouds. Fallen into disuse, your
weapons no longer shine, as if they were ashamed.
And you, Arjuna, no longer look resplendent with
them. Because you have lost your fame, your entire
appearance is changed, and you look like the ocean
drained of water. The strands of my hair hang
loose, disheveled by the dust of the insulting hand
with which Duhshasana dragged them. With no
one to protect them, left to the mercy of fortune,
they reproach your strength and courage. I wonder
whether you are still the same Dhanamjaya, 'winner
of wealth.'

A Kshatriya, 'warrior,' is one capable of protecting the 48
good; *kārmuka*, a 'bow,' is that which accomplishes
deeds. He who uses these words in a vague,
general sense is guilty of misusing them, without
understanding their correct etymology and the full
weight of their meaning.

Their splendor lost, reduced to mere existence, waiting for 49
you to restore their honor, in all this, as though they
shared in our grief, your virtues resemble us, son of
Pritha.

५० आक्षिप्यमाणं रिपुभिः प्रमादान्नागैरिवालूनसटं मृगेन्द्रम् ।
त्वां धूरियं योग्यतयाधिरूढा दीप्या दिनश्रीरिव तिग्मरश्मिम् ॥

५१ करोति यो ऽशेषजनातिरिक्तां संभावनामर्थवतीं क्रियाभिः ।
संसत्सु जाते पुरुषाधिकारे न पूरणी तं समुपैति संख्या ॥

५२ प्रियेषु यैः पार्थ विनोपपत्तेर्विचिन्त्यमानैः क्रममेति चेतः ।
तव प्रयातस्य जयाय तेषां क्रियादघानां मघवा विघातम् ॥

५३ मा गाश्चिरायैकचरः प्रमादं वसन्नसंबाधशिवे ऽपि देशे ।
मात्सर्यरागोपहतात्मनां हि स्खलन्ति साधुष्वपि मानसानि ॥

५४ तदाशु कुर्वन्वचनं महर्षेर्मनोरथान्नः सफलीकुरुष्व ।
प्रत्यागतं त्वास्मि कृतार्थमेव स्तनोपपीडं परिरब्धुकामा ॥

५५ उदीरितां तामिति याज्ञसेन्या नवीकृतोद्वाहितविप्रकाराम् ।
आसाद्य वाचं स भृशं दिदीपे काष्ठामुदीचीमिव तिग्मरश्मिः ॥

Because of your past fecklessness you were insulted by   50
our enemies, like a lion whose mane is trampled by
elephants. But now this yoke has fallen upon your
shoulders because you are a capable warrior, like
the sun that sustains the beauty of the day with his
brilliance.

When the subject of heroes is raised in the assembly, he   51
alone gains first rank who proves by his exploits an
effective capability beyond all other men.

Son of Pritha!* When you have set off on this mission for   52
victory, you are bound to think of us who are dear
to you, and your heart will grow sad for no apparent
reason. May Indra the bountiful dispel those sorrows
for you!

Although you will live alone for a long time in a secluded   53
place free of evil, do not be heedless, for the minds
of men gripped by envy and passion are apt to turn
violent even toward the good.[12]

Therefore, quickly fulfill the sage's command, and make   54
our wishes come true. I look forward to clasping
you to my breast when you have returned, your task
accomplished."

When he heard the words spoken by Yajnasena's   55
daughter,† words that revived and drove home the
Pandavas' humiliation at the hands of the enemy, the
hero burned with anger, as the sun blazes up when
reaching the north.

———

* A name of Kunti.
† Draupadi.

५६ अथाभिपश्यन्निव विद्विषः पुरः पुरोधसारोपितहेतिसंहतिः ।
बभार रम्यो ऽपि वपुः स भीषणं गतः क्रियां मन्त्र इवाभिचारि-
कीम् ॥

५७ अविलङ्घ्यविकर्षणं परैः प्रथितज्यारवकर्म कार्मुकम् ।
अगतावरिदृष्टिगोचरं शितनिस्त्रिंशयुजौ महेषुधी ॥

५८ यशसेव तिरोदधन्मुहुर्महसा गोत्रभिदायुधक्षतीः ।
कवचं च सरत्नमुद्वहञ्ज्वलितज्योतिरिवान्तरं दिवः ॥

५९ अलकाधिपभृत्यदर्शितं शिवमुर्वीधरवर्त्म संप्रयान् ।
हृदयानि समाविवेश स क्षणमुद्भ्राष्टदृशां तपोभृताम् ॥

६० अनुजगुरथ दिव्यं दुन्दुभिध्वानमाशाः
सुरकुसुमनिपातैर्व्योम्नि लक्ष्मीर्वितेने ।
प्रियमिव कथयिष्यन्नालिलिङ्ग स्फुरन्तीं
भुवमनिभृतवेलावीचिबाहुः पयोधिः ॥

Then, when the family priest had armed Arjuna with his   56
weapons, as if he saw his enemies before his very eyes,
the hero assumed a terrifying form, like a benign
sacred chant magically deployed for a murderous
deed.

Arjuna was equipped with a bow renowned for its exploits   57-59
and its great twang, one no enemy could withstand
once the hero had drawn it;[13] two great quivers no
enemy had ever seen,[14] with a sharp sword attached
to them; and glittering like a starlit sky, gem-studded
armor on which the cracks left from the blows of
Indra's thunderbolt were covered over with the hero's
own brilliant majesty.[15] As he set off on the auspicious
path to the Himalaya mountain, guided by the
servant of Kubera, for a moment the sight of the hero
moved even the hearts of the ascetics in the Dvaita
hermitage, and their eyes filled with tears.

The quarters of space echoed with celestial drumbeats.   60
The sky grew lovely, filled with flowers showered
by the gods. And as if he wished to whisper a sweet
secret in her ear, the ocean embraced the earth, who
quivered with joy as his arms, the restless waves,
lapped at her shore.[16]

CHAPTER 4

Autumn Landscape

१   ततः स कूजत्कलहंसमेखलां सपाकसस्याहितपाण्डुतागुणाम् ।
उपाससादोपजनं जनप्रियः प्रियामिवासादितयौवनां भुवम् ॥

२   विनम्रशालिप्रसवौघशालिनीरपेतपङ्काः ससरोरुहाम्भसः ।
ननन्द पश्यन्नुपसीम स स्थलीरुपायनीभूतशरदृणश्रियः ॥

३   निरीक्ष्यमाणा इव विस्मयाकुलैः पयोभिरुन्मीलितपद्मलोचनैः ।
हतप्रियादृष्टिविलासविभ्रमा मनो ऽस्य जह्रुः शफरीविवृत्तयः ॥

४   तुतोष पश्यन्कलमस्य सो ऽधिकं सवारिजे वारिणि रामणीयकम् ।
सुदुर्लभे नार्हति को ऽभिनन्दितुं प्रकर्षलक्ष्मीमनुरूपसंगमे ॥

५   नुनोद तस्य स्थलपद्मिनीगतं वितर्कमाविष्कृतफेनसंतति ।
अवाग्मकिञ्जल्कविभेदमुच्चकैर्विवृत्तपाठीनपराहतं पयः ॥

६   कृतोर्मिरेखं शिथिलत्वमायता शनैः शनैः शान्तरयेण वारिणा ।
निरीक्ष्य रेमे स समुद्रयोषितां तरङ्गितक्षौमविपाण्डु सैकतम् ॥

Like a lover courting a beloved girl in the bloom of youth,   1
    her girlfriends by her side, Arjuna, dear to all men,
    drew near a rural landscape, colored pale gold with
    ripened grain and laced with a girdle of chattering
    wild geese.[1]

He enjoyed the beauty of the natural scenery at the   2
    borders of the villages, a gift from autumn: rice fields
    free of mud, bowed down with abundant grain, and
    dotted with ponds blooming with lotus flowers.

Leaping minnows, more graceful than the beloved's   3
    darting glances, and intently watched by streams with
    lotus eyes opened wide, captivated his heart.

He found the rice plant lovelier in the water, surrounded   4
    by lotuses. Who does not appreciate the heightened
    beauty born of the rare union of complementary
    things?

The illusion of lotuses growing on land was dispelled when   5
    he suddenly saw water appearing, lined with foam,
    thick with pollen shaken from the stamens of lotuses
    by a catfish suddenly leaping up.

He was charmed by the sandy riverbanks scored by waves   6
    receding slowly with the thinning flow of water in
    autumn, looking like a length of rippling white silk.

७ मनोरमं प्रापितमन्तरं भ्रुवोरलंकृतं केसररेणुनाणुना ।
अलक्तताम्राधरपल्लवश्रिया समानयन्तीमिव बन्धुजीवकम् ॥

८ नवातपालोहितमाहितं मुहुर्महानिवेशौ परितः पयोधरौ ।
चकासयन्तीमरविन्दजं रजः परिश्रमाम्भःपुलकेन सर्पता ॥

९ कपोलसंश्लेषि विलोचनत्विषा विभूषयन्तीमवतंसकोत्पलम् ।
सुतेन पाण्डोः कलमस्य गोपिकां निरीक्ष्य मेने शरदः कृतार्थता ॥

१० उपारताः पश्चिमरात्रिगोचरादपारयन्तः पतितुं जवेन गाम् ।
तमुत्सुकाश्चक्कुरवेक्षणोत्सुकं गवां गणाः प्रसुतपीवरौधसः ॥

११ परीतमुक्षावजये जयश्रिया नदन्तमुच्चैः क्षतसिन्धुरोधसम् ।
ददर्श पुष्टिं दधतं स शारदीं सविग्रहं दर्पमिवाधिपं गवाम् ॥

१२ विमुच्यमानैरपि तस्य मन्थरं गवां हिमानीविशदैः कदम्बकैः ।
शरन्नदीनां पुलिनैः कुतूहलं गलद्दुकूलैर्जघनैरिवादधे ॥

१३ गतान्पशूनां सहजन्मबन्धुतां गृहाश्रयं प्रेम वनेषु बिभ्रतः ।
ददर्श गोपानुपधेनु पाण्डवः कृतानुकारानिव गोभिराजवे ॥

64

Her lovely lower lip, painted red with lac, rivaled the   7-9
midday flower,[2] flecked with fine pollen, that
decorated her forehead. The lotus pollen, rosy as the
morning sunlight, enveloping her voluptuous breasts,
shimmered from the drops of sweat appearing on
them. The brilliance of her eyes brightened the water
lily that decorated her ear and embraced her cheek.
In the woman who stood guard in the rice fields,
Pandu's son beheld autumn reaping its rewards in full.

He steadily gazed at the herds of cows returning from the   10
pasture in the late evening, gait slowed down by heavy
udders oozing milk as they longed to join their calves.

In the king bull, his body sleek in autumn, bellowing   11
loudly and pawing the riverbank, covered in glory
at his victory over his rival, Arjuna saw the pride of
autumn incarnate.

As the herds of cows, white as massed snow, were slowly   12
leaving the autumnal riverbanks, Arjuna saw in the
sands a charming likeness of women's torsos with
silken garments slipping from them.

The Pandava saw cowherds with their cattle, men who   13
loved the cows like their own siblings, and loved the
pastures as other men love the home, and he thought
the cattle must have learned their gentle ways from
their keepers.

१४ परिभ्रमन्मूर्धजषड्दुदाकुलैः स्मितोदयादर्शितदन्तकेसरैः ।
मुखैश्चलत्कुण्डलरश्मिरञ्जितैर्नवातपामृष्टसरोजचारुभिः ॥

१५ निबद्धनिःश्वासविकम्पिताधरा लता इव प्रस्फुरितैकपल्लवाः ।
व्यपोढपार्श्वैरपवर्तितत्रिका विकर्षणैः पाणिविहारहारिभिः ॥

१६ व्रजाजिरेष्वम्बुदनादशङ्किनीः शिखण्डिनामुन्मदयत्सु योषितः ।
मुहुः प्रणुन्नेषु मथां विवर्तनैर्नदत्सु कुम्भेषु मृदङ्गमन्थरम् ॥

१७ स मन्थरावल्गितपीवरस्तनीः परिश्रमक्लान्तविलोचनोत्पलाः ।
निरीक्षितुं नोपरराम बल्लवीरभिप्रनृत्ता इव वारयोषितः ॥

१८ पपात पूर्वां जहतो विजिह्मतां वृषोपभुक्तान्तिकसस्यसंपदः ।
रथाङ्गसीमन्तितसान्द्रकर्दमान्प्रसक्तसंपातपृथक्कृतान्पथः ॥

१९ जनैरुपग्राममनिन्द्यकर्मभिर्विविक्तभावेङ्गितभूषणैर्वृताः ।
भृशं ददर्शाश्रममण्डपोपमाः सपुष्पहासाः स निवेशवीरुधः ॥

The black curls of the cowherd women were bees   14–17
fluttering around faces lovely as lotuses lit up by the
rays of the morning sun. Their faces glittered with
swaying earrings, and when they smiled their teeth
appeared fine as lotus stamens. With their lower
lips trembling with suppressed breaths, the women
were like vines with leaves all fluttering, as they
pulled the ropes of butter churns with charming
motions of the hands, their hips gracefully moving
to and fro to the rhythm. In the courtyards of the
cow stalls, as the churning sticks turned round and
round, the buttermilk pots rumbled as deep as clay-
headed *mṛdaṅga* drums, and peahens went mad
with joy, thinking it was the sound of thunder.[3] And
Arjuna could not take his eyes off those women,
who seemed to dance like courtesans, their swelling
breasts heaving gently, eyes like lotuses wilted by the
exertion.

The roads were no longer impassable, and he flew along   18
them. Bulls cropped the ample grain growing in
roadside fields, cart wheels had raised ridges of caked
mud on the ground, like a parting in the hair, and a
steady flow of traffic had etched a rutted track.

In the villages Arjuna gazed reverently at huts made of   19
leaves, smiling with blossoms, and inhabited by people
ornamented by nothing more than their gestures of
perfect concentration as they went about their honest
tasks; and those homes appeared to him like the huts
of ascetics in a hermitage.

२० ततः स संप्रेक्ष्य शरदृणश्रियं शरदृणालोकनलोलचक्षुषम् ।
उवाच यक्षस्तमचोदितो ऽपि गां न हीङ्गितज्ञो ऽवसरे ऽवसीदति ॥

२१ इयं शिवाया नियतेरिवायतिः कृतार्थयन्ती जगतः फलैः क्रियाः ।
जयश्रियं पार्थ पृथूकरोतु ते शरत्प्रसन्नाम्बुरनम्बुवारिदा ॥

२२ उपैति सस्यं परिणामरम्यता नदीरनौद्धत्यमपङ्कता महीम् ।
नवैर्गुणैः संप्रति संस्तवस्थिरं तिरोहितं प्रेम घनागमश्रियः ॥

२३ पतन्ति नास्मिन्विशदाः पतत्त्रिणो धृतेन्द्रचापा न पयोदपङ्क्तयः ।
तथापि पुष्णाति नभः श्रियं परां न रम्यमाहार्यमपेक्षते गुणम् ॥

२४ विपाण्डुभिर्म्लानतया पयोधरैश्च्युताचिराभागुणहेमदामभिः ।
इयं कदम्बानिलभर्तुरत्यये न दिग्वधूनां कृशता न राजते ॥

२५ विहाय वाञ्छामुदिते मदात्ययादरक्तकण्ठस्य रुते शिखण्डिनः ।
श्रुतिः श्रयत्युन्मदहंसनिःस्वनं गुणाः प्रियत्वे ऽधिकृता न
संस्तवः ॥

Then the yaksha mountain-spirit, taking in the beauty 20
of autumn, without prompting addressed the hero,
whose eyes were dazzled by the sight of autumn's
bounty. A sensitive man always speaks out when the
time is right.[4]

"Son of Pritha! May this autumn season, of clear waters 21
and unraining clouds, and which brings to fruition the
work of men, like the maturing of a propitious fate,
enhance your all-conquering majesty!

Ripeness renders the crops beautiful, the rivers have 22
become calm, the earth is free of mud. New virtues
now draw our hearts away from the beauties of the
rainy season, so dear to us not long ago.

No white birds fly in the sky, no banks of clouds bear 23
rainbows, and yet the sky is supremely lovely. Innate
beauty does not depend on imported virtues for its
flourishing.[5]

White from lack of water, bereft of lightning, and grieving 24
at the loss of fragrant breezes wafted from *kadamba*
trees,[6] the quarters of the sky still look lovely, like
women who pine away, their golden necklaces
loosened, their breasts pale from grief at parting from
their lovers.

No longer pleased by the shrill peacock cry grown 25
cacophonous now that the mating season has ended,
the ear is now tuned to the passionate call of the wild
goose. Virtue, not familiarity, has the power to please.

२६ अमी पृथुस्तम्बभृतः पिशङ्गतां गता विपाकेन फलस्य शालयः ।
विकासि वप्राम्भसि गन्धसूचितं नमन्ति निघ्रातुमिवासितोत्पलम् ॥

२७ मृणालिनीनामनुरञ्जितं त्विषा विभिन्नमम्भोजपलाशशोभया ।
पयः स्फुरच्छालिशिखापिशङ्गितं द्रुतं धनुष्खण्डमिवाहिविद्विषः ॥

२८ विपाण्डु संव्यानमिवानिलोद्धृतं निरुन्धतीः सप्तपलाशजं रजः ।
अनाविलोन्मीलितबाणचक्षुषः सपुष्पहासा वनराजियोषितः ॥

२९ अदीपितं वैद्युतजातवेदसा सिताम्बुदच्छेदतिरोहितातपम् ।
ततान्तरं सान्तरवारिशीकरैः शिवं नभोवर्त्म सरोजवायुभिः ॥

३० सितच्छदानामपदिश्य धावतां रुतैरमीषां ग्रथिताः पतत्त्रिणाम् ।
प्रकुर्वते वारिदरोधनिर्गताः परस्परालापमिवामला दिशः ॥

३१ विहारभूमेरभिघोषमुत्सुकाः शरीरजेभ्यश्च्युतयूथपङ्क्तयः ।
असक्तमूर्धांसि पयः क्षरन्त्यमूरुपायनानीव नयन्ति धेनवः ॥

३२ जगत्प्रसूतिर्जगदेकपावनी व्रजोपकण्ठं तनयैरुपेयुषी ।
द्युतिं समग्रां समितिर्गवामसावुपैति मन्त्रैरिव संहिताहुतिः ॥

It looks as though these rice plants, bowed down by heavy   26
clusters of ripening golden grain, are bending to smell
the blue water lily blooming in the field canal, its
presence announced by its scent.

Tinged with the green of lotus plants, mingled with the   27–30
rosy glow of lotus petals, and painted gold with the
tips of stalks of paddy, the water in the rice fields looks
like a liquid fragment of the rainbow of Indra, the
serpent slayer.[7] The woods are lovely women: with
blue *bāṇa* flowers for bright eyes, they smile with their
flowers, and they cling to their breastcloths, the white
pollen of seven-leaf trees, snatched away by the wind.
The sky is beautiful, even though it is no longer lit up
by fiery lightning, even though it is sprayed with scant
drops of water borne by a breeze that has brushed past
lotuses, even though the sun is hidden by patches of
white cloud. Relieved to be freed from the banks of
rainclouds, the quarters of the clear sky are talking
to each other through the calls of wild geese flying
toward the water, the woods, and the sky, with white
wings beating.

Breaking away from the herd in their eagerness to reach   31
the stalls, these cows returning from the late evening
pasture ground bear udders freely flowing with milk,
a gift for their calves.

Cows joined with their calves at their return to the cow   32
pen, this herd, mother of the universe and its chief
source of blessing, takes on the perfect luster of a
sacrificial offering joined with sacred chants.[8]

३३ कृतावधानं जितबर्हिणध्वनौ सुरक्तगोपीजनगीतनिःस्वने ।
इदं जिघत्सामपहाय भूयसीं न सस्यमभ्येति मृगीकदम्बकम् ॥

३४ असावनास्थापरयावधीरितः सरोरुहिण्या शिरसा नमन्नपि ।
उपैति शुष्यन्कलमः सहाम्भसा मनोभुवा तप्त इवाभिपाण्डुताम् ॥

३५ अमी समुद्धूतसरोजरेणुना हता हतासारकणेन वायुना ।
उपागमे दुश्चरिता इवापदां गतिं न निश्चेतुमलं शिलीमुखाः ॥

३६ मुखैरसौ विद्रुमभङ्गलोहितैः शिखाः पिशङ्गीः कलमस्य बिभ्रती ।
शुकावलिर्व्यक्तशिरीषकोमला धनुःश्रियं गोत्रभिदो ऽनुगच्छति ॥

३७ इति कथयति तत्र नातिदूरा-
दथ दट्टशे पिहितोष्णरश्मिबिम्बः ।
विगलितजलभारशुक्लभासां
निचय इवाम्बुमुचां नगाधिराजः ॥

३८ तमतनुवनराजिश्यामितोपत्यकान्तं
नगमुपरि हिमानीगौरमासाद्य जिष्णुः ।
व्यपगतमदरागस्यानुससार लक्ष्मी-
मसितमधरवासो बिभ्रतः सीरपाणेः ॥

Engrossed by the herdswomen's melodious songs, sweeter   33
    than a peacock's call, a herd of female deer forgets its
    hunger and stops eating the grain in the paddy fields.

This rice plant must have been rebuffed by an indifferent   34
    lotus, for it bows down its head, turns deathly pale,
    and dries up, along with the water, as though burning
    with desire.[9]

Sucked in by a wind that whirls about the pollen of lotuses,   35
    mixed with drops of water, bees flutter blindly and
    lose their way, like scoundrels at a loss for strategy
    when misfortune strikes.

Flying with golden grains of rice held in beaks red as   36
    chunks of coral, this flock of parrots, green like a *śirīṣa*
    blossom, shimmers like Indra's rainbow."

As the yaksha spoke, a short distance away Arjuna caught   37
    sight of Himalaya, king of mountains, blocking the
    orb of the sun, like a shining white mass of clouds
    emptied of their burden of water.

As he climbed up the mountain, its crest white with snow   38
    and lower slopes dark with dense forests, Arjuna the
    conqueror was reminded of handsome Balarama, hero
    with the plough, with his black lower garment and
    face gone pale from losing the flush of wine.[10]

CHAPTER 5

The Magnificent Himalaya

१ अथ जयाय नु मेरुमहीभृतो रभसया नु दिगन्तदिदृक्षया ।
अभिययौ स हिमाचलमुच्छ्रितं समुदितं नु विलङ्घयितुं नभः ॥

२ तपनमण्डलदीपितमेकतः सततनैशतमोवृतमन्यतः ।
हसितभिन्नतमिस्रचयं पुरः शिवमिवानुगतं गजचर्मणा ॥

३ क्षितिनभःसुरलोकनिवासिभिः कृतनिकेतमदृष्टपरस्परैः ।
प्रथयितुं विभुतामभिनिर्मितं प्रतिनिधिं जगतामिव शंभुना ॥

४ भुजगराजसितेन नभःश्रिता कनकराजिविराजितसानुना ।
समुदितं निचयेन तडित्वतीं लघयता शरदम्बुदसंहतिम् ॥

५ मणिमयूखचयांशुकभासुराः सुरवधूपरिभुक्तलतागृहाः ।
दधतमुच्छशिलान्तरगोपुराः पुर इवोदितपुष्पवना भुवः ॥

६ अविरतोज्झितवारिविपाण्डुभिर्विरहितैरचिरद्युतितेजसा ।
उदितपक्षमिवारतनिःस्वनैः पृथुनितम्बविलम्बिभिरम्बुदैः ॥

Then he began to climb the high Himalaya, which soared   1
   above him as if poised to conquer Meru, the cosmic
   mountain, or eager to scan the limits of the horizon,
   or wishing to rise above the sky.[1]

Lit on one side by the disc of the sun, and engulfed on   2
   the other by the perpetual darkness of night, the
   mountain looked like the god Shiva, with the flayed
   hide of the elephant demon draped on his back,
   shattering the massed darkness before him with his
   triumphant laughter.[2]

Becoming a single abode for the inhabitants of the earth,   3
   the sky, and the world of the gods, normally invisible
   to one another, the Himalaya was a perfect image of
   the three worlds fashioned by Shiva to manifest his
   supreme power over the cosmos.[3]

Touching the sky with towering peaks white as the cosmic   4
   snake Shesha, and glittering with streaks of gold,
   the mountain looked more beautiful than a bank of
   autumn clouds lit with flashes of lightning.

The mountainside abounded in spaces that looked like   5
   pleasure cities of Indra's nymphs: deep clefts between
   the rocks were gateway towers; bowers of vines were
   houses; the massed rays of light streaming from
   precious stones shone like colorful silken banners, and
   there were luxuriant flower gardens.

White clouds, empty from incessantly showering rain,   6
   bereft of flashing lightning, the rumbling of thunder
   silenced, hung down from the broad slopes of the
   mountain, as if it had sprouted wings.

७ दधतमाकरिभिः करिभिः क्षतैः समवतारसमैरसमैस्तटैः ।
विविधकामहिता महिताम्भसः स्फुटसरोजवना जवना नदीः ॥

८ नवविनिद्रजपाकुसुमत्विषां द्युतिमतां निकरेण महाश्मनाम् ।
विहितसांध्यमयूखमिव क्वचिन्निचितकाञ्चनभित्तिषु सानुषु ॥

९ पृथुकदम्बककदम्बकराजितं ग्रथितमालतमालवनाकुलम् ।
लघुतुषारतुषारजलश्रुतं धृतसदानसदाननदन्तिनम् ॥

१० रहितरत्नचयान्न शिलोच्चयानपलताभवना न दरीभुवः ।
विपुलिनाम्बुरुहा न सरिद्बधूरकुसुमान्दधतं न महीरुहः ॥

११ व्यथितसिन्धुमनीरशनैः शनैरमरलोकवधूजघनैर्घनैः ।
फणभृतामभितो विततं ततं दयितरम्यलताबकुलैः कुलैः ॥

१२ ससुरचापमनेकमणिप्रभैरपपयोविशदं हिमपाण्डुभिः ।
अविचलं शिखरैरुपबिभ्रतं ध्वनितसूचितमम्बुमुचां चयम् ॥

The Himalaya's swift rivers had clumps of blooming 7
lotuses, salutary waters fit for a myriad uses, and
lovely banks—mines of gold—that were battered by
mountain elephants yet level at their fords.[4]

Covered with sheets of gold, and studded with large rubies 8
the color of newly blossomed hibiscus, the mountain's
peaks glowed as though lit up by rays of the setting
sun.

The Himalaya was covered with stands of spreading 9
kadamba trees and groves of *tamāla* trees. Melting
ice dripped slowly down its slopes, spraying rutting
elephants with their splendid trunks.

On that mountain were no cliffs without masses of gems, 10
no caves without bowers of vines, no rivers without
sandbanks like young women with lovely hips and
lotuses for their faces, and no trees without an
abundance of blooming flowers.

Celestial nymphs, their swelling hips laced with girdles, 11
gracefully swam in the mountain's rivers. There were
swarms of snakes, too, drawn by its beautiful vines
and *bakula* trees.

Only from their rumbling could one tell apart the 12
motionless clouds, white for lack of water and
sheltering a rainbow, from the mountain peaks on
which they rested, white with snow and glittering with
the brilliance of many-colored gems.

१३ विकचवारिरुहं दधतं सरः सकलहंसगणं शुचि मानसम् ।
शिवमगात्मजया च कृतेर्ष्यया सकलहं सगणं शुचिमानसम् ॥

१४ ग्रहविमानगणानभितो दिवं ज्वलयतौषधिजेन कृशानुना ।
मुहुरनुस्मरयन्तमनुक्षपं त्रिपुरदाहमुमापतिसेविनः ॥

१५ विततशीकरराशिभिरुच्छ्रितैरुपलरोधविवर्तिभिरम्बुभिः ।
दधतमुन्नतसानुसमुद्धतां धृतसितव्यजनामिव जाह्नवीम् ॥

१६ अनुचरेण धनाधिपतेरथो नगविलोकनविस्मितमानसः ।
स जगदे वचनं प्रियमादरान्मुखरतावसरे हि विराजते ॥

१७ अलमेष विलोकितः प्रजानां सहसा संहतिमंहसां विहन्तुम् ।
घनवर्त्म सहस्रधेव कुर्वन्हिमगौरैरचलाधिपः शिरोभिः ॥

80

That mountain was the home of sacred lake Manasa, full   13
of blossoming lotuses and royal wild geese. There
too dwelt Shiva, yogi pure of mind, along with his
attendant spirits, the *ganas,* and he was absorbed
in lovers' quarrels with the jealous Parvati, the
mountain's daughter.[5]

Every night illuminating, with fire born from its magic   14
herbs, the flying cars of the celestials and the planets
moving in the skies around it, the mountain reminded
the servants of Shiva, Uma's* husband, of the day he
burned down the three citadels of the demons.[6]

On the mountain's high peaks Jahnu's daughter,[7] the   15
river Ganga, flowed in a torrent as if waving a white
flywhisk fan, with surging waters that eddied around
the rocks in their course, throwing up a fine mist.[8]

The servant of Kubera, god of wealth, spoke affectionately   16
and sweetly to Arjuna as he stood filled with wonder at
the sight of the mountain. Eloquence excels when it is
timely.[9]

"The sight of this king of mountains, who seems to tear up   17
the sky into a thousand pieces with the thrusts of his
snow-white peaks, suffices to destroy a person's whole
store of sins, all at once.

---

* A name of the goddess Parvati.

१८ इह दुरधिगमैः किंचिदेवागमैः
सततमसुतरं वर्णयन्त्यन्तरम् ।
अमुमतिविपिनं वेद दिग्व्यापिनं
पुरुषमिव परं पद्मयोनिः परम् ॥

१९ रुचिरपल्लवपुष्पलतागृहैरुपलसज्जलजैर्जलराशिभिः ।
नयति संततमुत्सुकतामयं धृतिमतीरुपकान्तमपि स्त्रियः ॥

२० सुलभैः सदा नयवतायवता निधिगुह्यकाधिपरमैः परमैः ।
अमुना धनैः क्षितिभृतातिभृता समतीत्य भाति जगती जगती ॥

२१ अखिलमिदममुष्य गौरीगुरोस्त्रिभुवनमपि नैति मन्ये तुलाम् ।
अधिवसति सदा यदेनं जनैरविदितविभवो भवानीपतिः ॥

२२ वीतजन्मजरसं परं शुचि ब्रह्मणः पदमुपैतुमिच्छताम् ।
आगमादिव तमोपहादितः संभवन्ति मतयो भवच्छिदः ॥

Impenetrable, with immensely tall trees and dense forests,   18
    pervading space in every direction, this mountain
    is like Purusha, the all-pervasive supreme Person,
    whose inner truth is difficult to understand, since he
    is spoken of only in the most esoteric scriptures. And
    both great beings can be known only by the creator
    god, Brahma, seated on the lotus.

With its bowers of vines blooming with lovely shoots   19
    and flowers, and its lakes adorned with beautiful
    lotuses, the mountain constantly arouses longing in
    women, even when they are content in love and in the
    company of their lovers.[10]

Forever supplied by this mountain with vast riches that   20
    the pious and the saintly may easily command,
    treasure to delight Kubera himself, king of riches and
    of yakshas, guardians of wealth, the earth, with the
    Himalaya towering above her, surpasses the other two
    worlds in splendor.

I feel the three worlds together cannot equal this   21
    mountain. He is father of Gauri, the goddess
    Bhavani,[11] and home of her husband, Shiva, whose
    greatness is beyond human understanding.

Men who wish to attain the supreme, pure condition of   22
    *brahma,** unitary consciousness, free from old age and
    rebirth, may gain insight from this mountain, who
    dispels dark ignorance like scripture itself.

---

* The essential real underlying the phenomena of the universe.

२३ दिव्यस्त्रीणां सचरणलाक्षारागा रागायाते निपतितपुष्पापीडाः ।
पीडाभाजः कुसुमचिताः साशंसं शंसन्त्यस्मिन्सुरतविशेषं
शय्याः ॥

२४ गुणसंपदा समधिगम्य परं महिमानमत्र महिते जगताम् ।
नयशालिनि श्रिय इवाधिपतौ विरमन्ति न ज्वलितुमौषधयः ॥

२५ कुररीगणः कृतरवस्तरवः कुसुमानताः सकमलं कमलम् ।
इह सिन्धवश्च वरणावरणाः करिणां मुदे सनलदानलदाः ॥

२६ सादृश्यं गतमपनिद्रचूतगन्धै-
रामोदं मदजलसेकजं दधानः ।
एतस्मिन्मदयति कोकिलानकाले
लीनालिः सुरकरिणां कपोलकाषः ॥

२७ सनाकवनितं नितम्बरुचिरं चिरं सुनिनदैर्नदैर्वृतममुम् ।
मता फणवतो ऽवतो रसपरा परास्तवसुधा सुधाधिवसति ॥

२८ श्रीमल्लताभवनमोषधयः प्रदीपाः
शय्या नवानि हरिचन्दनपल्लवानि ।
अस्मिन्नतिश्रमनुदश्च सरोजवाताः
स्मर्तुं दिशन्ति न दिवः सुरसुन्दरीभ्यः ॥

Crumpled, stained with lac paint from designs decorating   23
the feet, strewn with floral chaplets dislodged in the
height of passion, and dotted with flowers, the beds of
celestial women betray the many moves of passionate
lovemaking.[12]

Having attained the acme of excellence through their   24
abundant virtues, the luminous herbs that grow
on this mountain worshiped by the world shine
continuously, day and night, like fortune steadily
favoring a king who practices right conduct and just
policy.

This mountain rings with the female osprey's cry, the trees   25
are bowed with flowers, the lotus blooms profusely,
and elephants delight in rivers shaded by trees and
lush with cooling, fragrant *uśīra* root.

On this mountain cuckoos are maddened out of season   26
by the fragrance, sweet as the scent of mango
blossoms in spring, of the streaming ichor that soaks
the bee dense trees where the gods' elephants have
rubbed their cheeks.[13]

Because it is home to celestial nymphs, its slopes are   27
beautiful, and it teems with murmuring streams,
sweet ambrosia, dear to Vasuki, the serpent who
guards the underworld,[14] scorns the earth, and makes
this mountain its permanent refuge.

Here bowers made of vines with magical herbs for lamps,   28
beds made of the young shoots of the sandalwood
tree, and lotus breezes that dispel the fatigue of
lovemaking, persuade the celestial beauties to forget
heaven itself.[15]

२९ ईशार्थमम्भसि चिराय तपश्चरन्त्या
यादोविलङ्घनविलोलविलोचनायाः ।
आलम्बताग्रकरमत्र भवो भवान्याः
श्रोत्रनिदाघसलिलाङ्गुलिना करेण ॥

३० येनापविद्धसलिलः स्फुटनागसद्मा
देवासुरैरमृतमम्बुनिधिर्ममन्थे ।
व्यावर्तनैरहिपतेरयमाहिताङ्कः
खं व्यालिखन्निव विभाति स मन्दराद्रिः ॥

३१ नीतोच्छ्रायं मुहुरशिशिररश्मेरुस्सै-
रानीलाभैर्विरचितपरभागा रत्नैः ।
ज्योत्स्नाशङ्कामिह वितरति हंसश्येनी
मध्ये ऽप्यह्नः स्फटिकरजतभित्तिच्छाया ॥

३२ दधत इव विलासशालि नृत्यं मृदु पतता पवनेन कम्पितानि ।
इह ललितविलासिनीजनभ्रूगतिकुटिलेषु पयःसु पङ्कजानि ॥

३३ अस्मिन्नगृह्यत पिनाकभृता सलील-
माबद्धवेपथुरधीरविलोचनायाः ।
विन्यस्तमङ्गलमहौषधिरीश्वरायाः
स्रस्तोरगप्रतिसरेण करेण पाणिः ॥

Here once the goddess Bhavani, who sought the god for   29
her husband, performed austerities for a long time,
standing in the water, eyes trembling from fear of
river creatures that jostled her legs, until Shiva,
source of all life, grasped her hand with his own hand
dripping with sweat.[16]

Splitting the sky asunder, this mountain looks like Mount   30
Mandara, whose slopes were grooved by the coils of
Vasuki, king of snakes, when the gods and demons,
seeking ambrosia, turned Mandara into a stick to
churn the milk ocean, draining its waters and exposing
the netherworld, the abode of the snakes.[17]

The radiance of the Himalaya's crystal and silver walls,   31
white as the feathers of wild geese, intensified by
the sun's rays, and beautifully contrasted by the
dark luster of glittering sapphires, often gives the
appearance of moonlight even in the middle of the
day.[18]

Here lotuses ruffled by a gentle breeze perform a lively   32
dance, it seems, in waters rippling softly like the
graceful play of a young woman's eyebrows.

On this mountain, with a hand from which the snake   33
that served as the ceremonial string was slipping
from his wrist, Shiva the archer once gently grasped
in marriage the trembling hand, wreathed with
auspicious magic herbs, of the goddess with restless
glances.[19]

३४ क्राम्द्विर्घनपदवीमनेकसंख्यै-
स्तेजोभिः शुचिमणिजन्मभिर्विविभिन्नः ।
उस्राणां व्यभिचरतीव सप्तसप्तेः
पर्यस्यन्निह निचयः सहस्रसंख्याम् ॥

३५ व्यधत्त यस्मिन्पुरमुच्चगोपुरं पुरां विजेतुर्धृतये धनाधिपः ।
स एष कैलास उपान्तसर्पिणः करोत्यकालास्तमयं विवस्वतः ॥

३६ नानारत्नज्योतिषां संनिपातैश्छन्नेष्वन्तःसानु वप्रान्तरेषु ।
बद्धां बद्धां भित्तिशङ्काममुष्मिन्रावानावान्मातरिश्वा निहन्ति ॥

३७ रम्या नवद्युतिरपैति न शाद्वलेभ्यः
श्यामीभवन्त्यनुदिनं नलिनीवनानि ।
अस्मिन्विचित्रकुसुमस्तबकाचितानां
शाखाभृतां परिणमन्ति न पल्लवानि ॥

३८ परिसरविषयेषु लीढमुक्ता हरिततृणोद्गमशङ्कया मृगीभिः ।
इह नवशुककोमला मणीनां रविकरसंवलिताः फलन्ति भासः ॥

३९ उत्फुल्लस्थलनलिनीवनादमुष्मा-
दुद्धूतः सरसिजसंभवः परागः ।
वात्याभिर्वियति विवर्तितः समन्ता-
दाधत्ते कनकमयातपत्रलक्ष्मीम् ॥

Mingling with innumerable rays of light streaming from   34
the crystals on this mountain, and reaching the sky,
the rays of the sun, its chariot drawn by seven horses,
fan out all around, seeming to multiply beyond their
normal count of a thousand.[20]

Here Mount Kailasa, the peak on which Kubera, god of   35
riches, has built a city with high gateway towers for
the delight of Shiva, destroyer of the demons' cities,
sends the sun, approaching near, to an untimely
setting.[21]

On this mountain's slopes, only a fierce wind, blowing   36
through the crevices between the rocks, dispels the
illusion of a solid wall created by the commingled
radiance of a multitude of many-colored gems.[22]

Here the grass never loses its fresh young sheen, lotus   37
plants remain forever dark green, and young shoots
never wither on trees blooming with clusters of many-
colored flowers.[23]

In the regions around the mountain slopes, mistaking   38
it for fresh green grass, female deer lick and then
draw back from the bright rays streaming from
emeralds, the soft green of a young parrot's wings, and
burgeoning from mixing with sunlight.

The pollen from beds of full-bloomed lotuses on the land,   39
stirred up by gusts of wind and whirled about in the
sky, takes shape as a lovely golden parasol.[24]

४० इह सनियमयोः सुरापगायामुषसि सयावकसव्यपादरेखा ।
कथयति शिवयोः शरीरयोगं विषमपदा पदवी विवर्तनेषु ॥

४१ संमूर्छतां रजतभित्तिमयूखजाले-
रालोलपादपलतान्तरनिर्गतानाम् ।
घर्मद्युतेरिह मुहुः पटलानि धाम्रा-
मादर्शमण्डलनिभानि समुल्लसन्ति ॥

४२ शुक्लैर्मयूखनिचयैः परिवीतमूर्ति-
र्वप्राभिघातपरिमण्डलितोरुदेहः ।
श्रृङ्गाण्यमुष्य भजते गणभर्तुरुक्षा
कुर्वन्वधूजनमनःसु शशाङ्कशङ्काम् ॥

४३ संप्रति लब्धजन्म शनकैः कथमपि लघुनि
क्षीणपयस्युपेयुषि भिदां जलधरपटले ।
खण्डितविग्रहं बलभिदो धनुरिह विविधाः
पूरयितुं भवन्ति विभवः शिखरमणिरुचः ॥

४४ स्नपितनवलतातरुप्रवालै-
रमृतलवस्नुतिशालिभिर्मयूखैः ।
सततमसितयामिनीषु शंभो-
रमलयतीह वनान्तमिन्दुलेखा ॥

On this mountain a trail of uneven footprints, the left   40
one alone marked with red lac paint, tells of the
conjoined bodies of Shiva and the goddess performing
circumambulations in rites of worship at dawn on the
bank of the river Ganga.[25]

Multiplied by rays of light from the mountain's silver   41
walls, and streaming through the interstices
of swaying tree limbs, discs of sunlight flash
intermittently like the broken pieces of a mirror.

His figure flooded by bright rays, his powerful body arced   42
in a curve as he bends down to butt the riverbanks,
the bull of Shiva, master of the *gaṇa* spirits, roams the
peaks of this mountain, and the women think it must
be the moon.[26]

Slowly struggling to take shape in a bank of airy clouds   43
that have disintegrated after showering rain, and
harboring only a few drops of water, the broken arc
of the rainbow, Indra's bow, can be filled out by the
radiance of the gems on the peaks of this mountain.

Even in the darkening half of the month the crescent   44
moon on Shambhu's* head perpetually brightens the
woods on this mountain, bathing the young shoots on
creepers and trees with rays dripping ambrosia.

---

* Shiva's.

४५ क्षिपति यो ऽनुवनं विततां बृहद्‌द्रुहतिकामिव रौचनिकीं रुचम् ।
अयमनेकहिरण्मयकंदरस्तव पितुर्दयितो जगतीधरः ॥

४६ सक्तिं जवादपनयत्यनिले लतानां
वैरोचनैर्द्विगुणिताः सहसा मयूखैः ।
रोधोभुवां मुहुरमुत्र हिरण्मयीनां
भासस्तडिद्विलसितानि विडम्बयन्ति ॥

४७ कषणकम्पनिरस्तमहाहिभिः क्षणविमत्तमतङ्गजवर्जितैः ।
इह मदस्रपितैरनुमीयते सुरगजस्य गतं हरिचन्दनैः ॥

४८ जलदजालघनैरसिताश्मनामुपहतप्रचयेह मरीचिभिः ।
भवति दीप्तिरदीपितकंदरा तिमिरसंवलितेव विवस्वतः ॥

४९ भव्यो भवन्नपि मुनेरिह शासनेन
क्षात्रे स्थितः पथि तपस्य हतप्रमादः ।
प्रायेण सत्यपि हितार्थकरे विधौ हि
श्रेयांसि लब्धुमसुखानि विनान्तरायैः ॥

Here is the mountain dear to your father, the god Indra,   45
abounding in caves full of gold and streaming the
golden gleam of yellow orpiment on its forests, as if it
were spreading a large cloak over them.[27]

On this mountain, when a strong wind suddenly pulls   46
apart closely twined creepers, the glitter of gold on the
riverbanks, doubled by the rays of the sun, flashes like
bolts of lightning.

On this mountain, from the state of young sandalwood   47
trees bathed in streams of elephant ichor; from the
snakes shaken off from the trees when he rubbed
against them, and the mountain's wild elephants
avoiding them, we can infer the trail of Airavata,
Indra's elephant.

Unable to mass together, and darkened by the rays   48
streaming from sapphires black as banks of
rainclouds, the sun's rays here are strangely prevented
from illuminating the mountain caves.

Even though you have calmed your mind with ascetic   49
vows, stand firm by the warrior code, following the
sage's instruction, and never let down your guard as
you perform austerities on this mountain! No matter
how praiseworthy a man's endeavor, the road to
success is generally fraught with obstacles.

५० मा भूवन्नपथहृतस्तवेन्द्रियाश्वाः
    संतापे दिशतु शिवः शिवां प्रसक्तिम् ।
    रक्षन्तस्तपसि बलं च लोकपालाः
    कल्याणीमधिकफलां क्रियां क्रियासुः ॥

५१ इत्युक्त्वा सपदि हितं प्रियं प्रियार्हे
    धाम स्वं गतवति राजराजभृत्ये ।
    सोत्कण्ठं किमपि पृथासुतः प्रदध्यौ
    संधत्ते भृशमरतिं हि सद्द्वियोगः ॥

५२ तमनतिशयनीयं सर्वतः सारयोगा-
    दविरहितमनेकेनाङ्कभाजा फलेन ।
    अकृशमकृशलक्ष्मीश्वेतसाशंसितं स
    स्वमिव पुरुषकारं शैलमभ्याससाद ॥

May those wild horses, your sense organs, not run 50
wild and lead you astray! May Shiva bless you with
renewed firmness of resolve when tormented by
austerity! May the guardian gods of the worlds
increase your power in the practice of ascetic vows,
and make your worthy endeavor bear ample and
auspicious fruit!"

Having spoken these pleasing and benevolent words 51
to Arjuna, the friendly servant of Kubera at once
returned to his home, and the son of Pritha was left to
melancholy reflection. Indeed, parting company with
good men is a source of deep unhappiness.

Arjuna, hero of perfect majesty, had reached the desired 52
destination, the mountain whose power was
unrivaled in every way, the repository of momentous
and imminent results, as though it were the very
embodiment of the heroic deeds he was about to
perform, matchless because of his extraordinary
strength, and rich with the promise of immediate and
resounding success for his undertaking.[28]

CHAPTER 6

Arjuna's Asceticism

१ रुचिराकृतिः कनकसानुमथो परमः पुमानिव पतितं पतताम् ।
धृतसत्पथस्त्रिपथगामभितः स तमारुरोह पुरूहूतसुतः ॥

२ तमनिन्द्यबन्दिन इवेन्द्रसुतं विहितालिनिक्कणजयध्वनयः ।
पवनेरिताकुलविजिह्मशिखा जगतीरुहो ऽवचकरुः कुसुमैः ॥

३ अवधूतपङ्कजपरागकणास्तनुजाह्नवीसलिलवीचिभिदः ।
परिरेभिरे ऽभिमुखमेत्य सुखाः सुहृदः सखायमिव तं मरुतः ॥

४ उदितोपलस्खलनसंवलिताः स्फुटहंससारसविराववयुजः ।
मुदमस्य माङ्गलिकतूर्यकृतां ध्वनयः प्रतेनुरनुवप्रमपाम् ॥

५ अवरुणतुङ्गसुरदारुतरौ निचये पुरः सुरसरित्पयसाम् ।
स ददर्श वेतसवनाचरितां प्रणतिं बलीयसि समृद्धिकरीम् ॥

६ प्रबभूव नालमवलोकयितुं परितः सरोजरजसारुणितम् ।
सरिदुत्तरीयमिव संहतिमत्स तरङ्गरङ्गि कलहंसकुलम् ॥

Walking toward the Ganga, river with three paths,* the   1
    son of Indra, a handsome man and devoted to the path
    of virtue, climbed the golden-peaked mountain like
    the supreme Person Vishnu mounting Garuda, king of
    birds.
Like skillful bards the trees sang victory songs by the   2
    humming of bees, and showered the hero with
    blossoms from branches that swayed in the breeze,
    bending slightly at their tips.
Showering lotus pollen and spraying water from the   3
    Ganga, cool breezes came forward to embrace him,
    like friends greeting a friend.
Echoing from striking high rocks and mingled with the   4
    piercing calls of wild geese and cranes, the thundering
    waters of the Ganga, crashing against its banks,
    delighted him like festive drums.[1]
He admired the reeds he saw before him as they bowed   5
    before the mighty torrent of the river of the gods,
    which had torn up the towering pine trees. Such
    humility was sure to ensure their flourishing.[2]
He did not tire of gazing at the flock of wild geese that   6
    enveloped the water like a woman's bodice, gilded
    with pollen from the lotuses that surrounded them.

* Heaven, earth, and the netherworld.

७ दधति क्षतीः परिणतद्विरदे मुदितालियोषिति मदस्रुतिभिः ।
अधिकां स रोधसि बबन्ध धृतिं महते रुजन्नपि गुणाय महान् ॥

८ अनुहेमवप्रमरुणैः समतां गतमूर्मिभिः सहचरं पृथुभिः ।
स रथाङ्गनामवनितां करुणैरनुबध्नतीमभिनन्द रुतैः ॥

९ सितवाजिने निजगदू रुचयश्चलवीचिरागरचनापटवः ।
मणिजालमम्भसि निमग्नमपि स्फुरितं मनोगतमिवाकृतयः ॥

१० उपलाहतोद्धततरङ्गधृतं जविना विधूतविततं मरुता ।
स ददर्श केतकशिखाविशदं सरितः प्रहासमिव फेनमपाम् ॥

११ बहु बर्हिचन्द्रकनिभं विदधे धृतिमस्य दानपयसां पटलम् ।
अवगाढमीक्षितुमिवेभपतिं विकसद्द्विलोचनशतं सरितः ॥

१२ प्रतिबोधजृम्भणविभिन्नमुखी पुलिने सरोरुहदृशा ददृशे ।
पतदच्छमौक्तिकमणिप्रकरा गलदश्रुबिन्दुरिव शुक्तिवधूः ॥

Arjuna was enchanted by the riverbank, scarred by the   7
slant thrusts of a wild elephant's tusks, yet delighting
the female bee with streams of ichor. The great confer
distinction even when inflicting pain.

He applauded the shelduck desperately searching for her   8
mate. She called out to him with piteous cries, unable
to tell him apart from the great waves tinted gold by
the mountain's golden slopes.[3]

Though they were hidden deep in the water, the brilliant   9
flash of a myriad gems, coloring the restless waves,
declared their presence to the hero with the white
horse, like changing facial expressions revealing the
flickering of inner emotions.

He saw the river's boisterous laughter in the foam, white   10
as the tip of the screwpine flower,* that bubbled up
on the waves as they dashed against rocks and was
dispersed by strong gusts of wind.

The many patches of elephant ichor gave him great   11
pleasure, iridescent as a peacock's tail, and looking
like a hundred eyes the river had opened to gaze at the
king elephant entering the water.

To the hero with eyes lovely as lotuses, pearl oysters lying   12
on a sandbank, burst wide open and pouring out
translucent pearls, looked like women yawning and
shedding tears on being awakened after a night's love-
making.

---

* *Ketaka,* a highly fragrant and thorny white flower.

१३ शुचिरप्सु विद्रुमलताविटपस्तनुसान्द्रफेनलवसंवलितः ।
स्मरदायिनः स्मरयति स्म भृशं दयिताधरस्य दशनांशुभृतः ॥

१४ उपलभ्य चञ्चलतरङ्गहृतं मदगन्धमुत्थितवतां पयसः ।
प्रतिदन्तिनामिव स संबुबुधे करियादसामभिमुखान्करिणः ॥

१५ स जगाम विस्मयमुदीक्ष्य पुरः सहसा समुत्पतिषोः फणिनः ।
प्रहितं दिवि प्रजविभिः श्वसितैः शरदभ्रविभ्रममपां पटलम् ॥

१६ स ततार सैकतवतीरभितः शफरीपरिस्फुरितचारुदृशः ।
ललिताः सखीरिव बृहज्जघनाः सुरनिम्नगामुपयतीः सरितः ॥

१७ अधिरुह्य पुष्पभरनम्रशिखैः परितः परिष्कृततलां तरुभिः ।
मनसः प्रसत्तिमिव मूर्ध्नि गिरेः शुचिमाससाद स वनान्तभुवम् ॥

१८ अनुसानु पुष्पितलताविततिः फलितोरुभूरुहविविक्तवनः ।
धृतिमात्तान तनयस्य हरेस्तपसे ऽधिवस्तुमचलामचलः ॥

१९ प्रणिधाय तत्र विधिनाथ धियं दधतः पुरातनमुनेर्मुनिताम् ।
श्रममादधावसुकरं न तपः किमिवावसादकरमात्मवताम् ॥

A branch of bright coral in the water, entwined with a   13
    delicate streak of bubbling foam, keenly reminded
    him of his beloved's lower lip, kindler of desire, joined
    with the luster of her teeth.

Only by the scent of ichor wafted by the surging waves   14
    could he tell the wild elephants apart from the large
    river creatures, whom they confronted like rival
    elephants when they came out of the water.

He looked up with wonder at a jet of water, beautiful as a   15
    white autumn cloud, shooting up in the air before him,
    propelled by the great hisses of a snake that reared up
    all of a sudden.

He crossed streams flanked by sandbanks rushing to meet   16
    the Ganga, river of the gods, like graceful girlfriends
    with swelling hips and bewitching eyes in the form of
    darting minnows.

Ascending the mountain's summit, he arrived as though at   17
    mental calm itself, at a lovely wooded place, beautiful
    with trees growing all around, bowed down with the
    weight of flowers.

The mountain, with secluded forests of great fruit trees   18
    and peaks covered with blossoming creepers, kindled
    in Indra's son an unshakeable resolve to settle there to
    practice austerity.

When Arjuna, who had been a sage in the ancient past,   19
    steadied his mental flux and took up ascetic practice
    there, according to the precepts of yoga, he was not
    fatigued by the rigors of austerity. Hardship cannot
    weary the man of self-control.[4]

२० शमयन्धृतेन्द्रियशमैकसुखः शुचिभिर्गुणैरघमयं स तमः ।
प्रतिवासरं सुकृतिभिर्ववृधे विमलः कलाभिरिव शीतरुचिः ॥

२१ अधरीचकार च विवेकगुणादगुणेषु तस्य धियमस्तवतः ।
प्रतिघातिनीं विषयसङ्गरतिं निरुपप्लवः शमसुखानुभवः ॥

२२ मनसा जपैः प्रणतिभिः प्रयतः समुपेयिवानधिपतिं स दिवः ।
सहजेतरौ जयशमौ दधती बिभरांबभूव युगपन्महसी ॥

२३ शिरसा हरिन्मणिनिभः स वहन्कृतजन्मनो ऽभिषवणेन जटाः ।
उपमां ययावरुणदीधितिभिः परिमृष्टमूर्धनि तमालतरौ ॥

२४ धृतहेतिरप्यधृतजिह्ममतिश्चरितैर्मुनीनधरयञ्शुचिभिः ।
रजयांचकार विरजाः स मृगान्किमिवेशते रमयितुं न गुणाः ॥

His sole pleasure disciplining the senses, he destroyed   20
dark impurity with his shining virtues.[5] Free of
blemish, he flourished day by day with acts of
austerity, like the cool-rayed moon, dispeller of
darkness, waxing with its digits.

As he controlled vicious thoughts by the virtue of insight,   21
a joyous tranquility boundlessly spread over him and
overcame all harmful passion.

When the self-controlled Arjuna worshiped Indra, king of   22
the gods, with meditation, sacred chants, and ritual
prostrations,[6] he displayed two kinds of splendor, one
innate, the other acquired, of martial power and of
peace.

Shining like an emerald and bearing on his head a mass of   23
tawny hair matted from his ritual baths, he resembled
a dark *tamāla* tree, its top engulfed by the red rays of
the morning sun.

Though he bore arms, he bore malice toward none, and   24
because he surpassed sages with his pure conduct, he
charmed the beasts of the forest though far beyond
pleasure himself. Is there anyone whom virtue cannot
win over?

२५ अनुकूलपातिनमचण्डगतिं किरता सुगन्धिमभितः पवनम् ।
अवधीरितार्तवगुणं सुखतां नयता रुचां निचयमंशुमतः ॥

२६ नवपल्लवाञ्जलिभृतः प्रचये बृहतस्तरूनामयतावनतिम् ।
स्तृणता तृणैः प्रतिनिशं मृदुभिः शयनीयतामुपयतीं वसुधाम् ॥

२७ पतितैरपेतजलदान्नभसः पृषतैरपां शमयता च रजः ।
स दयालुनेव परिगाढकृशः परिचर्य्यायानुजगृहे तपसा ॥

२८ महते फलाय तदवेक्ष्य शिवं विकसन्निमित्तकुसुमं स पुरः ।
न जगाम विस्मयवशं वशिनां न निहन्ति धैर्यमनुभावगुणः ॥

२९ तदभूरिवासरकृतं सुकृतैरुपलभ्य वैभवमनन्यभवम् ।
उपतस्थुरास्थितविषादधियः शतयज्वनो वनचरा वसतिम् ॥

३० विदिताः प्रविश्य विहितानतयः शिथिलीकृते ऽधिकृतकृत्यविधौ ।
अनपेतकालमभिरामकथाः कथयांबभूवुरिति गोत्रभिदे ॥

३१ शुचिवल्कवीततनुरन्यतमस्तिमिरच्छिदामिव गिरौ भवतः ।
महते जयाय मघवन्ननघः पुरुषस्तपस्यति तपञ्जगतीम् ॥

३२ स बिभर्ति भीषणभुजंगभुजः पृथु विद्विषां भयविधायि धनुः ।
अमलेन तस्य धृतसच्चरिताश्रितेन चातिशयिता मुनयः ॥

It wafted a favorable, soft, scented breeze around him,   25–27
and tempered the sun's hot rays, rendered pleasing
to the eye in defiance of the season. It made the tall
trees bow with young sprouts as hands cupped in
reverence, for him to pluck flowers. Every night
it strewed soft grass on the earth, turning it into a
comfortable bed for him. And it settled the dust with
raindrops showered from a cloudless sky. In all these
ways, austerity itself served the emaciated Arjuna, as
if moved to compassion for him.

Although he saw that auspicious omen blossoming before   28
him, heralding wonderful fruit, he did not yield to
amazement, for power—a virtue in the case of men of
self-control—does not destroy equanimity.

Troubled by the extraordinary, commanding power that   29
Arjuna had amassed with austerities practiced only
a few days, *guhyaka* foresters, inhabitants of the
mountain, went to the palace of Indra, performer of a
hundred horse sacrifices.

Ushered in, they saluted him; and without delay, since   30
they had left their appointed tasks, they gave him
news that warmed his heart.

"Bountiful Indra! Clad in shining bark cloth, burning   31
the universe like a second sun, a blameless man is
practicing austerity on your mountain, seeking a great
victory!

That man has terrifying arms, like snakes, and he bears a   32
great bow that strikes terror in his enemies. Yet in his
pure conduct he surpasses the most virtuous sages.

३३ मरुतः शिवा नवतृणा जगती विमलं नभो रजसि वृष्टिरपाम् ।
गुणसंपदानुगुणतां गमितः कुरुते ऽस्य भक्तिमिव भूतगणः ॥

३४ इतरेतरानभिभवेन मृगास्तमुपासते गुरुमिवान्तसदः ।
विनमन्ति चास्य तरवः प्रचये परवान्स तेन भवतेव नगः ॥

३५ उरु सत्त्वमाह विपरिश्रमता परमं वपुः प्रथयतीव जयम् ।
शमिनो ऽपि तस्य नवसंगमने विभुतानुषङ्ग्रि भयमेति जनः ॥

३६ ऋषिवंशजः स यदि दैत्यकुले यदि वान्वये महति भूमिभृताम् ।
चरतस्तपस्तव वनेषु सहा न वयं निरूपयितुमस्य गतिम् ॥

३७ विगणय्य कारणमनेकगुणं निजयाथवा कथितमल्पतया ।
असदप्यदः सहितुमर्हसि नः क्व वनेचराः क्व निपुणा मतयः ॥

३८ अधिगम्य गुह्यकगणादिति तन्मनसः प्रियं प्रियसुतस्य तपः ।
निजुगोप हर्षमुदितं मघवा नयवर्त्मगाः प्रभवतां हि धियः ॥

३९ प्रणिधाय चित्तमथ भक्ततया विदिते ऽप्यपूर्व इव तत्र हरिः ।
उपलब्धुमस्य नियमस्थिरतां सुरसुन्दरीरिति वचो ऽभिदधे ॥

The winds are favorable, the earth is newly carpeted with   33
     grass, the sky is clear, and yet showers settle the dust.
     It is as though the elements themselves, captivated by
     his virtues, were worshiping him.

Wild beasts, abandoning their mutual hostility, sit at his   34
     feet like students around a teacher; when he picks
     flowers, trees bow down to him of their own accord,
     and the mountain serves him even as it serves you.

His tireless effort points at immense strength; his   35
     magnificent figure proclaims imminent success. Even
     though he is an ascetic, practicing a vow of peace, his
     commanding presence fills men's hearts with fear.

Whatever his lineage, whether son of a seer or one born   36
     to a demon or the scion of an illustrious dynasty of
     kings, we are unable to discover why he is performing
     asceticism in your forest.

A host of reasons could have motivated this endeavor,   37
     and we are creatures of little understanding. Please
     consider these things, and forgive our words, even
     if they might prove wrong. After all, we are mere
     foresters, not men of superior intellect."

Learning from the foresters of his dear son's austerities,   38
     pleasing to his heart, Indra the bountiful concealed
     his rising joy, for the minds of kings are guided by
     considerations of statesmanship.[7]

Then Indra focused his mind, and though fully aware   39
     of Arjuna's devotion, he pretended ignorance, for
     he wished to test the firmness of the ascetic-hero's
     resolve. He spoke these words to the apsarases,
     celestial nymphs who graced his court.

४० सुकुमारमेकमणु मर्मभिदामतिदूरगं युतममोघतया ।
अविपक्षमस्त्रमपरं कतमद्द्विजयाय यूयमिव चित्तभुवः ॥

४१ भववीतये हतबृहत्तमसामवबोधवारि रजसः शमनम् ।
परिपीयमाणमिव वो ऽसकलैरवसादमेति नयनाञ्जलिभिः ॥

४२ बहुधा गतां जगति भूतसृजा कमनीयतां समभिहृत्य पुरा ।
उपपादिता विदधता भवतीः सुरसद्मयानसुमुखी जनता ॥

४३ तदुपेत्य विघ्नयत तस्य तपः कृतिभिः कलासु सहिताः सचिवैः ।
हृतवीतरागमनसां ननु वः सुखसङ्गिनं प्रति सुखावजितिः ॥

४४ अविमृश्यमेतदभिलष्यति स द्विषतां वधेन विषयाभिरतिम् ।
भववीतये न हि तथा स विधिः क्व शरासनं क्व च विमुक्तिपथः ॥

४५ पृथुधाम्नि तत्र परिबोधि च मा भवतीभिरन्यमुनिवद्द्विकृतिः ।
स्वयशांसि विक्रमवतामवतां न वधूष्वघानि विमृशन्ति धियः ॥

"Tiny, delicate, deployed one at a time, striking from afar,   40
immensely effective, irresistible—what other weapon
of the love god can lead to so sure a victory as you?[8]
You drink up with your half-closed eyes, as if with cupped   41
hands, the water of enlightenment, which stills the
dust of passion of the greatest ascetics, who have
quelled dark, base tendencies, striving to end the cycle
of birth-and-death.[9]
From the moment the creator god fashioned you long   42
ago, assembling in one place the fragments of beauty
scattered about the universe, men have been eager to
journey to the world of the gods.
Therefore, go to him, accompanied by your partners, the   43
gandharvas, those skilled musicians, and put an end
to his austerities! Indeed, conquering this man, who
seeks pleasure, should be a simple task for you, who
have seduced the hearts of men who have overcome
passion!
It is certain this man seeks sensual pleasures by defeating   44
his enemies, for the observances he has undertaken
cannot lead to release from the cycle of birth-and-
death. What does the warrior's bow have to do with
the path to liberation?
You need not fear this fierce warrior will curse you in   45
anger, in the manner of ordinary ascetics. Always
intent on protecting his reputation, a hero would
never harm a woman."

४६ आशंसितापचितिचारु पुरः सुराणा-
मादेशमित्यभिमुखं समवाप्य भर्तुः ।
लेभे परां द्युतिममर्त्यवधूसमूहः
संभावना ह्यधिकृतस्य तनोति तेजः ॥

४७ प्रणतिमथ विधाय प्रस्थिताः सद्मनस्ताः
स्तनभरनमिताङ्गीरङ्गनाः प्रीतिभाजः ।
अचलनलिनलक्ष्मीहारि नालं बभूव
स्तिमितममरभर्तुर्द्रष्टुमक्ष्णां सहस्रम् ॥

The immortal women glowed with transcendent beauty as   46
    they received their lord's command, their loveliness
    increased by the honor bestowed upon them before
    the gods. It is the master's praise that makes the
    servant shine.[10]
As the women bowed to him on leaving the palace,   47
    bending under the weight of their breasts, the
    thousand eyes of the king of immortals, unblinking
    for wonder like a thousand motionless lotuses, were
    not enough for gazing at the nymphs he had favored.

CHAPTER 7

The Journey of the Apsarases and Gandharvas

१ श्रीमद्भिः सरथगजैः सुराङ्गनानां
गुप्तानामथ सचिवैस्त्रिलोकभर्तुः ।
संमूर्छन्नलघुविमानरन्ध्रभिन्नः
प्रस्थानं समभिदधे मृदङ्गनादः ॥

२ सोत्कण्ठैरमरगणैरनुप्रकीर्णा-
न्निर्याय ज्वलितरुचः पुरान्मघोनः ।
रामाणामुपरि विवस्वतः स्थितानां
नासेदे चरितगुणत्वमातपत्रैः ॥

३ धूतानामभिमुखपातिभिः समीरै-
रायासादविशदलोचनोत्पलानाम् ।
आनिन्ये मदजनितां श्रियं वधूना-
मुष्णांशुद्युतिजनितः कपोलरागः ॥

४ तिष्ठद्भिः कथमपि देवतानुभावा-
दाकृष्टैः प्रजविभिरायतं तुरंगैः ।
नेमीनामसति विवर्तने रथौघै-
रासेदे वियति विमानवत्प्रवृत्तिः ॥

116

Then the roll of drums, echoing and spreading in the 1
vast spaces of the gods' flying cars, announced the
departure of Indra's nymphs with the gandharvas,
their partners and guardians, riding on elephants and
in sumptuous chariots.[1]

Leaving Indra's shining city, where crowds of immortals 2
had gathered, eager to see them, the women found
their parasols quite useless, since they were flying
above the sun.

Winds blowing against their faces tossed them about, 3
lotus eyes glazed over with weariness. The sun's hot
rays furnished the women with the glow of wine-
flushed cheeks.

Securely held up in the sky by the magic of the gods, the 4
gandharvas' chariots were speedily drawn by swift
horses. With no need for the fellies of their wheels to
turn, those chariots flew forward like the gods' aerial
cars.

५ कान्तानां कृतपुलकः स्तनाङ्गरागे
वक्त्रेषु च्युततिलकेषु मौक्तिकाभः ।
संपेदे श्रमसलिलोद्गमो विभूषां
रम्याणां विकृतिरपि श्रियं तनोति ॥

६ राजद्भिः पथि मरुतामभिन्नरूपै-
रुल्कार्चिःस्फुटगतिभिर्ध्वजांशुकानाम् ।
तेजोभिः कनकनिकाषराजिगौरै-
रायामः क्रियत इव स्म सातिरेकः ॥

७ रामाणामवजितमाल्यसौकुमार्ये
संप्राप्ते वपुषि सहत्वमातपस्य ।
गन्धर्वैरधिगतविस्मयैः प्रतीये
कल्याणी विधिषु विचित्रता विधातुः ॥

८ सिन्दूरैः कृतरुचयः सहेमकक्ष्याः
स्रोतोभिस्त्रिदशगजा मदं क्षरन्तः ।
साद्दश्यं ययुररुणांशुरागभिन्नै-
र्वर्षद्भिः स्फुरितशतह्रदैः पयोदैः ॥

९ अत्यर्थं दुरुपसदादुपेत्य दूरं
पर्यन्तादहिममयूखमण्डलस्य ।
आशानामुपरचितामिवैकवेणीं
रम्योर्मि त्रिदशनदीं ययुर्बलानि ॥

The sweat, which made the down on their saffron-painted   5
    breasts stiffen, erased the forehead marks on their
    faces and, shining like pearls, became an ornament
    in itself for the women. Even disorder only adds to a
    beauty's loveliness.

Blazing a trail of light that tore through the sky like an   6
    unbroken line of sparks from firebrands, and glittering
    like streaks of gold left behind on a touchstone, the
    entourage's silk banners seemed to stretch endlessly
    into the horizon.

Amazed that the women's bodies, more delicate than a   7
    flower garland, could withstand the sun's heat, the
    gandharvas understood the creator's extraordinary
    benevolence in endowing his creations with a variety
    of attributes.

Painted with designs of red lead, bound with golden   8
    saddle chains, flowing with ichor from every orifice,
    the celestial elephants looked like clouds glittering
    with lightning, shot through with the sun's vermilion
    rays, and showering rain.

Drawing away from the hot sun's unapproachable disc, the   9
    army reached the Ganga, river of the gods, her lovely
    waves a single braid of hair bound by the nymphs of
    the directions.

१०
आमत्तभ्रमरकुलाकुलानि धुन्व-
न्नुद्धूतग्रथितरजांसि पङ्कजानि ।
कान्तानां गगननदीतरङ्गशीतः
संतापं विरमयति स्म मातरिश्वा ॥

११
संभिन्नैरिभतुरगावगाहनेन
प्राप्योर्वीरनुपदवीं विमानपङ्क्तीः ।
तत्पूर्वं प्रतिविदधे सुरापगाया
वप्रान्तस्खलितविवर्तनं पयोभिः ॥

१२
क्रान्तानां ग्रहचरितात्पथो रथाना-
मक्षाग्रक्षतसुरवेश्मवेदिकानाम् ।
निःसङ्गं प्रधिभिरुपाददे विवृत्तिः
संपीडक्षुभितजलेषु तोयदेषु ॥

१३
तन्मानामुपदधिरे विषाणभिन्नाः
प्रह्लादं सुरकरिणां घनाः क्षरन्तः ।
युक्तानां खलु महतां परोपकारे
कल्याणी भवति रुजत्स्वपि प्रवृत्तिः ॥

१४
संवाता मुहुरनिलेन नीयमाने
दिव्यस्त्रीजघनवरांशुके विवृत्तिम् ।
पर्यस्यत्पृथुमणिमेखलांशुजालं
संजज्ञे युतकमिवान्तरीयमूर्वोः ॥

The wind shook lotuses swarming with drunken bees and   10
    tossed up lotus pollen, rolled up in balls. Cool from
    brushing against the sky-river's waves, it brought
    relief to the women wearied by the heat.

Churned up by elephants and horses plunging in, the   11
    sky-river's waves struck the long line of flying cars[2]
    moving in her tracks, and so for the first time ever,
    found themselves rolling back from a bank.

Once the chariots had left the path of the planets, where   12
    their axles had knocked against the bases of the gods'
    mansions, the rims of the chariot wheels began to turn
    freely, churning the water in every cloud they met.

Pierced by the elephants' tusks, the clouds began to   13
    shower rain, reviving them as they wilted from the
    heat. Is it not true that those set on helping others will
    be kind even to those who hurt them?

Every time the nymphs' fine silk skirts were blown aside   14
    by the gusting wind, the rays of light radiating from
    the great gems on their girdle belts became a skirt to
    cover up their thighs.

१५ प्रत्याद्रीकृततिलकास्तुषारपातैः
प्रह्लादं शमितपरिश्रमा दिशन्तः ।
कान्तानां बहुमतिमाययुः पयोदा
नाल्पीयान्बहु सुकृतं हिनस्ति दोषः ॥

१६ यातस्य ग्रथिततरङ्गसैकताभे
विच्छेदं विपयसि वारिवाहजाले ।
आतेनुस्त्रिदशवधूजनाङ्गभाजां
संधानं सुरधनुषः प्रभा मणीनाम् ॥

१७ संसिद्धाविति करणीयसंनिबद्धै-
रालापैः पिपतिषतां विलङ्घ्य वीथीम् ।
आसेदे दशशतलोचनध्वजिन्या
जीमूतैरपिहितसानुरिन्द्रकीलः ॥

१८ आकीर्ण मुखनलिनैर्विलासिनीना-
मुद्धूतस्फुटविशदातपत्रफेना ।
सा तूर्यध्वनितगभीरमापतन्ती
भूभर्तुः शिरसि नभोनदीव रेजे ॥

१९ सेतुत्वं दधति पयोमुचां विताने
संरम्भादभिपततो रथाङ्गवेन ।
आनिन्युर्नियमितरश्मिभुग्रघोणाः
कृच्छ्रेण क्षितिमवनामिनस्तुरंगाः ॥

122

Though the clouds with their cool spray made their 15
    painted forehead ornaments run, they pleasantly
    relieved their fatigue and so earned the beautiful
    women's esteem. A small fault does not negate a great
    favor.

When the rainbow's arc broke on a bank of clouds emptied 16
    of rain, white as wavy sand, the light streaming from
    the gems of the nymphs' jewels supplied its missing
    curve.

Discussing strategies for the success of their mission, 17
    Indra's army traversed the path of the birds and
    reached Indrakila's cloud-covered peak.

Covered with the lotuses that were the women's faces, 18
    flecked with the foam of the unfurled white parasols
    raised above them, deeply rumbling with the beat of
    drums, the army seemed like the sky-river itself as it
    landed on the mountain peak.

Straining forward, muzzles curved back from the pull 19
    of the reins, the horses labored to bring the chariots
    safely to earth as they flew headlong over a bridge
    formed by a bank of clouds.

२० माहेन्द्रं नगमभितः करेणुवर्याः
पर्यन्तस्थितजलदा दिवः पतन्तः ।
साहृश्यं निलयननिष्कम्पपक्षै-
राजगर्मुर्जलनिधिशायिभिर्नगेन्द्रैः ॥

२१ उत्सङ्गे समविषमे समं महाद्रेः
क्रान्तानां वियदभिपातलाघवेन ।
आ मूलादुपनदि सैकतेषु लेभे
सामग्रीं खुरपदवी तुरंगमाणाम् ॥

२२ सध्वानं निपतितनिर्झरासु मन्द्रैः
संमूर्छन्प्रतिनिनदैरधित्यकासु ।
उद्गीवैर्घनरवशङ्कया मयूरैः
सोत्कण्ठं ध्वनिरुपशुश्रुवे रथानाम् ॥

२३ संभिन्नामविरलपातिभिर्मयूखै-
र्नीलानां भृशमुपमेखलं मणीनाम् ।
विच्छिन्नामिव वनिता नभोऽन्तराले
वप्राम्भःस्रुतिमवलोकयांबभूवुः ॥

२४ आसन्नद्विपपदवीमदानिलाय
क्रुध्यन्तो धियमवमत्य धूर्गतानाम् ।
सव्याजं निजकरिणीभिरात्तचित्ताः
प्रस्थानं सुरकरिणः कथंचिदीषुः ॥

124

Flanked by clouds as they flew down from the sky toward   20
    Indra's mountain peak, the gandharva army's prize
    elephants looked like the mountains lying still on the
    ocean floor, with motionless wings.[3]

Flying with ease in the sky, the horses had strained to keep   21
    a steady course on the uneven terrain of the mountain
    slopes, but they left a perfectly even track on the
    sandy riverbank at the foot of the mountain.

Peacocks, craning their necks, eagerly listened, hearing   22
    thunder in the rumble of the chariots, amplified by
    deep echoes on highlands where roaring cataracts
    came crashing down.[4]

Suffused at the foot by blue rays of light steadily streaming   23
    from sapphires on the mountain slope, a highland
    waterfall appeared to the women as if it were cut off
    and suspended in the sky.

Enraged by the scent of ichor carried by the wind from the   24
    track of wild elephants nearby, the gods' elephants
    refused to obey the driver's command; only when
    enticed and distracted by their mates were they
    persuaded to move.

२५ नीरन्ध्रं पथिषु रजो रथाङ्गनुन्नं
पर्यस्यन्नवसलिलारुणं वहन्ती ।
आतेने वनगहनानि वाहिनी सा
घर्मान्तक्षुभितजलेव जह्नुकन्या ॥

२६ संभोगक्षमगहनामथोपगङ्गं
बिभ्राणां ज्वलितमणीनि सैकतानि ।
अध्यूषुश्श्रुतकुसुमाचितां सहाया
वृत्रारेरविरलशार्दूलां धरित्रीम् ॥

२७ भूभर्तुः समधिकमादधे तदोर्व्याः
श्रीमत्तां हरिसखवाहिनीनिवेशः ।
संसक्तौ किमसुलभं महोदयाना-
मुच्छ्रायं नयति यदृच्छयापि योगः ॥

२८ सामोदाः कुसुमतरुश्रियो विविक्ताः
संपत्तिः किसलयशालिनीलतानाम् ।
साफल्यं ययुरमराङ्गनोपभुक्ताः
सा लक्ष्मीरुपकुरुते यया परेषाम् ॥

२९ क्रान्तो ऽपि त्रिदशवधूजनः पुरस्ता-
ल्लीनाहिश्वसितविलोलपल्लवानाम् ।
सेव्यानां हतविनयैरिवावृतानां
संपर्कं परिहरति स्म चन्दनानाम् ॥

Enveloped in thick dust kicked up on the roads by chariot   25
  wheels, dust red like river waters swelling after the
  first rains, the army spread over the dense forests like
  the river Ganga flowing turbid at summer's end.

Indra's companions camped on a spot on the Ganga's   26
  bank, a piece of ground perfectly suited for
  enjoyment, furnished with sand glittering with gems,
  abounding in green grass, and carpeted with fallen
  flowers.

That mountain land glowed with heightened beauty   27
  when Indra's army had set up camp there. Nothing
  is beyond the reach of those who associate with
  magnanimous people; even a chance relationship can
  yield beneficent results.

The lovely celestial women took pleasure in the trees   28
  blooming with fragrant flowers, the mountain camp's
  secluded spots, and its bounty of creepers bursting
  with young shoots, and all thereby reaped the benefit
  of their existence. The true purpose of wealth is to be
  of service to others.

Though exhausted, the nymphs were careful not to lean   29
  against the sandalwood trees before them, for the
  leaves fluttered with the hisses of the snakes coiled
  around their trunks, like deceivers who insinuate
  themselves with eminent men.

३० उत्सृष्टध्वजकुथकङ्कटा धरित्री-
मानीता विदितनयैः श्रमं विनेतुम् ।
आक्षिप्तद्रुमगहना युगान्तवातैः
पर्यस्ता गिरय इव द्विपा विरेजुः ॥

३१ प्रस्थानश्रमजनितां विहाय निद्रा-
मामुक्ते गजपतिना सदानपङ्के ।
शय्यान्ते कुलमलिनां क्षणं विलीनं
संरम्भच्युतमिव शृङ्खलं चकाशे ॥

३२ आयस्तः सुरसरिदोघरुद्धवर्त्मा
संप्राप्तुं वनगजदानगन्धि रोधः ।
मूर्धानं निहितशिताङ्कुशं विधुन्व-
न्यन्तारं न विगणयांचकार नागः ॥

३३ आरोढुः समवनतस्य पीतशेषे
साशङ्कं पयसि समीरिते करेण ।
संमार्जन्नरुणमदसुती कपोलौ
सस्यन्दे मद इव शीकरः करेणोः ॥

३४ आघ्राय क्षणमतितृष्यतापि रोषा-
दुत्तीरं निहितविवृत्तलोचनेन ।
संपृक्तं वनकरिणां मदाम्बुसेकै-
र्नाचेमे हिममपि वारि वारणेन ॥

When the expert trainers had removed banners and   30
    saddlecloths and plates of armor from the celestial
    elephants, and coaxed them to rest lying down on the
    ground, the elephants took on the ruined majesty
    of mountains lying scattered about, their forests
    swept away by hurricane winds, at the time of cosmic
    dissolution.

A king elephant, waking from the sleep of exhaustion,   31
    rose from his bed, leaving it wet with sweet ichor, and
    the row of bees for a moment alighting looked like his
    chain falling as he hastily got up.

The celestial river's swelling current blocked the path of   32
    an elephant straining to cross to the other bank, which
    smelt of the ichor of wild elephants. When the driver
    drove the sharp goad into his head, he merely shook it
    off and paid no heed.

Another elephant bent down to drink from the river,   33
    but did not finish for fear of his driver. The water he
    sprayed with his trunk rubbed off the red streams of
    ichor flowing down his cheeks, then took their place.

Instantly smelling the ichor of wild elephants in the water,   34
    an elephant refused to drink it, although it was cool
    and he was very thirsty. Eyes rolling in rage, he stared
    at the other bank.

३५ प्रश्योतन्मदसुरभीणि निम्नगायाः
क्रीडन्तो गजपतयः पयांसि कृत्वा ।
किञ्जल्कव्यवहितताम्रदानलेखै-
रुत्तेरुः सरसिजगन्धिभिः कपोलैः ॥

३६ आकीर्ण बलरजसा घनारुणेन
प्रक्षोभैः सपदि तरङ्गितं तटेषु ।
मातङ्गोन्मथितसरोजरेणुपिङ्गं
माञ्जिष्ठं वसनमिवाम्बु निर्बभासे ॥

३७ श्रीमद्द्विनियमितकन्धरापरान्तैः
संसक्तैरगुरुवनेषु साङ्घहारम् ।
संप्रापे निसृतमदाम्बुभिर्गजेन्द्रैः
प्रस्यन्दिप्रचलितगण्डशैलशोभा ॥

३८ निःशेषं प्रशमितरेणु वारणानां
स्रोतोभिर्मदजलमुज्झतामजस्रम् ।
आमोदं व्यवहितभूरिपुष्पगन्धो
भिन्नैलासुरभिमुवाह गन्धवाहः ॥

३९ साटङ्कश्यं दधति गभीरमेघघोषै-
रुन्निद्रक्षुभितमृगाधिपश्रुतानि ।
आतेनुश्चकितचकोरनीलकण्ठा-
न्कच्छान्तानमरमहेभबृंहितानि ॥

Playing in the river, the bull elephants perfumed the water   35
    with streaming ichor. When they came out, their
    cheeks smelled of lotuses, and lotus filaments covered
    the streaks of ichor.[5]

Covered with the copper-red dust kicked up by the army,   36
    ruddy with the pollen of lotuses trampled down by the
    elephants, striking the banks in sudden waves where
    it had been stirred up, the river shone like a cloth dyed
    red with madder.[6]

Handsome bull elephants, chained by the neck and hind   37
    legs, streaming ichor as they stirred gracefully among
    the black aloe trees, looked like rocks dripping water,
    just rolled down from mountain cliffs.

Mixing it with the fragrance of various flowers, the wind   38
    wafted the scent of elephant ichor, sweet smelling like
    crushed cardamom, profusely streaming from every
    opening, settling the dust everywhere.

Sounding like the deep thunder of clouds, the trumpeting   39
    of the gods' mighty elephants awakened lions and put
    them on their guard, echoed across the riverbanks,
    and threw the *cakora* partridges and peacocks into
    confusion.[7]

४० शाखावसक्तकमनीयपरिच्छदाना-
मध्वश्रमातुरवधूजनसेवितानाम्।
जज्ञे निवेशनविभागपरिष्कृतानां
लक्ष्मीः पुरोपवनजा वनपादपानाम्॥

With beautiful garments hanging from their branches,   40
   the travel-weary nymphs resting against them, and the
   divisions of the celestial army surrounding them, the
   forest trees looked like trees in a city pleasure park.

CHAPTER 8

Playing in the Woods and the River Ganga

७ करौ धुनाना नवपल्लवाकृती वृथा कृथा मानिनि मा परिश्रमम् ।
उपेयुषी कल्पलताभिशङ्कया कथं न्वितस्त्रस्यति षट्पदावलिः ॥

८ जहीहि कोपं दयितो ऽनुगम्यतां पुरानुशेते तव चञ्चलं मनः ।
इति प्रियं कांचिदुपैतुमिच्छतीं पुरो ऽनुनिन्ये निपुणः
सखीजनः ॥

९ समुन्नतैः काशदुकूलशालिभिः परिक्वणत्सारसपङ्क्तिमेखलैः ।
प्रतीरदेशैः स्वकलत्रचारुभिर्विभूषिताः कुञ्जसमुद्रयोषितः ॥

१० विदूरपातेन भिदामुपेयुषश्रुताः प्रवाहादभितः प्रसारिणः ।
प्रियाङ्कशीताः शुचिमौक्तिकत्विषो वनप्रहासा इव वारिबिन्दवः ॥

११ सखीजनं प्रेम गुरूकृतादरं निरीक्षमाणा इव नम्रमूर्तयः ।
स्थिरद्विरेफाञ्जनशारितोदरैर्विसारिभिः पुष्पविलोचनैर्लताः ॥

१२ उपेयुषीणां बृहतीरधित्यका मनांसि जहुः सुरराजयोषिताम् ।
कपोलकाषैः करिणां मदारुणैरुपाहितश्यामरुचश्च चन्दनाः ॥

१३ स्वगोचरे सत्यपि चित्तहारिणा विलोभ्यमानाः प्रसवेन
शाखिनाम् ।
नभश्चराणामुपकर्तुमिच्छतां प्रियाणि चक्रुः प्रणयेन योषितः ॥

"Why tire yourself, proud girl? It is no use waving your   7–8
arms that look like tender shoots. How will you drive
away this swarm of bees flying toward you, thinking
you a vine of paradise?⁴ Give up your anger, take pity
on your lover before your fickle heart regrets it!"
Knowing that she wanted to go to her lover, clever
girlfriends pacified a young woman even before a
quarrel had begun, paving the way for her to approach
him.⁵

The forest streams on the highlands looked like beautiful   9–12
women. Their high banks, lovely as the hips of the
nymphs, were draped in *kāśa* flowers that were white
silk garments, and laced with girdles of chattering
wild geese. There drops of water fractured as they fell
from great heights and encircled the earth in a lover's
cool embrace. The woods seemed to laugh with those
drops, bright as pearls. There were vines, stalks bent
down a little, as though they were women gazing at
their girlfriends with deep affection, with wide-open
flower-eyes flecked dark with motionless bees. And
the sandalwood trees were stained dark with the flow
of ichor from the cheeks of elephants rubbing against
them. With all these charms the highlands enchanted
the apsarases as they climbed up.

Sorely tempted by the delightful flowers within reach on   13
the trees, yet eager to please their lovers, the loving
women let the gandharvas help them gather the
blossoms.

139

१४ प्रयच्छतोच्चैः कुसुमानि मानिनी विपक्षगोत्रं दयितेन लम्भिता ।
न किंचिदूचे चरणेन केवलं लिलेख बाष्पाकुललोचना भुवम् ॥

१५ प्रिये ऽपरा यच्छति वाचमुन्मुखी निबद्धदृष्टिः शिथिलाकुलोच्चया ।
समादधे नांशुकमाहितं वृथा विवेद पुष्पेषु न पाणिपल्लवम् ॥

१६ सलीलमासक्तलतान्तभूषणं समासजन्त्या कुसुमावतंसकम् ।
स्तनोपपीडं नुनुदे नितम्बिना घनेन कश्चिज्जघनेन कान्तया ॥

१७ कलत्रभारेण विलोलनीविना गलद्दुकूलस्तनशालिनोरसा ।
बलिव्यपायस्फुटरोमराजिना निरायतत्वादुदरेण ताम्यता ॥

१८ विलम्बमानाकुलकेशपाशया कयाचिदाविष्कृतबाहुमूलया ।
तरुप्रसूनान्यपदिश्य सादरं मनोऽधिनाथस्य मनः समादे ॥

१९ व्यपोहितुं लोचनतो मुखानिलैरपारयन्तं किल पुष्पजं रजः ।
पयोधरेणोरसि काचिदुन्मनाः प्रियं जघानोन्नतपीवरस्तनी ॥

२० इमान्यमूनीत्यपवर्जिते शनैर्यथाभिरामं कुसुमाग्रपल्लवे ।
विहाय निःसारतयेव भूरुहान्पदं वनश्रीर्वनितासु संदधे ॥

One apsaras was upset when her lover, even while offering 14
flowers he had plucked, called her by her rival's name,
out loud. She said nothing, but with eyes brimming
with tears, simply stood scratching the ground with
her toe.[6]

Another, standing with uplifted face, eyes riveted on the 15
lover speaking to her, did not feel the knot loosening,
or draw the skirt around her as it slipped down, or
notice the slim hand she stretched out in vain for the
flowers.

Another, gracefully arranging a chaplet of blossoms laced 16
with shoots on her hair, pressed her breasts against
her lover, and leaned on him with the weight of her
swelling hips and buttocks.

Yet another, coyly pretending to reach for a flower, stood 17-18
up, and her skirt's knot loosened, straining at broad,
full hips; the silk cloth slipped from her breasts,
showing a fine line of hair on the taut belly, where the
three graceful folds disappeared as she stretched; her
hairdo fell disheveled, cascading down her back, half a
breast showing on one side—and the lover's heart was
won.

A lover deliberately took his time, blowing away the pollen 19
from his lady's eyes. Desire aroused, she pressed her
high, plump breasts against his chest.

"I want this one—no, that one!"—When the nymphs had 20
gathered, one after another, the loveliest flowers and
shoots from every branch, the beauty of the forest left
the trees, bankrupt in their bareness, and settled on
the young women.

२१ प्रवालभङ्गारुणपाणिपल्लवः परागपाण्डूकृतपीवरस्तनः ।
महीरुहः पुष्पसुगन्धिराददे वपुर्गुणोच्छायमिवाङ्गनाजनः ॥

२२ वरोरुभिर्वारणहस्तपीवरैश्चिराय खिन्नान्नवपल्लवश्रियः ।
समे ऽपि यातुं चरणाननीश्वरान्मदादिव प्रस्खलतः पदे पदे ॥

२३ विसारिकाञ्चीमणिरश्मिलब्धया मनोहरोच्छायनितम्बशोभया ।
स्थितानि जित्वा नवसैकतद्युतिं श्रमातिरिक्तैर्जघनानि गौरवैः ॥

२४ समुच्छ्वसत्पङ्कजकोशकोमलैरुपाहितश्रीण्युपनीवि नाभिभिः ।
दधन्ति मध्येषु वलीविभङ्गिषु स्तनातिभारादुदराणि नम्रताम् ॥

२५ समानकान्तीनि तुषारभूषणैः सरोरुहैरस्फुटपत्रपङ्क्तिभिः ।
चितानि घर्माम्बुकणैः समन्ततो मुखान्यनुत्फुल्लविलोचनानि च ॥

२६ विनिर्यतीनां गुरुखेदमन्थरं सुराङ्गनानामनुसानु वर्त्मनः ।
सविस्मयं रूपयतो नभश्चरान्निवेश तत्पूर्वमिवेक्षणादरः ॥

२७ अथ स्फुरन्मीनविधूतपङ्कजा विपङ्कतीरस्खलितोर्मिसंहतिः ।
पयो ऽवगाढुं कलहंसनादिनी समाजुहावेव वधूः सुरापगा ॥

२८ प्रशान्तघर्माभिभवः शनैर्विवान्विलासिनीभ्यः परिमृष्टपङ्कजः ।
ददौ भुजालम्बमिवात्तशीकरस्तरङ्गमालान्तरगोचरो ऽनिलः ॥

Smelling sweeter with the scent of flowers, shootlike　　21
　　hands redder from breaking off twigs, full breasts
　　gilded with pollen, the women seemed to have simply
　　added to their own charms.
The women's feet, tender as young shoots, were burdened　　22-26
　　by thighs plump as elephant trunks. They struggled
　　to walk even on level ground, faltering at every
　　step as though they were drunk. Their heavy hips,
　　weighed down by weariness, shone brighter than fresh
　　sandbanks. The charming swell of the buttocks was
　　illumined by light streaming from the girdle's gems.
　　Bellies, beautiful at the knot of the skirt, revealed
　　navels soft as the hearts of blooming lotuses. Weighed
　　down by full breasts, torsos curved gently at the
　　waist's undulating folds. Faces with half-closed eyes,
　　studded with perspiration, looked as lovely as lotuses
　　with half-open petals covered with dewdrops. Gazing
　　with wonder at these charms of the nymphs as they
　　slowly, wearily emerged from the path on the slopes,
　　the gandharva lovers realized for the first time the
　　true value of eyesight.[7]
Then, with the sweet call of wild geese, the flutter of　　27
　　lotuses jostled by glittering fish, and waves rolling
　　onto banks free of mud, the divine river Ganga invited
　　the women to enter her water.[8]
A cooling breeze from off the billows, brushing past the　　28
　　lotuses and bearing water droplets, blew gently,
　　offering the weary women, it seemed, a helping hand.

२९ गतैः सहावैः कलहंसविक्रमं कलत्रभारैः पुलिनं नितम्बिभिः ।
    मुखैः सरोजानि च दीर्घलोचनैः सुरस्त्रियः साम्यगुणान्निरासिरे ॥

३० विभिन्नपर्यन्तगमीनपङ्क्तयः पुरो विगाढाः सखिभिर्मरुत्वतः ।
    कथंचिदापः सुरसुन्दरीजनैः सभीतिभिस्तत्प्रथमं प्रपेदिरे ॥

३१ विगाढमात्रे रमणीभिरम्भसि प्रयत्नसंवाहितपीवरोरुभिः ।
    विभिद्यमाना विससार सारसानुदस्य तीरेषु तरङ्गसंहतिः ॥

३२ शिलाघनैर्नाकसदामुरःस्थलैर्बृहन्निवेशैश्च वधूपयोधरैः ।
    तटाभिनीतेन विभिन्नवीचिना रुषेव भेजे कलुषत्वमम्भसा ॥

३३ विधूतकेशाः परिलोलितस्रजः सुराङ्गनानां प्रविलुप्तचन्दनाः ।
    अतिप्रसङ्गाद्द्विहितागसो मुहुः प्रकम्पमीयुः सभया इवोर्मयः ॥

३४ विपक्षचित्तोन्मथना नखव्रणास्तिरोहिता विभ्रममण्डनेन ये ।
    हृतस्य शेषानिव कुङ्कुमस्य तान्विकत्थनीयान्दधुरन्यथा स्त्रियः ॥

The gait of wild geese could not compare with the 29
    apsarases' graceful walk, nor the sandbanks with
    their hips weighed down by swelling buttocks, nor the
    lotuses with their faces with long, curving eyes.

The gandharvas, Indra's companions, plunged in first, 30
    scattering the fish and driving them toward the river's
    banks. Hesitantly following their lovers, the lovely
    nymphs took their first timid dip in the water.

No sooner did the beautiful women plunge in, guiding 31
    their plump thighs with effort, than the parted waves
    flowed outward, stirring up the cranes flocking on the
    opposite bank.

Breaking on the gandharvas' rock-hard chests and the 32
    nymphs' ample breasts, the waves were thrown onto
    the river's banks, and the water grew turbid as though
    enraged.

The waves quivered more than ever, as if afraid of having 33
    offended the nymphs with their audacious behavior,
    for they had rumpled the women's hair, put their
    garlands in disarray, and rubbed off the sandalwood
    cream from their breasts.

Before, decorative designs had hidden nail wounds from 34
    the night's lovemaking, those sources of pride that
    arouse pangs of envy in rivals; but now the women
    displayed them openly on their bodies, pretending
    they were traces of the red saffron cream the water
    had washed away.

३५ सरोजपत्रे नु विलीनषड्दे विलोलदृष्टेः स्विदमू विलोचने ।
शिरोरुहाः स्विन्नतपक्ष्मसंततेर्द्विरेफवृन्दं नु निशब्दनिश्चलम् ॥

३६ अगूढहासस्फुटदन्तकेसरं मुखं स्विदेतद्द्विकसन्नु पङ्कजम् ।
इति प्रलीनां नलिनीवने सखीं विदांबभूवुः सुचिरेण योषितः ॥

३७ प्रियेण संग्रथ्य विपक्षसंनिधावुपाहितां वक्षसि पीवरस्तने ।
स्रजं न काचिद्द्विजहौ जलाविलां वसन्ति हि प्रेम्णि गुणा न
वस्तुनि ॥

३८ असंशयं न्यस्तमुपान्तरक्ततां यदेव रोढुं रमणीभिरञ्जनम् ।
हृते ऽपि तस्मिन्सलिलेन शुक्लतां निरास रागो नयनेषु न
श्रियम् ॥

३९ द्युतिं वहन्तो वनितावतंसका हृताः प्रलोभादिव वेगिभिर्जलैः ।
उपप्लुतास्तत्क्षणशोचनीयतां च्युताधिकाराः सचिवा इवाययुः ॥

४० विपत्तलेखा निरलक्तकाधरा निरञ्जनाक्षीरपि बिभ्रतीः श्रियम् ।
निरीक्ष्य रामा बुबुधे नभश्चरैरलंकृतं तद्वपुषैव मण्डनम् ॥

"Are these the bee-laden petals of a lotus, or the eyes of   35-36
the girl with darting glances? Are these her curved
lashes, or a still, silent swarm of bees? Is this her
mouth with its filamentlike teeth displayed in a wide
smile, or a blooming lotus?" Assailed by such doubts
as these, the young women looked long for their
girlfriend in her camouflage, a bed of lotuses.[9]

A young woman clung to her garland, although ruined by   37
the water, for her lover had woven it himself and put
it on her voluptuous breasts with her rival looking on.
An object is valued for the sentiment attached to it,
and not for itself.

The reason the women had lined their eyes with mascara   38
must have been to cover the redness at their corners,
not to beautify the eyes. For now that the water had
washed it off, the redness chased the whiteness from
the eyes, but not their beauty.[10]

The nymphs' bright floral chaplets were snatched away by   39
the swift currents as if from greed, and as they floated
away they became instantly pitiable, like powerful
ministers toppled from office by greedy fools.

When the gandharvas saw the nymphs glowing with   40
beauty, although the river water had washed away the
leaf designs of aloe and musk from their cheeks, the
lac gloss from their lips, and the mascara from their
eyes, they realized the women's bodies beautified
their cosmetics, not the other way around.

४१ तथा न पूर्वं कृतभूषणादरः प्रियानुरागेण विलासिनीजनः ।
यथा जलार्द्रो नखमण्डनश्रिया ददाह दृष्टीश्च विपक्षयोषिताम् ॥

४२ शुभाननाः साम्बुरुहेषु भीरवो विलोलहाराश्चलफेनपङ्क्तिषु ।
नितान्तगौर्यो हृतकुङ्कुमेष्वलं न लेभिरे ताः परभागमूर्मिषु ॥

४३ हृदाम्भसि व्यस्तवधूकराहते रवं मृदङ्गध्वनिधीरमुज्झति ।
मुहुः स्तनैस्तालसमं समाददे मनोरमं नृत्यमिव प्रवेपितम् ॥

४४ श्रिया हसद्भिः कमलानि सस्मितैरलंकृताम्बुः प्रतिमागतैर्मुखैः ।
कृतानुकूल्या सुरराजयोषितां प्रसादसाफल्यमवाप जाह्नवी ॥

४५ परिस्फुरन्मीनविघट्टितोरवः सुराङ्गनास्त्रासविलोलदृष्टयः ।
उपाययुः कम्पितपाणिपल्लवाः सखीजनस्यापि विलोकनीयता-
म् ॥

४६ भयादिवाश्लिष्य झषाहते ऽम्भसि प्रियं मुदानन्दयति स्म
मानिनी ।
अकृत्रिमप्रेमरसाहितैर्मनो हरन्ति रामाः कृतकैरपीहितैः ॥

Not even when decked out in jewels did those graceful 41
women burn their rivals' eyes with their lovers'
passion, as they did now, with water-drenched
bodies beautified by nail wounds from the night's
lovemaking.[11]

The timid nymphs could not excel the waves in beauty: 42
their faces were radiant, their strands of pearls
swayed, their complexions were superbly fair, but the
waves had lotuses, and surging foam, and the saffron
washed away from their bodies.[12]

As the women slapped the water, it resounded with the 43
deep tones of a *mṛdaṅga* drum, and their breasts
swayed rhythmically, keeping time to the beat, as
though performing a charming dance.

Her water graced by the reflection of the nymphs' smiling 44
faces, whose glowing beauty put its lotuses to shame,
the river Ganga reaped the benefit of her clarity.

Because glittering fish were nudging their thighs, the 45
apsarases' eyes grew wide with fear, and their hands
were trembling—and they charmed even their
girlfriends' eyes.

As fish darted about her in the water, a young woman 46
delighted her lover by throwing her arms around him
as though frightened, though she really wanted to
embrace him. Women charm their lovers' hearts even
with feigned gestures when prompted by genuine
feeling.

४७ तिरोहितान्तानि नितान्तमाकुलैरपां विगाहादलकैः प्रसारिभिः ।
यययुर्वधूनां वदनानि तुल्यतां द्विरेफवृन्दान्तरितैः सरोरुहैः ॥

४८ करौ धुनाना नवपल्लवाकृती पयस्यगाधे किल जातसंभ्रमा ।
सखीषु निर्वाच्यमधाच्छ्र्यद्दूषितं प्रियाङ्कसंश्लेषमवाप⁷ मानिनी ॥

४९ प्रियैः सलिलं करवारिवारितः प्रवृद्धनिःश्वासविकम्पितस्तनः ।
सविभ्रमाधूतकराग्रपल्लवो यथार्थतामाप विलासिनीजनः ॥

५० उदस्य धैर्यं दयितेन सादरं प्रसादितायाः करवारिवारितम् ।
मुखं निमीलन्नयनं नतभ्रुवः श्रियं सपत्नीवदनादिवाददे ॥

५१ विहस्य पाणौ विधृते धृताम्भसि प्रियेण वध्वा मदनार्द्रचेतसः ।
सखीव काञ्ची पयसा घनीकृता बभार वीतोच्चयबन्धमंशुकम् ॥

५२ निरञ्जने साचिविलोकितं दृशावयावकं वेपथुरोष्ठपल्लवम् ।
नतभ्रुवो मण्डयति स्म विग्रहे बलिक्रिया चातिलकं तदास्पदम् ॥

५३ निमीलदाकेकरलोलचक्षुषां प्रियोपकण्ठं कृतगात्रवेपथुः ।
निमज्जतीनां श्वसितोद्धतस्तनः श्रमो नु तासां मदनो नु पप्रथे ॥

Half hidden by long, spreading curls disheveled from   47
 swimming, the nymphs' faces in the water looked like
 lotuses covered by swarms of black bees.

As if afraid of the deep water a proud beauty waved   48
 her lovely arms and embraced her lover, disarming
 criticism from friends and escaping blame for
 boldness.[13]

As their lovers splashed them playfully with handfuls of   49
 water, the women's breasts rose with heaving breaths
 and their shootlike hands fluttered gracefully, fully
 earning them the epithet of "charmers."

One lover yielded and graciously appeased a girl, who   50
 closed her eyes when he splashed her with a handful
 of water. And her face grew lovely, as though it had
 drained all the beauty from her rival's face.

Another grasped his beloved's hands with a laugh as she   51
 cupped them to splash him with water. Her heart
 melted, and her skirt, knot loosened, began to slip but
 her girdle, tightened by the water, came to her aid like
 a friend to hold it up.

On one woman's face, the sidelong glances of a lover's   52
 quarrel beautified eyes bereft of mascara; a tremor,
 the lips bereft of lac gloss; a furrow, the forehead
 where the forehead mark had been erased.

As the women swam in the river close to their lovers, their   53
 curved eyes—usually restless—were closed, their
 limbs quivered, and their breasts heaved with sighs.
 Were they overcome by the weariness of exercise, or
 by desire?

५४ प्रियेण सिक्ता चरमं विपक्षतश्चुकोप काचिन्न तुतोष सान्त्वनैः ।
जनस्य रूढप्रणयस्य चेतसः किमप्यमर्षो ऽनुनये भृशायते ॥

५५ इत्थं विहृत्य वनिताभिरुदस्यमानं
पीनस्तनोरुजघनस्थलशालिनीभिः ।
उत्सर्पितोर्मिचयलङ्घिततीरदेश-
मौत्सुक्यनुन्नमिव वारि पुरः प्रतस्थे ॥

५६ तीरान्तराणि मिथुनानि रथाङ्गनाम्नां
नीत्वा विलोलितसरोजवनश्रियस्ताः ।
संरेजिरे सुरसरिज्जलधौतहारा-
स्तारावितानतरला इव यामवत्यः ॥

५७ संक्रान्तचन्दनरसाहितवर्णभेदं
विच्छिन्नभूषणमणिप्रकरांशुचित्रम् ।
बद्धोर्मि नाकवनितापरिभुक्तमुक्तं
सिन्धोर्बभार सलिलं शयनीयलक्ष्मीम् ॥

A gandharva provoked his partner's anger by splashing   54
her with water only after he had splashed her rival,
and no amount of coaxing could bring her around.
When a woman is deeply in love, the lover's entreaties
somehow only serve to make her angrier still.

Tossed up in play by the women with full breasts and wide   55
hips, the river water climbed up on the banks with
swelling waves, surging forward as if it were driven by
desire.

The women had driven the shelldrake couples to opposite   56
riverbanks and disturbed the lovely beds of lotuses.
And now, with their strands of pearls gleaming from
being washed in the waters of the divine Ganga, they
shone like nights radiant with canopies of stars.[14]

Stained by mixing with sandalwood cream and flecked by   57
the sparkling gems spilled from broken jewelry, the
undulating river, once the women had finished playing
and left, looked like a rumpled bed after a night of
lovemaking.

CHAPTER 9

The Lovemaking of the Apsarases and Gandharvas

१ वीक्ष्य रन्तुमनसः सुरनारीरात्तचित्रपरिधानविभूषाः ।
तत्प्रियार्थमिव यातुमथास्तं भानुमानुपपयोधि ललम्बे

२ मध्यमोपलनिभे लसदंशावेकतश्रुतिमुपेयुषि भानौ ।
द्यौरुवाह परिवृत्तिविलोलां हारयष्टिमिव वासरलक्ष्मीम् ॥

३ अंशुपाणिभिरतीव पिपासुः पद्मजं मधु भृशं रसयित्वा ।
क्षीबतामिव गतः क्षितिमेष्यँल्लोहितं वपुरुवाह पतंगः ॥

४ गम्यतामुपगते नयनानां लोहितायति सहस्रमरीचौ ।
आससाद विरहय्य धरित्रीं चक्रवाकहृदयान्यभितापः ॥

५ मुक्तमूललघुरुज्झितपूर्वः पश्चिमे नभसि संभृतसान्द्रः ।
सामि मज्जति रवौ न विरेजे खिन्नजिह्व इव रश्मिसमूहः ॥

६ कान्तदूत्य इव कुङ्कुमताम्राः सायमण्डनमभि ऽ त्वरयन्त्यः ।
सादरं ददृशिरे वनिताभिः सौधजालपतिता रविभासः ॥

७ अग्रसानुषु नितान्तपिशङ्गैर्भूरुहान्मृदुकरैरवलम्ब्य ।
अस्तशैलगहनं नु विवस्वानाविवेश जलधिं नु महीं नु ॥

When the nymphs were ready for lovemaking, dressed in   1
   brightly colored garments and sumptuously arrayed
   in jewels, the sun began to sink into the ocean as if it
   wished to do them a favor.[1]

The sky put on the fleeting beauty of the evening   2
   twilight, like a swaying strand of pearls, with the sun
   suspended on one side, shining like a great pendant
   gem with its gleaming rays.

Its great thirst quenched by deep draughts of lotus honey,   3
   drunk from cupped hands that were its rays, the
   sun turned red and sank low on the horizon, like a
   drunken man falling down.

When the thousand-rayed sun turned red and became   4
   pleasing to men's eyes, burning heat left the earth
   and entered the hearts of shelldrakes, doomed to part
   every night from their mates.

Losing strength when losing their refuge, when they had   5
   left the east, the rays of the sun in the western sky,
   half-sunk in the ocean, grew somber like clients at
   the loss of their patron, reduced to insignificance,
   abandoned by old friends, and broken by grief.[2]

The women warmly greeted the sun's rays reddening the   6
   windows of the mansions, rays that urged them to
   begin their evening toilet, like maidservants sent as
   messengers by their lovers.

Feebly clutching at the trees on the sunset mountain's   7
   tablelands with rays that had turned a deep red, did
   the sun plunge into the mountain's dense forests, or
   into the ocean, or the earth?[3]

८ आकुलश्चलपतत्त्रिकुलानामारवैरनुदितौषसरागः ।
आययावहरिदश्विपाण्डुस्तुल्यतां दिनमुखेन दिनान्तः ॥

९ आस्थितः स्थगितवारिदपङ्क्या संध्यया गगनपश्चिमभागः ।
सोर्मिविद्रुमवितानविभासा रञ्जितस्य जलधेः श्रियमूहे ॥

१० प्राञ्जलावपि जने नतमूर्ध्नि प्रेम तत्प्रवणचेतसि हित्वा ।
संध्ययानुविदधे विरमन्त्या चापलेन सुजनेतरमैत्री ॥

११ औषसातपभयादपलीनं वासरच्छविविरामपटीयः ।
संनिपत्य शनकैरिव निम्नादन्धकारमुदवाप समानि ॥

१२ एकतामिव गतस्य विवेकः कस्यचिन्न महतो ऽप्युपलेभे ।
भास्वता निदधिरे भुवनानामात्मनीव पतितेन विशेषाः ॥

१३ इच्छतां सह वधूभिरभेदं यामिनीविरहिणां विहगानाम् ।
आपुरेव मिथुनानि वियोगं लभ्यते न खलु कालनियोगः ॥

१४ यच्छति प्रतिमुखं दयितायै वाचमन्तिकगते ऽपि शकुन्तौ ।
नीयते स्म नतिमुज्झितहर्षं पङ्कजं मुखमिवाम्बुरुहिण्या ॥

१५ रञ्जिता नु विविधास्तरुशैला नामितं नु गगनं स्थगितं नु ।
पूरिता नु विषमेषु धरित्री संहृता नु ककुभस्तिमिरेण ॥

Pale from lack of sunlight, noisy with the calls of flocks   8
    of birds flying about, and untinged by the crimson
    twilight, evening resembled dawn.

Suffused with the evening twilight spreading over massed   9
    clouds, the western sky looked beautiful, like the
    ocean colored by the glow of coral hidden beneath the
    waves.

As she vanished, forsaking the fervent devotee who   10
    worshiped her with palms cupped and head bowed
    low in reverence, the fickle evening twilight mimicked
    the false friendship of a wicked man.

Gone into hiding for fear of the morning sunlight, gaining   11
    strength with the fading daylight, and emerging
    slowly from the depths, darkness pervaded the earth's
    level spaces.

The eye could no longer distinguish great from small.   12
    All things merged into one in the darkness. It was as
    though the setting sun had gathered into itself the
    marks of distinction of every object in the universe.

Although they longed to stay together, the shelldrake and   13
    his mate, doomed to part every night, were inevitably
    separated. No one can resist what time has ordained.[4]

Hearing the shelldrake crying out to his beloved, unable to   14
    see her even though she was close by, the lotus plant
    bowed her flower face in grief.

Did darkness dye the various trees and mountains black?   15
    Did it drag the sky down or completely engulf it? Did
    it level the earth's uneven surfaces? Did it obliterate
    the regions of space?[5]

१६ रात्रिरागमलिनानि विकासं पङ्कजानि रहयन्ति विहाय ।
स्पष्टतारकमियाय नभः श्रीर्वस्तुमिच्छति निरापदि सर्वः ॥

१७ व्यानशे शशधरेण विमुक्तः केतकीकुसुमकेसरपाण्डुः ।
चूर्णमुष्टिरिव लम्बितकान्तिर्वासवस्य दिशमंशुसमूहः ॥

१८ उज्झती शुचिमिवाशु तमिस्रामन्तिकं व्रजति तारकराजे ।
दिक्प्रसादगुणमण्डनमूहे रश्मिमहासविशदं मुखमैन्द्री ॥

१९ नीलनीरजनिभे हिमगौरं शैलरुद्धवपुषः सितरश्मेः ।
खे रराज निपतत्करजालं वारिधेः पयसि गाङ्गमिवाम्भः ॥

२० द्यां निरुन्धदतिनीलघनाभं ध्वान्तमुद्यतकरेण पुरस्तात् ।
क्षिप्यमाणमसितेतरभासा शंभुनेव करिचर्म चकासे ॥

२१ अन्तिकान्तिकगतेन्दुविसृष्टे जिह्लतां जहति दीधितिजाले ।
निःसृतस्तिमिरभारनिरोधादुच्छ्वसन्निव रराज दिगन्तः ॥

२२ लेखया विमलविद्रुमभासा संततं तिमिरमिन्दुरुदासे ।
दंष्ट्रया कनकटङ्कपिशङ्ग्या मण्डलं भुव इवादिवराहः ॥

Leaving the folded lotuses, their color dulled by the   16
twilight's red, beauty moved to the star-studded night
sky. Everyone prefers a home in a flourishing place.

Dazzling rays streaming from the moon, white as the   17
pollen on a screwpine flower, spread over Indra's
region of the sky, the east, like a handful of fragrant
camphor showered by a lover on his beloved.

At the approach of the moon, husband of the stars, the   18
eastern direction quickly tossed the darkness off, like
a woman shaking off the sorrow of separation from
her lover, and put on a face bright with a smile and
adorned with joyful clarity.

The snow-white rays of the moon, streaming from behind   19
the mountain, shone against a sky the color of a blue
lotus, like the waters of the Ganga merging with the
ocean.

Propelled by the moon's rays streaming from the east, and   20
enveloping the sky like a dark blue cloud, the darkness
shimmered like the hide Shiva tossed up when he had
killed the demon elephant.[6]

As the moon approached ever closer, with its web of rays   21
burgeoning and fanning out, the eastern region of the
sky began to shine as if heaving a sigh of relief, freed of
the oppressive burden of darkness.

Tossing up the dense darkness with a single digit that   22
shimmered like translucent coral, the moon looked
like the primeval boar lifting the earth's sphere with a
tawny tusk that shone like a golden chisel.[7]

२३ दीपयन्नथ नभः किरणौचैः कुङ्कुमारुणपयोधरगौरः ।
हेमकुम्भ इव पूर्वपयोधेरुन्ममज्ज शनकैस्तुहिनांशुः ॥

२४ उद्धतेन्दुमविभिन्नतमिस्रां पश्यति स्म रजनीमवितृप्तः ।
व्यंशुकस्फुटमुखीमतिजिह्वां व्रीडया नववधूमिव लोकः ॥

२५ न प्रसादमुचितं गमिता द्यौर्नोद्धृतं तिमिरमद्रिवनेभ्यः ।
दिङ्मुखेषु न च धाम विकीर्णं भूषितैव रजनी हिमभासा ॥

२६ मानिनीजनविलोचनपातानुष्णबाष्पकलुषान्प्रतिगृह्लन् ।
मन्दमन्दमुदितः प्रययौ खं भीतभीत इव शीतमयूखः ॥

२७ श्लिष्यतः प्रियवधूरुपकण्ठं तारकास्ततकरस्य हिमांशोः ।
उद्बभन्निभिरराज समन्तादङ्गराग इव लोहितरागः ॥

२८ प्रेरितः शशधरेण करौघः संहतान्यपि नुनोद तमांसि ।
क्षीरसिन्धुरिव मन्दरभिन्नः काननान्यविरलोच्चतरूणि ॥

२९ शारतां गमितया शशिपादैश्छायया विटपिनां प्रतिपेदे ।
न्यस्तशुक्लबलिचित्रतलाभिस्तुल्यता वसतिवेश्ममहीभिः ॥

Then the moon, shining with the red-gold glow of a   23
woman's breast decorated with saffron cream, slowly
rose from the eastern ocean like a golden jar, lighting
up the sky with its rays.[8]

With the moon risen but darkness not quite dispelled,   24
people eagerly gazed at the night the way a
bridegroom gazes at his new bride who reveals her
face when the veil is drawn aside, yet bashfully turns
away.

The sky did not regain its natural clarity, darkness was   25
not dispelled from the woods on the mountain, nor
did light spread over the regions of space. Yet the cool
moon became an ornament for the night.[9]

The moon rose slowly and hesitantly in the sky, as if   26
fearing to be greeted by the volley of cutting looks,
clouded by hot tears, of women angered in lovers'
quarrels.

As the moon enfolded his wives, the stars, into the close   27
embrace of his outstretched arms, his rays, the rosy
flush of passion encircled him like overflowing saffron
cream worn by the women.

The brilliant white rays sent out by the moon dispelled the   28
darkness, massed though it was, like the ocean of milk
churned by Mount Mandara, tossing up dense forests
of tall trees falling from the mountain.[10]

In the moonlight, the mottled shade under the trees   29
looked like the floors of roof terraces in houses,
speckled with white grains of rice and other votive
offerings.

३० आतपे धृतिमता सह वध्वा यामिनीविरहिणा विहगेन ।
सेहिरे न किरणा हिमरश्मेर्दुःखिते मनसि सर्वमसह्याम् ॥

३१ गन्धमुद्धतरजःकणवाही विक्षिपन्निकसतां कुमुदानाम् ।
आदुधाव परिलीनविहंगा यामिनीमरुदपां वनराजीः ॥

३२ संविधातुमभिषेकमुदासे मन्मथस्य लसदंशुजलौघः ।
यामिनीवनितया ततचिह्नः सोत्पलो रजतकुम्भ इवेन्दुः ॥

३३ ओजसापि खलु नूनमनूनं नासहायमुपयाति जयश्रीः ।
यद्विभुः शशिमयूखसखः सन्नाददे विजयि चापमनङ्गः ॥

३४ सद्मनां विरचनाहितशोभैरागतप्रियकथैरपि दूत्यम् ।
संनिकृष्टरतिभिः सुरदारैर्भूषितैरपि विभूषणमीषे ॥

३५ न स्रजो रुरुचिरे रमणीभ्यश्चन्दनानि विरहे मदिरा वा ।
साधनेषु हि रतेरुपधत्ते रम्यतां प्रियसमागम एव ॥

In the company of his mate the shelldrake had found   30
   pleasure even in the hot sunlight, yet doomed to part
   from her every night, he found the moon's cool rays
   unbearable. All things are painful when the heart is
   heavy.

Wafting the scent of opening water lilies thick with pollen,   31
   and bearing drops of water, the night breeze gently
   shook the mountain's forests with their sleeping birds.

Now the moon, rays shimmering and dark spot clearly   32
   visible, became a silver urn decorated with a blue
   water lily, lifted up by Lady Night for the love god's
   ritual bath before setting out on his campaign of
   conquest.

To be sure, victory does not favor a man with military   33
   strength but lacking allies. That is why the love
   god, powerful though he is, did not lift his bow
   for conquest before recruiting the moon's rays as
   helpmates.

As the time for lovemaking neared, although their   34
   mansions were already sumptuously decked out,
   the celestial nymphs wanted to decorate them yet
   again; although they had already heard from their
   lovers, they longed for the maids to bring them more
   messages; although their evening toilet was complete,
   they wanted to dress themselves up all over again.

While awaiting their lovers the women found no pleasure   35
   in flower garlands or fragrant sandalwood cream or
   wine. It is the presence of the lover that gives the
   accessories of lovemaking the power to charm.

३६ प्रस्थिताभिरधिनाथनिवासं ध्वंसितप्रियसखीवचनाभिः ।
मानिनीभिरपहस्तितधैर्यः सादयन्नपि मदो ऽवललम्बे ॥

३७ कान्तवेश्म बहु संदिशतीभिर्यातमेव रतये रमणीभिः ।
मन्मथेन परिलुप्तमतीनां प्रायशः स्खलितमप्युपकारि ॥

३८ आशु कान्तमभिसारितवत्या योषितः पुलकरुद्धकपोलम् ।
निर्जिगाय मुखमिन्दुमखण्डं खण्डपत्रतिलकाकृति कान्त्या ॥

३९ उच्यतां स वचनीयमशेषं नेश्वरे परुषता सखि साध्वी ।
आनयैनमनुनीय कथं वा विप्रियाणि जनयन्ननुनेयः ॥

४० किं गतेन न हि युक्तमुपैतुं कः प्रिये सुभगमानिनि मानः ।
योषितामिति कथासु समेतैः कामिभिर्बहुरसा धृतिरूहे ॥

४१ योषितः पुलकरोधि दधत्या घर्मवारि नवसंगमजन्म ।
कान्तवक्षसि बभूव पतन्त्या मण्डनं लुलितमण्डनतैव ॥

The angry young women en route to their lovers'   36
houses, piqued by a quarrel and brushing aside
their girlfriends' advice, surrendered themselves to
drunkenness, even though it defeated their purpose,
making them unsteady and weakening their resolve.

Engrossed in composing messages to their lovers about   37
the night of love that lay ahead, the nymphs found
themselves arrived at their rendezvous. As a rule,
even mistakes help love-crazed persons to realize the
desired goal.

As one woman quickly ran toward her lover, the down   38
rising on her cheek, although its painted decorations
and forehead mark were smudged, her bright face
outshone the full moon.

"Tell him everything I have said; leave nothing out."   39-40
"Friend, it is not wise to be so hard on your lord."
"Well then, entreat him, and bring him to me!" "Of
what use is entreaty, when you have hurt him so?"
"Then what is the use of approaching him? Don't
go!" "Proud girl, so lovely in your anger, why are
you so angry with him?" When the gandharva lovers
overheard such conversation among the women as
they drew near, they savored the delight of an entire
spectrum of moods.[11]

When a nymph eagerly fell upon her lover's chest, and   41
sweat broke out at the pleasure of the first embrace
and enveloped her tingling breast, the smudged
ornament became an ornament in itself.[12]

४२ शीधुपानविधुरासु निगृह्णन्मानमाशु शिथिलीकृतलज्जः ।
संगतासु दयितैरुपलेभे कामिनीषु मदनो नु मदो नु ॥

४३ द्वारि चक्षुरधिपाणि कपोलौ जीवितं त्वयि कुतः कलहो ऽस्याः ।
कामिनामिति वचः पुनरुक्तं प्रीतये नवनवत्वमियाय ॥

४४ साचि लोचनयुगं नमयन्ती रुन्धती दयितवक्षसि पातम् ।
सुभ्रुवो जनयति स्म विभूषां संगतावुपरराम च लज्जा ॥

४५ सव्यलीकमवधीरितखिन्नं प्रस्थितं सपदि कोपपदेन ।
योषितः सुहृदिव स्म रुणद्धि प्राणनाथमभिबाष्पनिपातः ॥

४६ शङ्किताय कृतबाष्पनिपातामीर्ष्यया विमुखितां दयिताय ।
मानिनीमभिमुखाहितचित्तां शंसति स्म घनरोमविभेदः ॥

४७ लोलदृष्टि वदनं दयितायाश्चुम्बति प्रियतमे रभसेन ।
ब्रीडया सह विनीवि नितम्बादंशुकं शिथिलतामुपपेदे ॥

४८ ह्रीतया गलितनीवि निरस्यन्नन्तरीयमवलम्बितकाञ्चि ।
मण्डलीकृतपृथुस्तनभारं सस्वजे दयितया हृदयेशः ॥

Whose handiwork could one see in those passionate   42
women when, overcome by draughts of wine, they
joined their lovers, quickly losing their modesty and
surrendering their pride—the work of the love god,
the intoxicator, or of intoxication itself?[13]

"Her eyes are fixed on the door, her chin is propped in her   43
hand, her life depends on you. Why must you quarrel
with her?" These words of the messenger, repeated
to please them, gave the lovers renewed pleasure each
time they were spoken.

Forcing her to lower her eyes and glance sideways at her   44
lover and keeping her from falling into his arms,
bashfulness adorned the lovely woman, but then
gracefully withdrew when the time came for making
love.

The guilty lover, dejected because his pleas had been   45
rebuffed, feigned anger and suddenly turned to go.
But he was stopped, as if by her trusted girlfriend, by
the flowing tears his woman faced him with.

The jealous woman turned away from her lover in anger,   46
tears flowing down her face, for she suspected him of
infidelity; but the down rising on her skin declared her
love for him was as complete as ever.[14]

When a lover seized his beloved's face with its restless   47
glances and kissed her, the skirt, its knot loosened,
slipped down from her hips, along with her modesty.[15]

When the lover pulled her skirt off, unraveling its knot,   48
it was barely held up by the girdle. Embarrassed, the
girl embraced him tightly, her breasts rounded into
globes.

४९ आहृता नखपदैः परिरम्भाश्चुम्बितानि घनदन्तनिपातैः ।
सौकुमार्यगुणसंभृतकीर्तिर्वाम एव सुरतेष्वपि कामः ॥

५० पाणिपल्लवविधूननमन्तः सीत्कृतानि नयनार्धनिमेषाः ।
योषितां रहसि गद्गदवाचामस्तनतामुपययुर्मदनस्य ॥

५१ पातुमाहितरतीन्यभिलेषुस्तर्षयन्त्यपुनरुक्तरसानि ।
सस्मितानि वदनानि वधूनां सोत्पलानि च मधूनि युवानः ॥

५२ कान्तसंगमपराजितमन्यौ वारुणीरसनशान्तविवादे ।
मानिनीजन उपाहितसंधौ संदधे धनुषि नेषुमनङ्गः ॥

५३ कुप्यताशु भवतानतचित्ताः कोपितांश्च वरिवस्यत यूनः ।
इत्यनेक उपदेश इव स्म स्वाद्यते युवतिभिर्मधुवारः ॥

५४ भर्तृभिः प्रणयसंभ्रमदत्तां वारुणीमतिरसां रसयित्वा ।
ह्रीविमोहविरहादुपलेभे पाटवं नु हृदयं नु वधूभिः ॥

५५ स्वादितः स्वयमथैधितमानं लम्भितः प्रियतमैः सह पीतः ।
आसवः प्रतिपदं प्रमदानां नैकरूपरसतामिव भेजे ॥

Embraces were treasured for the marks of a lover's nails,　49
and kisses for love bites deeply incised. The love god
may be famed for his delicate ways, but in the throes
of passion he is coarse.[16]

The waving of hands like sprays of flowers, the sharp　50
intake of breath, the half-closed eyes as the women
moaned in private—all became weapons in the arsenal
of Madana, god of love.

The young men longed to drink in their lovers' smiling　51
faces and the wine laced with water lilies. Both
inflamed their passion, both offered new delights with
each mouthful, and both only increased their thirst.[17]

Lovemaking quelled anger; draughts of wine ended love　52
quarrels. The proud women made peace with their
lovers, and the love god had no further need to aim his
arrows at them.

With every draught, the young women relished ever　53
further instruction from the wine: "Quarrel with your
young man! Be quick to relent! When he is stung,
placate him with devotion!"

Savoring the wine offered by their lovers, the sweeter　54
for being given with tender passion, the women lost
their modesty and innocence. Were they just showing
off their inborn cleverness, or their newly acquired
expertise in the arts of love?

The wine acquired a new flavor, it seemed, with each　55
draught: first drunk by the women on their own, then
given by their lovers with great tenderness, and later
drunk together with their men.

५६ भ्रूविलाससुभगाननुकर्तुं विभ्रमानिव वधूनयनानाम् ।
आददे मृदुविलोलपलाशैरुत्पलैश्चषकवीचिषु कम्पः ॥

५७ ओष्ठपल्लवविदंशरुचीनां हृद्यतामुपययौ रमणानाम् ।
फुल्ललोचनविनीलसरोजैरङ्गनास्यचषकैर्मधुवारः ॥

५८ प्राप्यते गुणवतापि गुणानां व्यक्तमाश्रयवशेन विशेषः ।
तत्तथा हि दयिताननदत्तं व्यानशे मधु रसातिशयेन ॥

५९ वीक्ष्य रत्नचषकेष्वतिरिक्तां कान्तदन्तपदमण्डनलक्ष्मीम् ।
जज्झिरे बहुमताः प्रमदानामोष्ठयावकनुदो मधुवाराः ॥

६० लोचनाधरकृताहृतरागा वासिताननविशेषितगन्धा ।
वारुणी परगुणात्मगुणानां व्यत्ययं विनिमयं नु वितेने ॥

६१ तुल्यरूपमसितोत्पलमक्ष्णोः कर्णगं निरुपकारि विदित्वा ।
योषितः सुहृदिव प्रविभेजे लम्भितेक्षणरुचिर्मदरागः ॥

६२ क्षीणयावकरसो ऽप्यतिपानैः कान्तदन्तपदसंभृतशोभः ।
आययावतितरामिव वध्वाः सान्द्रतामधरपल्लवरागः ॥

Floating water lilies quivered in the rippling wine in   56
the goblet, their petals fluttering gently as though
mimicking the graceful coquetry of the women's eyes
and the charming play of their eyebrows.

The gandharva lovers, eager to taste the beloved's lip in a   57
love bite, took greatest delight in wine quaffed from
the goblets that were their women' faces, where eyes
blossomed like blue lotuses.

The right vessel confers greater distinction on the virtues   58
of the virtuous. That is why the wine drunk right from
the beloved's mouth was especially delicious.

When they saw, reflected in the jeweled goblets, how the   59
wine had washed the lac from their lips and made the
bite marks from the lovers' teeth, those bright red
ornaments, shine so bright, the women esteemed the
draughts even more.

It erased the red gloss from the women's lips and made   60
their eyes red with intoxication. It scented the
nymphs' mouths, whose sweet scent intensified its
fragrance. Was it by accident, or by design, that the
wine drunk by the apsarases exchanged its attributes
with theirs?

Knowing the blue water lily tucked behind the ear looked   61
too much like one lady's eyes and so did little for her,
intoxication's flush made her eyes shine bright and so
helped, like a friend, distinguish them from the flower.

Even though repeated draughts of wine had rubbed off   62
the soft shimmer of red lac from one girl's lower lip,
growing moist and full from the lover's bite, the lip
seemed to grow lovelier.

६३ रागकान्तनयनेषु नितान्तं विद्रुमारुणकपोलतलेषु ।
सर्वगापि दददृशे वनितानां दर्पणेष्विव मुखेषु मदश्रीः ॥

६४ बद्धकोपविकृतीरपि रामाश्रुतिभिमततामुपनिन्ये ।
वश्यतां मधुमदो दयितानामात्मवर्गहितमिच्छति सर्वः ॥

६५ वाससां शिथिलतामुपनाभि ह्रीनिरासमपदे कुपितानि ।
योषितां विदधती गुणपक्षे निर्ममार्ज मदिरा वचनीयम् ॥

६६ भर्तृषूपसखि निक्षिपतीनामात्मनो मधुमदोद्ग्रमितानाम् ।
व्रीडया विफलया वनितानां न स्थितं न विगतं हृदयेषु ॥

६७ रुन्धती नयनवाक्यविकासं सादितोभयकरा परिरम्भे ।
व्रीडितस्य ललितं युवतीनां क्षीबता बहुगुणैरनुजह्रे ॥

६८ योषिदुद्धतमनोभवरागा मानवत्यपि ययौ दयिताङ्कम् ।
कारयत्यनिभृता गुणदोषे वारुणी खलु रहस्यविभेदम् ॥

६९ आहिते नु मधुना मधुरत्वे चेष्टितस्य गमिते नु विकासम् ।
आबभौ नव इवोद्धतरागः कामिनीष्ववसरः कुसुमेषोः ॥

The lovely flush of intoxication had spread all over their   63
bodies, and yet it was in the women's faces, as in a
mirror, that it found its clearest manifestation, in eyes
red with passion and cheeks the color of coral.

Although the nymphs were piqued by quarrels with the   64
gandharvas, their beauty made them all the more
alluring to their lovers. Their drunkenness, by
contrast, gave the men the upper hand, helping them
to seduce the reluctant women. Everyone wants their
own sort to prosper.[18]

The skirt loosened at the navel, the loss of modesty, the   65
unprovoked fits of anger—by transforming all these
into virtues, wine saved the women from blame.

When the nymphs, emboldened by wine, flung themselves   66
on their lovers, while their girlfriends watched,
bashfulness, rendered useless, neither remained in
their hearts nor left them.

It prevented their eyes from opening fully, it hindered   67
their speech, it paralyzed their arms in embraces; in
all these ways drunkenness mimicked the women's
graceful modesty.

Driven by mounting passion, a nymph threw her arms   68
around her lover, forgetting her anger at his offenses.
Indifferent to virtue and blame, wine makes one's
secrets public.

Whether the wine had merely aroused their desire for   69
sweet love play or brought it to full bloom, in the
height of passion the young women became a fresh
target for the love god's flower arrows.

७० मा गमन्मदविमूढधियो नः प्रोज्झ्य रन्तुमिति शङ्कितनाथाः ।
योषितो न मदिरां भृशमीषुः प्रेम पश्यति भयान्यपदे ऽपि ॥

७१ चित्तनिर्वृतिविधायि विविक्तं मन्मथो मधुमदः शशिभासः ।
संगमश्च दयितैः स्म नयन्ति प्रेम कामपि भुवं प्रमदानाम् ॥

७२ धाष्ट्र्यलङ्घितयथोचितभूमौ निर्दयं विलुलितालकमाल्ये ।
मानिनीरतिविधौ कुसुमेषुर्मत्तमत्त इव विभ्रममाप ॥

७३ शीधुपानविधुरेषु वधूनां निघ्नतामुपगतेषु वपुःषु ।
ईहितं रतिरसाहितभावं वीतलक्ष्यमपि कामिषु रेजे ॥

७४ अन्योन्यरक्तमनसामथ बिभ्रतीनां
चेतोभुवो हरिसखाप्सरसां निदेशम् ।
वैबोधिकध्वनिविभावितपश्चिमार्धा
सा संहृतेव परिवृत्तिमियाय रात्रिः ॥

७५ निद्राविनोदितनितान्तरतिक्लमाना-
मायामिमङ्गलनिनादविबोधितानाम् ।
रामासु भाविविरहाकुलितासु यूनां
तत्पूर्वतामिव समादधिरे रतानि ॥

Suspicious of their lovers, the ladies thought, "He might   70
leave me for another woman if I am befuddled with
wine," and so they hesitated to drink too much. Love
sees dangers lurking everywhere.

Delightful seclusion, the god of love, wine's intoxication,   71
moonlight, and union with their lovers—all this took
the women's passion to new heights.

When the proud women crossed the limits of propriety   72
in the moves of passion, the floral chaplets in their
hair swaying wildly, the god of love reeled about like a
drunkard in their bold lovemaking.

Overcome by the wine, the nymphs yielded their bodies   73
to their lovers, and their ardent caresses at the height
of passion were arousing even when they missed their
mark.[19]

Then, announced by the herald's call, the night came to an   74
end, cut short, as it were, for Indra's minions and the
celestial nymphs, who were carrying out the love god's
command, driven by mutual passion.

Awakening to the resounding, auspicious songs of the   75
bards, the fatigue of the night's long bouts of love
dispelled by sleep, the young men began to make
love with renewed passion to their women, who were
distressed at the thought of parting from their lovers.

७६ कान्ताजनं सुरतखेदनिमीलिताक्षं
संवाहितुं समुपयानिव मन्दमन्दम् ।
हर्म्येषु माल्यमदिरापरिभोगगन्धा-
नाविश्चकार रजनीपरिवृत्तिवायुः ॥

७७ आमोदवासितचलाधरपल्लवेषु
निद्राकषायितविपाटललोचनेषु ।
व्यामृष्टपत्त्रतिलकेषु विलासिनीनां
शोभां बबन्ध वदनेषु मदावशेषः ॥

७८ गतवति नखलेखालक्ष्यतामङ्गरागे
समददयितपीतातात्राम्रबिम्बाधराणाम् ।
विरहविधुरमिष्टा सत्सखीवाङ्गनानां
हृदयमवललम्बे रात्रिसंभोगलक्ष्मीः ॥

.e night's many pleasures— 76
.nd lovemaking—across the
.iansions, a gentle morning breeze
the lovely nymphs, who lay with eyes
eary from lovemaking, as if to massage them.
the leaf designs and forehead marks were erased 77
om the lovely women's faces, traces of intoxication
furnished them with beauty, scenting the trembling,
frond-like lips with wine, and reddening eyes muddied
by sleep.
The women grew despondent at the imminent parting. 78
But displayed in full lips grown pale from the lovers'
passionate kisses, and in bodies where fragrant creams
had been rubbed off, fully revealing the marks of
the lovers' nails, the voluptuous glow of the night's
lovemaking comforted their hearts like a loving
girlfriend.[20]

CHAPTER 10

A Failed Seduction

१ अथ परिमलजामवाप्य लक्ष्मीमवयवदीपितमण्डनश्रियस्ताः ।
वसतिमभिविहाय रम्यहावाः सुरपतिसूनुविलोभनाय जग्मुः ॥

२ द्रुतपदमभियातुमिच्छतीनां गमनपरिक्रमलाघवेन तासाम् ।
अवनिषु चरणैः पृथुस्तनीनामलघुनितम्बतया चिरं निषेदे ॥

३ निहितसरसयावकैर्बभासे चरणतलैः कृतपद्धतिर्वधूनाम् ।
अविरलवितेव शक्रगोपैररुणितनीलतृणोलपा धरित्री ॥

४ ध्वनिरगविवरेषु नूपुराणां पृथुरशनागुणशिञ्जितानुयातः ।
प्रतिरववितो वनानि चक्रे मुखरसमुत्सुककहंससारसानि ॥

५ अवचयपरिभोगवन्ति हिंस्रैः सहचरितान्यमृगाणि काननानि ।
अभिदधुरभितो मुनिं वधूभ्यः समुदितसाध्वसविक्लवं च चेतः ॥

६ नृपतिमुनिपरिग्रहेण सा भूः सुरसचिवाप्सरसां जहार तेजः ।
उपहितपरमप्रभावधाम्नां न हि जयिनां तपसामलङ्घ्यमस्ति ॥

Then Indra's nymphs, grown lovelier from lovemaking,   1
  brightening their cosmetic decoration with the beauty
  of their limbs and moving with graceful gestures, left
  their camp and set off to seduce Indra's son.
Used to flying with ease in the sky, the women endowed   2
  with ample breasts expected to move quickly, but
  weighed down by swelling hips, their feet lingered on
  the ground.
The soles of their feet, wet with decorative lac paint, left   3
  a trail of prints on the ground carpeted with green
  grasses. Drenched with the crimson dye, the ground
  looked as though it were bedecked with *indragopa* rain
  mites.[1]
The sound of anklets, mixed with the jingle of girdle   4
  chains and amplified by echoing in the mountain's
  caves, prompted the wild geese and cranes in the
  woods to utter cries of longing.[2]
The grove's trees were within easy reach for the celestials   5
  to pluck and enjoy. Naturally hostile beasts dwelt
  there in harmony. These signs, and hearts that grew
  faint for awe, told the celestial women the sage was
  near.
That mountain hermitage, abode of the princely ascetic,   6
  eclipsed the vitality and beauty of the gandharvas
  and apsarases with its flourishing. There is nothing
  that cannot be accomplished by the austerity of a
  conquering warrior when endowed with supernatural
  power and majesty.

७ सचकितमिव विस्मयाकुलाभिः शुचिसिकतास्वतिमानुषाणि
ताभिः ।
क्षितिषु दद्दशिरे पदानि जिष्णोरुपहितकेतुरथाङ्गलाञ्छनानि ॥

८ अतिशयितवनान्तरद्युतीनां फलकुसुमावचये ऽपि तद्विधानाम् ।
ऋतुरिव तरुवीरुधां समृद्ध्या युवतिजनैर्जगृहे मुनिप्रभावः ॥

९ मृदितकिसलयः सुराङ्गनानां ससलिलवल्कलभारभुग्नशाखः ।
बहुमतिमधिकां ययावशोकः परिजनतापि गुणाय सद्गुणानाम् ॥

Wonderstruck, the young women gazed with fear at the 7
superhuman footprints, marked with the emblems of
flag and chariot wheel,³ that Arjuna the conqueror had
left on the white sands.

Though the fruit had been picked and the flowers plucked, 8
the grove's trees and plants were the same as they had
been before and more lush than those in other woods.
From their luxuriance, the young women inferred the
extraordinary power of the sage, like a season by its
signs.

Its young shoots crushed and its bough bending with the 9
weight of the ascetic's wet bark garment, the *aśoka*
tree earned the great esteem of the celestial women.
The slightest help to a great man serves to elevate a
person.

१० यमनियमकृशीकृतस्थिराङ्गः परिदृष्टे विधृतायुधः स ताभिः ।
अनुपमशमदीप्ततागरीयान्कृतपदपङ्क्तिरथर्वणेव वेदः ॥

११ शशधर इव लोचनाभिरामैर्गगननविसारिभिरंशुभिः परीतः ।
शिखरनिचयमेकसानुसद्धा सकलमिवापि दधन्महीधरस्य ॥

१२ सुरसरिति परं तपो ऽधिगच्छन्विधृतपिशङ्गबृहज्जटाकलापः ।
हविरिव विततः शिखासमूहैः समभिलषन्नुपवेदि जातवेदाः ॥

१३ सदृशमतनुमाकृतेः प्रयलं तदनुगुणामपरैः क्रियामलङ्घ्याम् ।
दधदलघु तपः क्रियानुरूपं विजयवतीं च तपःसमां समृद्धिम् ॥

१४ चिरनियमकृशो ऽपि शैलसारः शमनिरतो ऽपि दुरासदः प्रकृत्या ।
ससचिव इव निर्जने ऽपि तिष्ठन्मुनिरपि तुल्यरुचिस्त्रिलोकभर्तुः ॥

186

His body was lean and firm from the mental disciplines and ritual observances of austerity,[4] and yet he bore weapons. Majestic, with an unparalleled combination of the glow of tranquility and the warrior's fiery power, he seemed to them like the *Atharva Veda* with its potent mantras.[5] Haloed by gentle rays that spread in the sky, he shone like the moon. Although he was dwelling on a single mountain peak, his presence filled the entire mountain range. Practicing superhuman austerity on the bank of the Ganga, with a great mass of tawny matted hair piled on his head, he resembled fire on the sacrificial altar, blazing up with a multitude of flames to receive the offering. His formidable undertaking matched his impressive figure; his incomparable actions matched his great undertaking; his extraordinary austerities suited his martial purpose, and his aura of sovereign power matched his potent austerities, aimed at conquering his enemies.[6] Though emaciated from long ascetic observances, he was strong as a mountain; though committed to tranquility, he was invincible by nature; though alone in a remote place, he was resplendent like a king accompanied by his retinue; and though an ascetic, he shone with the majesty of Indra, lord of the three worlds.[7]

१५ तनुमवजितलोकसारधाम्नीं त्रिभुवनगुप्तिसहां विलोकयन्त्यः ।
अवययुरमरस्त्रियो ऽस्य यत्नं विजयफले विफलं तपोऽधिकारे ॥

१६ मुनिदनुतनयान्विलोभ्य सद्यः प्रतनुबलान्यधितिष्ठतस्तपांसि ।
अलघुनि बहु मेनिरे च ताः स्वं कुलिशभृता विहितं पदे
नियोगम् ॥

१७ अथ कृतकविलोभनं विधित्सौ युवतिजने हरिसूनुदर्शनेन ।
प्रसभमवततार चित्तजन्मा हरति मनो मधुरा हि यौवनश्रीः ॥

१८ सपदि हरिसखैर्वधूनिदेशाद्ध्वनितमनोरमवल्लकीमृदङ्गैः ।
युगपदृतुगणस्य संनिधानं वियति वने च यथायथं वितेने ॥

१९ सजलजलधरं नभो विरेजे विवृतिमियाय रुचिस्तडिल्लतानाम् ।
व्यवहितरतिविग्रहैर्वितेने जलगुरुभिः स्तनितैर्दिगन्तरेषु ॥

२० परिसुरपतिसूनुधाम सद्यः समुपदधन्मुकुलानि मालतीनाम् ।
विरलमपजहार बद्धबिन्दुः सरजसतामवनेरपां निपातः ॥

२१ प्रतिदिशमभिगच्छताभिमृष्टः ककुभविकाससुगन्धिनानिलेन ।
नव इव विबभौ सचित्तजन्मा गतधृतिराकुलितश्च जीवलोकः ॥

The sight of the hero—surpassing as he did every other   15
　being in the universe with the power and majesty of
　his figure, and clearly capable of protecting the three
　worlds—convinced the celestial nymphs that his
　strenuous ascetic efforts were wasted on an unworthy
　cause—mere victory over his enemies.

Jaded from long experience of easily seducing sages and   16
　demons practicing austerity for trivial purposes, the
　nymphs cherished the task assigned to them by Indra,
　aimed at last at a challenging target.

Even as they prepared for their mission of seducing the   17
　ascetic hero, at the very sight of him they fell madly
　in love. What heart can resist the sweet charms of
　youth?

At once, at the nymphs' command, the gandharvas,   18
　Indra's companions, began to sing sweetly to the
　accompaniment of vinas and drums; and they
　conjured up all six seasons to manifest themselves all
　at once, yet separately, in the woods and sky.[8]

The sky shimmered with water-laden clouds, lit up by   19
　flashes of lightning. Deep, low rumbling thunder
　pervaded all space, bringing lovers' quarrels to an
　end.[9]

A sudden shower made the jasmine in Arjuna's hermitage   20
　burst into bud and settled the dust on the ground.[10]

Caressed by breezes blowing from every direction, laden   21
　with the scent of *kakubha* blossoms, the world of
　living beings, shaken and bewildered by the advent of
　desire, seemed all brand new.

२२ व्यथितमपि भृशं मनो हरन्ती परिणतजम्बुफलोपभोगगृह्णा ।
परभृतयुवतिः स्वनं वितेने नवनवयोजितकण्ठरागरम्यम् ॥

२३ अभिभवति मनः कदम्बवायौ मदमधुरे च शिखण्डिनां निनादे ।
जन इव न धृतेश्चचाल जिष्णुर्न हि महतां सुकरः समाधिभङ्गः ॥

२४ धृतबिसवलयावलिर्वहन्ती कुमुदवनैकदुकूलमात्तबाणा ।
शरदमलतले सरोजपाणौ घनसमयेन वधूरिवाललम्बे ॥

२५ समदशिखिरुतानि हंसनादैः कुमुदवनानि कदम्बपुष्पवृष्ट्या ।
श्रियमतिशयिनीं समेत्य जग्मुर्गुणमहतां महते गुणाय योगः ॥

२६ सरजसमपहाय केतकीनां प्रसवमुपान्तिकनीपरेणुकीर्णम् ।
प्रियमधुरसनानि षट्पदाली मलिनयति स्म विनीलबन्धनानि ॥

२७ मुकुलितमतिशय्य बन्धुजीवं धृतजलबिन्दुषु शाद्वलस्थलीषु ।
अविरलवपुषः सुरेन्द्रगोपा विकचपलाशचयश्रियं समीयुः ॥

The delightful variety of tunes sung by the sweet-voiced   22
female cuckoo, joyful from savoring ripe rose apples,
were utterly charming, however much they troubled
the heart.

Though a *kadamba*-scented breeze overpowered the   23
heart and the peacock's cries were sweet with passion,
Arjuna still did not lose his composure as a boor
would. The mental concentration of great men is not
easy to break.[11]

The rainy season grasped the pale lotus hand of autumn,   24
his bride, who wore a stack of lotus-stalk bracelets and
a silken garment made of a bed of water lilies, and held
a *bāṇa* flower for a bridal arrow.[12]

The passionate cries of peacocks sounded sweeter, joined   25
with the calls of wild geese; a shower of *kadamba*
blossoms heightened the beauty of the lotus bed. The
union of excellent things begets greater excellence.[13]

A swarm of bees, greedy for honey, left the screwpine   26
flower, brimming with pollen and coated with pollen
from nearby *nīpa* flowers, and settled like a large dark
spot on *asana** blossoms with blue-black stalks.

Fat velvety red rain mites, lovelier than midday flower   27
buds, swarmed on earth covered with rain-soaked
grass, looking like a beautiful cluster of full-bloomed
crimson flame-of-the-forest flowers.[14]

---

* The Indian kino tree.

२८ अविरलफलिनीवनप्रसूनः कुसुमितकुन्दसुगन्धिगन्धवाहः ।
गुणमसमयजं चिराय लेभे विरलतुषारकणस्तुषारकालः ॥

२९ निचयिनि लवलीलताविकासे जनयति लोध्रसमीरणे च हर्षम् ।
विकृतिमुपययौ न पाण्डुसूनुश्चलति नयान्न जिगीषतां हि चेतः ॥

३० कतिपयसहकारपुष्परम्यस्तनुतुहिनो ऽल्पविनिद्रसिन्दुवारः ।
सुरभिमुखहिमागमान्तशंसी समुपययौ शिशिरः स्मरैकबन्धुः ॥

३१ कुसुमनगवनान्युपैतुकामा किसलयिनीमवलम्ब्य चूतयष्टिम् ।
क्वणदलिकुलनूपुरा निरासे नलिनवनेषु पदं वसन्तलक्ष्मीः ॥

३२ विकसितकुसुमाधरं हसन्तीं कुरबकराजिवधूं विलोकयन्तम् ।
दद‌शुरिव सुराङ्गना निषण्णं सशरमनङ्गमशोकपल्लवेषु ॥

Winter, heavy with snow, acquired for a while an   28
   unseasonable charm from abundantly blooming rosy
   milkweed bushes,[15] and breezes bearing the scent of
   the full-bloomed jasmine.*
The *lavalī* vine, laden with blossoms, and the *lodhra*-   29
   scented breeze were delightful, but Pandu's son was
   not distracted. Warriors whose minds are set on
   conquest do not swerve from the path of proper moral
   and political conduct.
A few mango and five-leaved chaste trees[16] began to   30
   bloom, and the snow began to melt. Late winter, sole
   helpmate of the love god, had arrived, signaling the
   end of the cold season and the beginning of fragrant
   springtime.
Eager to embrace the forests full of flowering trees, the   31
   beauty of spring, perched upon a mango branch
   covered with shoots, and wearing jingling anklets in
   the form of humming bees, placed her first step in the
   beds of lotuses.[17]
Indra's nymphs caught sight of the god of love. He was   32
   seated with bow and arrows, hidden among the
   sprouts of the *aśoka* trees, and gazing at a row of
   crimson and white amaranth flowers† that looked like
   a young woman's blossom lips opening in a smile.

---

* *Kunda* or downy jasmine, blooming in early winter.
† *Kurabaka,* a tree blooming in the spring.

३३ मुहुरनुपतता विधूयमानं विरचितसंहति दक्षिणानिलेन ।
अलिकुलमलकाकृतिं प्रपेदे नलिनमुखान्तविसर्पि पङ्कजिन्याः ॥

३४ श्वसनचलितपल्लवाधरोष्ठे नवनिहितेर्ष्यमिवावधूनयन्ती ।
मधुसुरभिणि षड्पदेन पुष्पे मुख इव शाललतावधूश्चुचुम्बे ॥

३५ प्रभवति न तदा परो विजेतुं भवति जितेन्द्रियता यदात्मरक्षा ।
अवजितभुवनस्तथा हि लेभे सिततुरगे विजयं न पुष्पमासः ॥

३६ कथमिव तव संमतिर्भवित्री सममृतुभिर्मुनिनावधीरितस्य ।
इति विरचितमल्लिकाविकासः स्मयत इव स्म मधुं
निदाघकालः ॥

३७ बलवदपि बलं मिथोविरोधि प्रभवति नैव विपक्षनिर्जयाय ।
भुवनपरिभवी न यत्तदानीं तमृतुगणः क्षणमुन्मनीचकार ॥

३८ श्रुतिसुखमुपवीणितं सहायैर्विरललाञ्छनहारिणश्च कालाः ।
अविहितहरिसूनुविक्रियाणि त्रिदशवधूषु मनोभवं वितेनुः ॥

Fluttering around the flower that was the face of the   33
    lotus plant-woman, and clustering together while
    repeatedly buffeted by the southern breeze, a swarm
    of bees became locks of hair framing a woman's face.

Even though it was brushed off as if in a fit of anger, a bee   34
    kissed the *śāla** branch on the flower that was her
    wine-scented mouth, the lower lip a shoot fluttering
    with each heaving breath.

Enemies cannot conquer a man well guarded by restraint   35
    of the senses. And so the season of spring, conqueror
    of the entire universe, could not overpower Arjuna,
    hero with the white horse.

The summer season seemed to be mocking the spring with   36
    laughter composed of white jasmine blooms,† saying,
    "How can you win the world's respect when you have
    been insulted by this ascetic, just like all the other
    seasons?"

An army divided by dissension can never conquer   37
    the enemy. That is why the seasons of the year,
    conquerors of the whole world, were unable to disturb
    Arjuna even for a moment.[18]

Failing to affect Arjuna in any way whatever, the sweet   38
    songs of the gandharvas, sung to the accompaniment
    of the vina, and the charming seasons, offering a
    panoply of delights, kindled desire in the celestial
    nymphs.[19]

---

* Also *sarja* or sal.
† *Mallikā*, the summer-blooming jasmine.

३९ न दलति निचये तथोत्पलानां न च विषमच्छदगुच्छयूथिकासु ।
अभिरतिमुपलेभिरे यथासां हरितनयावयवेषु लोचनानि ॥

४० मुनिमभिमुखतां निनीषवो याः समुपययुः कमनीयतागुणेन ।
मदनमुपदधे स एव तासां दुरधिगमा हि गतिः प्रयोजनानाम् ॥

४१ प्रकृतमनुससार नाभिनेयं प्रविकसदङ्गुलि पाणिपल्लवं वा ।
प्रथममुपहितं विलासि चक्षुः सिततुरगे न चचाल नर्तकीनाम् ॥

४२ अभिनयमनसः सुराङ्गनाया निहितमलक्तकवर्तनाभिताम्रम् ।
चरणमभिपपात षड्पदाली धृतनवलोहितपङ्कजाभिशङ्का ॥

४३ अविरलमलसेषु नर्तकीनां द्रुतपरिषिक्तमलक्तकं पदेषु ।
सवपुषमिव चित्तरागमूहुर्नमितशिखानि कदम्बकेसराणि ॥

४४ नृपसुतमभितः समन्मथायाः परिजनगात्रतिरोहिताङ्गयष्टेः ।
स्फुटमभिलषितं बभूव वध्वा वदति हि संवृतिरेव कामितानि ॥

४५ अभिमुनि सहसा हृते परस्या घनमरुता जघनांशुकैकदेशे ।
चकितमवसनोरु सत्रपायाः प्रतियुवतीरपि विस्मयं निनाय ॥

No clusters of blooming water lilies or bunches of seven-   39
   leaf flowers or blossoms delighted them as much as
   Arjuna's eyes.

The nymphs had been sent to seduce the ascetic with their   40
   beauty, but it was they who fell in love with him. How
   unpredictable is the outcome of any undertaking!

As they danced, the women's seductive eyes failed to   41
   express the requisite emotions, or follow the cue of
   hand gestures articulated by graceful movements
   of the fingers. Once the women's gaze had fallen on
   Arjuna, it simply refused to move.[20]

As one nymph executed a dance step, a line of bees flew   42
   toward her foot, painted red with lac, mistaking it for
   a newly bloomed red lotus.[21]

The filaments of *kadamba* flowers lying on the ground,   43
   their tips crushed, absorbed the melted red lac paint
   dripping from the dancers' feet while they performed
   sensuous steps, as if their passionate desire for the
   ascetic had taken material form.[22]

Overcome by bashfulness when face to face with Arjuna,   44
   one infatuated woman tried to hide behind her friend,
   but her gesture exposed her passion rather than hid
   it. Concealment is the very thing that reveals one's
   hidden desires.

One woman was overcome with embarrassment when   45
   her skirt was suddenly blown aside by a strong gust
   of wind. The beauty of the girl in distress, thighs fully
   bared, struck even her girlfriends with wonder.

४६ धृतबिसवलये निधाय पाणौ मुखमधिरूषितपाण्डुगण्डलेखम् ।
नृपसुतमपरा स्मराभितापादमधुमदालसलोचनं निदध्यौ ॥

४७ सखि दयितमिहानयेति सा मां प्रहितवती कुसुमेषुणाभितप्ता ।
हृदयमहृदया न नाम पूर्वं भवदुपकण्ठमुपागतं विवेद ॥

४८ चिरमपि कलितान्यपारयन्त्या परिगदितुं परिशुष्यता मुखेन ।
गतघृण गमितानि सत्सखीनां नयनयुगैः सममार्द्रतां मनांसि ॥

४९ अचकमत सपल्लवां धरित्रीं मृदुसुरभिं विरहय्य पुष्पशय्याम् ।
भृशमरतिमवाप्य तत्र चास्यास्तव सुखशीतमुपैतुमङ्कमिच्छा ॥

५० तदनघ तनुरस्तु सा सकामा व्रजति पुरा हि परासुतां त्वदर्थे ।
पुनरपि सुलभं तपो ऽनुरागी युवतिजनः खलु नाप्यते ऽनुरूपः ॥

५१ जिहिहि कठिनतां प्रयच्छ वाचं ननु करुणामृदु मानसं मुनीनाम् ।
उपगतमवधीरयन्त्यभव्याः स निपुणमेत्य कयाचिदेवमूचे ॥

Tormented by desire, another nymph propped up her face,   46
beautiful cheeks gilt with cosmetic creams, on a hand
encircled by a lotus-stalk bracelet, and gazed steadily
at the handsome prince, the languorous beauty of
whose eyes owed nothing to the intoxication of wine.
Approaching Arjuna, a young woman delivered this clever   47-51
speech: "Tormented by love, my mistress sent me to
you, saying, 'Friend, bring my lover to me!' It looks
as though, although she has lost her heart to you, she
does not know that it has already reached you with
her message of love. Cruel man! Unable to watch
her struggling to utter with her grief-parched throat
the words of a message of her own composition that
she has rehearsed many times, our very hearts, her
girlfriends' hearts, are moved to tears, along with our
eyes. She gave up her soft, perfumed, flower-strewn
bed, finding it easier to lie on earth strewn with green
shoots; now even that is unbearable to her—only in
your arms' embrace will she find the cooling comfort
she longs for.[23] Good sir, please make her dreams
come true, for she is in danger of dying on account of
unrequited love for you. There will surely be many
other opportunities for pursuing austerities, but it
is not easy to find a worthy young woman who truly
loves you. Relent toward her, do not be so hard-
hearted! Pledge your love to her! After all, ascetics are
said to have hearts soft with compassion! And only
unfortunate men would reject the good fortune that
has come to them of its own accord."

५२ सललितचलितत्रिकाभिरामा शिरसिजसंयमनाकुलैकपाणिः ।
सुरपतितनये ऽपरा निरासे मनसिजजैत्रशरं विलोचनार्धम् ॥

५३ कुसुमितमवलम्ब्य चूतमुच्चैस्तनुरिभकुम्भपृथुस्तनानताङ्गी ।
तदभिमुखमनङ्गचापयष्टिर्विसृतगुणेव समुन्ननाम काचित् ॥

५४ सरभसमवलम्ब्य नीलमन्या विगलितनीवि विलोलमन्तरीयम् ।
अभिपतितुमनाः ससाध्वसेव च्युतरशनागुणसंदितावतस्थे ॥

५५ यदि मनसि शमः किमङ्ग चापं शठ विषयास्तव वल्लभा न मुक्तिः ।
भवतु दिशति नान्यकामिनीभ्यस्तव हृदये हृदयेश्वरावकाशम् ॥

५६ इति विषमितचक्षुषाभिधाय स्फुरदधरोष्ठमसूयया कयाचित् ।
अगणितगुरुमानलज्जयासौ स्वयमुरसि श्रवणोत्पलेन जघ्ने ॥

५७ सविनयमपराभिसृत्य साचि स्मितसुभगैकलसत्कपोललक्ष्मीः ।
श्रवणनियमितेन तं निदध्यौ सकलमिवासकलेन लोचनेन ॥

५८ करुणमभिहितं त्रपा निरस्ता तदभिमुखं च विमुक्तमश्रु ताभिः ।
प्रकुपितमभिसारणे ऽनुनेतुं प्रियमियती ह्यबलाजनस्य भूमिः ॥

Another young woman, an enchantress with gracefully   52
swaying hips, and one hand busied in gathering up her
disheveled hair, cast a sidelong glance, the love god's
all-powerful arrow, at Indra's son.

A nymph, bent slightly by breasts that swelled like an   53
elephant's temples, held aloft a flowering mango
branch before Arjuna, arching it like the love god's
bow, drawn and ready to shoot.

Yet another, clutching the blue skirt slipping from her   54
waist as its knot unraveled, hastily rose to approach
the ascetic but stood rooted to the spot, as if in
consternation, but in reality because her feet had
gotten entangled in her girdle's string.

"You deceiver! If you truly are committed to tranquility,   55-56
why do you carry a bow? Surely, you are in love with
the objects of sense, not with liberation from birth
and death. Or perhaps some woman already rules
your heart, and will not let another share that space
with her?"—Speaking thus with eyes narrowed and
lower lip trembling from envy, throwing to the winds
pride, modesty, and regard for elders, another girl
boldly struck Arjuna on the chest with the lotus that
decorated her ear.

Another girl quietly drew by his side, one cheek sweetly   57
dimpled in a smile, and gazed at him as if taking in his
whole form with a single sidelong glance.

Completely abandoning modesty, the nymphs tried   58
pleading with the ascetic, and they shed tears before
him. Pleas and tears are, after all, the last weapons in a
woman's arsenal for wooing an indifferent lover.

५९ असकलनयनेक्षितानि लज्जा गतमलसं परिपाण्डुता विषादः ।
इति विविधमियाय तासु भूषां प्रभवति मण्डयितुं वधूरनङ्गः ॥

६० अलसपदमनोरमं प्रकृत्या जितकलहंसवधूगति प्रयातम् ।
स्थितमुरुजघनस्थलातिभारादुदितपरिश्रमजिह्मितेक्षणं वा ॥

६१ भृशकुसुमशरेषुपातमोहादनवसितार्थपदाकुलो ऽभिलापः ।
अधिकविततलोचनं वधूनामयुगपदुन्नमितभ्रु वीक्षितं च ॥

६२ रुचिकरमपि नार्थवद्बभूव स्तिमितसमाधिशुचौ पृथातनूजे ।
ज्वलयति महतां मनांस्यमर्षे न हि लभते ऽवसरं
सुखाभिलाषः ॥

६३ स्वयं संराध्यैवं शतमखमखण्डेन तपसा
परोच्छित्त्या लभ्यामभिलषति लक्ष्मीं हरिसुते ।
मनोभिः सोद्रेगैः प्रणयविहतिध्वस्तरुचयः
सगन्धर्वा धाम त्रिदशवनिताः स्वं प्रतिययुः ॥

Sidelong glances and bashfulness, a lazy gait, pale   59
   complexions, and dejected faces—all these things
   enhanced the nymphs' beauty. All things become
   ornaments for a woman in love.²⁴

The graceful languor of the nymphs' walk, lovelier   60-62
   than the gait of the wild goose; the way the women
   paused, eyes flickering from the weariness caused
   by the weight of wide hips; their indistinct, unclear
   words, spoken under the spell of the love god's
   arrows; wide-eyed glances, with one eyebrow raised—
   charming gestures all, but none had the least effect
   on Pritha's son, yogi pure of mind, firmly established
   in contemplation. When the hearts of great men are
   burning with righteous anger, there is no room in
   them for the love of pleasure.²⁵

And so, while Arjuna looked forward to auspicious success   63
   in the form of the annihilation of his enemies, earned
   by steadfastly honoring Indra with the practice of
   austerities, the celestial nymphs went home with their
   gandharva partners, hearts plunged in dejection, their
   glowing loveliness dimmed by thwarted desire.

CHAPTER 11

Indra Tests Arjuna

१ अथामर्षान्निसर्गाच्च जितेन्द्रियतया तया ।
आजगामाश्रमं जिष्णोः प्रतीतः पाकशासनः ॥

२ मुनिरूपो ऽनुरूपेण सूनुना दद‍ृशे पुरः ।
द्राघीयसा वयोतीतः परिक्लान्तः किलाध्वना ॥

३ जटानां कीर्णया केशैः संहत्या परितः सितैः ।
पृक्तयेन्दुकरैरह्वः पर्यन्त इव संध्यया ॥

४ विशदभ्रूयुगच्छन्नवलितापाङ्गलोचनः ।
प्रालेयावततिम्लानपलाशाब्ज इव ह्रदः ॥

५ आसक्तभरनीकाशैरङ्गैः परिकृशैरपि ।
आद्घूनः सद्‌ग्रहिण्येव प्रायो यष्ट्यावलम्बितः ॥

६ गूढो ऽपि वपुषा राजन्धाम्ना लोकाभिभाविना ।
अंशुमानिव तन्वभ्रपटलच्छन्नविग्रहः ॥

७ जरतीमपि बिभ्राणस्तनुमप्राकृताकृतिः ।
चकाराक्रान्तलक्ष्मीकः ससाध्वसमिवाश्रमम् ॥

८ अभितस्तं पृथासूनुः स्नेहेन परितस्तरे ।
अविज्ञाते ऽपि बन्धौ हि बलात्प्रह्लादते मनः ॥

Pleased with Arjuna's anger against his enemies, a great   1
warrior's inborn attribute, and equally pleased with
his success in restraining the senses, Indra came to the
hero's hermitage.[1]

The god took on the guise of an aged man fatigued by   2-7
a long journey and appeared before his handsome
son living the life of a hermit. His tawny mass of
matted hair was everywhere sprinkled with gray, like
the evening twilight mingled with the moon's rays.
The wrinkled corners of his eyes, shaded by white
eyebrows, made him look like a lake where the petals
of lotuses are wilted by hoarfrost. Potbellied in spite
of an emaciated frame, he leaned heavily on a staff,
as if on a devoted wife. Even through this disguise his
figure radiated a light that overpowered the world,
like the sun barely veiled by a thin layer of clouds. His
aged yet superhuman figure eclipsed the beauty of the
hermitage, filling it with fear.

Pritha's son was overwhelmed by affection upon seeing   8
Indra. The sight of a kinsman brings joy to one's heart
even if he goes unrecognized.

९ आतिथेयीमथासाद्य सुतादपचितिं हरिः ।
विश्रम्य विष्टरे नाम व्याजहारेति भारतीम् ॥

१० त्वया साधु समारम्भि नवे वयसि यत्तपः ।
ह्रियते विषयैः प्रायो वर्षीयानपि माद्दशः ॥

११ श्रेयसीं तव संप्राप्ता गुणसंपदमाकृतिः ।
सुलभा रम्यता लोके दुर्लभं हि गुणार्जनम् ॥

१२ शरदम्बुधरच्छायागत्वर्यो यौवनश्रियः ।
आपातरम्या विषयाः पर्यन्तपरितापिनः ॥

१३ अन्तकः पर्यवस्थाता जन्मिनः संततापदः ।
इति त्याज्ये भवे भव्यो मुक्तावुत्तिष्ठते मनः ॥

१४ चित्तवानसि कल्याणी यत्त्वां मतिरुपस्थिता ।
विरुद्धः केवलं वेषः संदेहयति मे मनः ॥

१५ युयुत्सुनेव कवचं किमामुक्तमिदं त्वया ।
तपस्विनो हि वसते केवलाजिनवल्कले ॥

After accepting the rites of hospitality offered by his son,   9
Indra pretended to rest on his seat, and then he spoke.

"You do well to practice austerities at this tender age. As a   10
rule, even elderly men like me are seduced by sensual
enjoyments.

Your handsome figure is made all the more handsome   11
by your virtue. Physical beauty is easily found in the
world, but a virtuous man is a rare thing indeed.

The charms of youth are as transient as the shadow of an   12
autumn cloud. The objects of the senses may please
for a while, but in the end they only torment.

Death is the destined end of man, who is constantly beset   13
by misfortune. Convinced that the cycle of birth and
death is a condition to be cast off, the worthy man
applies himself to the goal of liberation.

Your excellent resolve tells me that you are a man of   14
understanding. It is only your incongruous attire that
makes my heart doubt.

Why are you clad in armor, as though you were ready for   15
battle? Ascetics wear only deerskin and bark.

१६ प्रपित्सोः किं च ते मुक्तिं निःस्पृहस्य कलेवरे ।
महेषुधी धनुर्भीमं भूतानामनभिद्रुहः ॥

१७ भयंकरः प्राणभृतां मृत्योर्भुज इवापरः ।
असिस्तव तपःस्थस्य न समर्थयते शमम् ॥

१८ जयमत्रभवान्नूनमरातिष्वभिलाषुकः ।
क्रोधलक्ष्म क्षमावन्तः क्रायुधं क्व तपोधनाः ॥

१९ यः करोति वधोदर्का निःश्रेयसकरीः क्रियाः ।
ग्लानिदोषच्छिदः स्वच्छाः स मूढः पङ्क्त्यत्यपः ॥

२० मूलं दोषस्य हिंसादेरर्थकामौ स्म मा पुषः ।
तौ हि तत्त्वावबोधस्य दुरुच्छेदावुपप्लवौ ॥

२१ अभिद्रोहेण भूतानामर्जयन्नत्वरीः श्रियः ।
उदन्वानिव सिन्धूनामापदामेति पात्रताम् ॥

२२ या गम्याः सत्सहायानां यासु खेदो भयं यतः ।
तासां किं यन्न दुःखाय विपदामिव संपदाम् ॥

२३ दुरासदानरीनुग्राभ्धृतेर्विश्वासजन्मनः ।
भोगान्भोगानिवाहेयानध्यास्यापन्न दुर्लभा ॥

If you are truly a person of detachment, seeking   16–17
liberation, with no interest in protecting your body
and no wish to harm living beings, why do you carry
a fierce bow and two great quivers? And if you are
indeed the ascetic that you claim to be, this sword of
yours, as terrifying to mortals as a third arm of the god
of death, fails to convince me of your commitment to
nonviolence.

There is no doubt that victory over your enemies is your   18
ultimate goal. What does an ascetic, a man of peace,
have to do with weapons, symbols of rage?

He who turns actions designed to engender liberation   19
into means of slaughter is as foolish as the man who
muddies pure water, sole remedy for the malady of
thirst.

Do not cultivate wealth and desire, root causes of violence   20
and other evils! Both are insurmountable obstacles to
insight into the true nature of things.

The man who amasses transient wealth by injuring   21
creatures becomes a receptacle for all misfortunes,
like the ocean for all rivers.

As with misfortunes, so it is with riches; nothing about   22
them does not lead to pain. A man cannot deal with
either without the support of good friends. Both exact
exhausting labor, and both are a constant source of
fear.

Sensual pleasures are like the coils of a snake, terrible,   23
intractable enemies of the contentment that comes
from freedom from anxiety. Whoever pursues them is
sure to be ruined.

२४ नान्तरज्ञाः श्रियो जातु प्रियैरासां न भूयते ।
आसक्तास्तास्वमी मूढा वामशीला हि जन्तवः ॥

२५ को ऽपवादः स्तुतिपदे यदशीलेषु चञ्चलाः ।
साधुवृत्तानपि क्षुद्रा विक्षिपन्त्येव संपदः ॥

२६ कृतवानन्यदेहेषु कर्ता च विधुरं मनः ।
अप्रियैरिव संयोगो विप्रयोगः प्रियैः सह ॥

२७ शून्यमाकीर्णतामेति तुल्यं व्यसनमुत्सवैः ।
विप्रलम्भो ऽपि लाभाय सति प्रियसमागमे ॥

२८ तदा रम्याण्यरम्याणि प्रियाः शल्यं तदासवः ।
तदैकाकी सबन्धुः सन्निष्टेन रहितो यदा ॥

२९ युक्तः प्रमाद्यसि हितादपेतः परितप्यसे ।
यदि नेष्टात्मनः पीडा मा सज्जि भवता जने ॥

३० जन्मिनो ऽस्य स्थितिं विद्वाँल्लक्ष्मीमिव चलाचलाम् ।
भवान्मा स्म वधीन्न्याय्यं न्यायाधारा हि साधवः ॥

३१ विजहीहि रणोत्साहं मा तपः साधु नीनशः ।
उच्छेदं जन्मनः कर्तुमेधि शान्तस्तपोधन ॥

212

Riches are not discriminating; no one is really dear to   24
them. But fools become attached to riches. What
perverse creatures men are!

Nothing would detract from the praise of riches if they   25
were fickle only toward those without virtue, but
wealth is unscrupulous enough to cast aside even men
of good conduct.

Parting from what you love and meeting with what you   26
dislike have pained your heart in former lives, and will
pain it again.

When a man is in the company of loved ones, poverty   27
becomes plenty, misfortune turns into a festival, and
even being deceived seems like a favor.

When a man has been deprived of what he holds dear,   28
pleasant things become unpleasant, dear life itself
becomes a thorn, and, for all the friends he may have,
he is left utterly alone.

When you possess the beneficial things you desire, you are   29
wild with joy; when you lose them, you are tormented.
If you dislike pain for your own self, then do not let
yourself become the cause of another's pain.

You know that the human condition is as unstable as   30
fortune. So do not destroy what is right, for good men
depend on righteous conduct.

Give up your determination for war, do not utterly destroy   31
your great ascetic power. Cleave to peace, ascetic, so
that you may destroy the cycle of birth!

३२ जीयन्तां दुर्जया देहे रिपवश्चक्षुरादयः ।
जितेषु ननु लोको ऽयं तेषु कृत्स्नस्त्वया जितः ॥

३३ परवानर्थसंसिद्धौ नीचवृत्तिरपत्रपः ।
अविधेयेन्द्रियः पुंसां गौरवैति विधेयताम् ॥

३४ श्वस्त्वया सुखसंवित्तिः स्मरणीयाधुनातनी ।
इति स्वप्नोपमान्मत्वा कामान्मा गास्तदङ्गताम् ॥

३५ श्रद्धेया विप्रलब्धारः प्रिया विप्रियकारिणः ।
सुदुस्त्यजास्त्यजन्तो ऽपि कामाः कष्टा हि शत्रवः ॥

३६ विविक्ते ऽस्मिन्नगे भूयः प्लाविते जह्नुकन्यया ।
प्रत्यासीदति मुक्तिस्त्वां पुरा मा भूरुदायुधः ॥

३७ व्याहृत्य मरुतां पत्याविति वाचमवस्थिते ।
वचः प्रश्रयगम्भीरमथोवाच कपिध्वजः ॥

३८ प्रसादरम्यमोजस्वि गरीयो लाघवान्वितम् ।
साकाङ्क्षमनुपस्कारं विष्वग्गति निराकुलम् ॥

३९ न्यायनिर्णीतसारत्वान्निरपेक्षमिवागमे ।
अप्रकम्प्यतयान्येषामाम्नायवचनोपमम् ॥

214

Conquer the enemies in your body, so difficult to   32
  overcome—the senses, beginning with the eye. When
  you have subdued these, you will have conquered the
  whole world.
A man intent on amassing wealth, with no control of his   33
  senses, shameless, and given to base deeds, becomes a
  slave to other men, no better than an ox.
Today's pleasurable experience will fade into mere   34
  memory tomorrow. Understand that desires are like
  dreams; do not fall a prey to them!
Sensual pleasures win one's trust and yet are deceitful,   35
  pleasant yet the cause of pain, and hard to give up
  even when they depart of their own accord—they are
  perverse enemies indeed!
On this secluded mountain peak, perennially bathed by   36
  the river Ganga, Jahnu's daughter, liberation will
  come to you very soon. Put aside your weapons!"
With this, the lord of the storm gods* ended his speech.   37
  Then Arjuna, hero with the monkey banner, delivered
  a speech dignified by courtesy.
"Your speech is pleasingly clear, yet complex; brief, yet   38
  profound; tightly constructed, yet not elliptical; of
  wide implication, yet not confused.
Since it is firmly founded on the tenets of logic, it appears   39
  to be independent of scripture; and yet, because
  it is irrefutable, it strikes the hearer as having the
  authority of scripture.

---

* Indra's companions, the Maruts, storm gods.

४० अलङ्घ्यत्वाज्जनैरन्यैः क्षुभितोदन्वदूर्जितम् ।
   औदार्यादर्थसंपत्तेः शान्तं चित्तमृषेरिव ॥

४१ इदमीदृग्गुणोपेतं लब्धावसरसाधनम् ।
   व्याकुर्यात्कः प्रियं वाक्यं यो वक्ता नेदृगाशयः ॥

४२ न ज्ञातं तात यत्नस्य पौर्वापर्यममुष्य ते ।
   शासितुं येन मां धर्मं मुनिभिस्तुल्यमिच्छसि ॥

४३ अविज्ञातप्रबन्धस्य वचो वाचस्पतेरिव ।
   व्रजत्यफलतामेव नयद्रुह इवेहितम् ॥

४४ श्रेयसो ऽप्यस्य ते तात वचसो नास्मि भाजनम् ।
   नभसः स्फुटतारस्य रात्रेरिव विपर्ययः ॥

४५ क्षत्रियस्तनयः पाण्डोरहं पार्थो धनंजयः ।
   स्थितः प्रास्तस्य दायादैर्भ्रातुर्ज्येष्ठस्य शासने ॥

४६ कृष्णद्वैपायनादेशाद्विभर्मि व्रतमीदृशम् ।
   भृशमाराधने यत्तः स्वाराध्यस्य मरुत्वतः ॥

४७ दुरक्षान्दीव्यता राज्ञा राज्यमात्मा वयं वधूः ।
   नीतानि पणतां नूनमीदृशी भवितव्यता ॥

216

Since it cannot be overcome by opponents, it is powerful   40
    as the stormy ocean, yet through its thoughtful
    nobility and its success in achieving its goal, it is
    tranquil as the mind of a sage.

Could a speaker who does not possess your qualities of   41
    mind have made so pleasing a speech, endowed with
    so many good figures of speech and so well suited to
    the occasion?

Father, you do not know the circumstance of my   42
    undertaking, and that is why you seek to instruct me
    in a code of conduct proper to ascetics![2]

The words of one unaware of the context of his topic—he   43
    might be Brihaspati, lord of speech, himself—become
    as useless as the efforts of a warrior who defies
    political wisdom.

Father, well intentioned as they are, your words are no   44
    more appropriate for me than a starlit sky for the day.

I am a warrior, Dhanamjaya, son of Pandu by Pritha, and   45
    I stand at the command of my eldest brother, who has
    been exiled from his kingdom by our kinsmen, our
    rivals.[3]

At the command of the sage Krishna Dvaipayana, I have   46
    taken up this mode of life, the practice of austerity,
    focusing my efforts on propitiating Indra, whose favor
    is easily won.

The king, gambling with loaded dice in a rigged match,   47
    wagered his kingdom, himself, us, his brothers, and
    his wife. Such, I suppose, was our destiny.

४८ तेनानुजसहायेन द्रौपद्या च मया विना ।
भृशमायामियामासु यामिनीष्वभितप्यते ॥

४९ हतोत्तरीयां प्रसभं सभायामागतह्रियः ।
मर्मच्छिदा नो वचसा निरतक्षन्नरातयः ॥

५० उपाधत्त सपत्नेषु कृष्णाया गुरुसंनिधौ ।
भावमानयने सत्याः सत्यंकारमिवान्तकः ॥

५१ तामैक्षन्त क्षणं सभ्या दुःशासनपुरःसराम् ।
अभिसायार्कमावृत्तां छायामिव महातरोः ॥

५२ अयथार्थक्रियारम्भैः पतिभिः किं तवेक्षितैः ।
अरुध्येतामितीवास्या नयने बाष्पवारिणा ॥

५३ सोढवान्नो दशामन्त्यां ज्यायानेव गुणप्रियः ।
सुलभो हि द्विषां भङ्गो दुर्लभा सत्त्ववाच्यता ॥

५४ स्थित्यतिक्रान्तिभीरूणि स्वच्छान्याकुलितान्यपि ।
तोयानि तोयराशीनां मनांसि च मनस्विनाम् ॥

In my absence he passes the long watches of the nights 48
  tormented by grief, along with his younger brothers
  and Draupadi.
Our enemies shamed us in the assembly, taking our upper 49
  robes by force, and then cutting us with wounding
  words.
The god of death put the notion into our enemies' hearts 50
  of disrobing the virtuous Draupadi, dark lady, in the
  presence of our elders, as if she were to become the
  security, taken in advance, for the Pandavas' paying
  up what they had lost.[4]
The courtiers could look at her only for a moment, as she 51
  entered the assembly hall, dragged by Duhshasana—
  she was like the shadow, turning back, of a great tree
  as it faces the evening sun.[5]
'What use is it to look at your husbands, whose actions 52
  belie their title of *pati*, "husband, protector?"'—it was
  as if with this in mind that her eyes blurred with tears.
It was the eldest among us, a lover of virtue, who tolerated 53
  our final disgrace, for it is easy to defeat one's enemies,
  but hard to retain one's good name among good men.
The waters of oceans and the minds of honorable men are 54
  averse to overstepping their bounds and remain pure
  even when agitated.

५५ धार्तराष्ट्रैः सह प्रीतिर्वैरमसमास्वसूयत ।
असन्मैत्री हि दोषाय कूलच्छायेव सेविता ॥

५६ अपवादादभीतस्य समस्य गुणदोषयोः ।
असद्वृत्तेरहोवृत्तं दुर्विभावं विधेरिव ॥

५७ ध्वंसेत हृदयं सद्यः परिभूतस्य मे परैः ।
यद्यमर्षः प्रतीकारं भुजालम्बं न लम्भयेत् ॥

५८ अवधूयारिभिर्नीता हरिणैस्तुल्यवृत्तिताम् ।
अन्योन्यस्यापि जिह्रीमः किं पुनः सहवासिनाम् ॥

५९ शक्तिवैकल्यनम्रस्य निःसारत्वाल्लघीयसः ।
जन्मिनो मानहीनस्य तृणस्य च समा गतिः ॥

६० अलङ्घ्यं तत्तदुद्वीक्ष्य यद्यदुच्चैर्महीभृताम् ।
प्रियतां ज्यायसीं मा गान्महतां केन तुङ्गता ॥

६१ तावदाश्रीयते लक्ष्म्या तावदस्य स्थिरं यशः ।
पुरुषस्तावदेवासौ यावन्मानान्न हीयते ॥

६२ स पुमानर्थवज्जन्मा यस्य नाम्नि पुरःस्थिते ।
नान्यामङ्गुलिमभ्येति संख्यायामुद्यताङ्गुलिः ॥

It was our very friendship with the sons of Dhritarashtra   55
that generated their enmity toward us. Associating
with bad men, like resorting to a crumbling riverbank
for shelter, is sure to end in disaster.

A scoundrel's actions are as unfathomable as the ways of   56
fate, for both are unafraid of ill repute and indifferent
to virtue and vice.

My heart would have instantly burst to be overpowered by   57
enemies in this way, had not my indignation given me
the thought of revenge to rely upon.

Ousted by the enemy, we have been forced to live like   58
deer in the forest. We are ashamed even to face one
another, much less our friends.

A man who has lost his pride suffers the fate of a blade of   59
grass, bowed down for want of strength, and of no
consequence because of a lack of substance.

It is not surprising that great men treasure loftiness, for   60
they have learned that the highest parts of a mountain
are the most difficult to scale.

Only so long does prosperity accompany a man, only so   61
long does his fame endure, only so long is he a real
man, as he does not lose his honor.

That man is born to some purpose, if the finger that is   62
raised to count his name as first among men is never
followed by another finger.[6]

६३ दुरासदवनज्यायानाम्यस्तुङ्गो ऽपि भूधरः ।
न जहाति महौजस्कं मानप्रांशुमलङ्घ्यता ॥

६४ गुरून्कुर्वन्ति ते वंश्यानन्वर्था तैर्वसुंधरा ।
येषां यशांसि शुभ्राणि ह्रेपयन्तीन्दुमण्डलम् ॥

६५ उदाहरणमाशीःषु प्रथमे ते मनस्विनाम् ।
शुष्के ऽशनिरिवामर्षो यैररातिषु पात्यते ॥

६६ न सुखं प्रार्थये नार्थमुदन्वद्वीचिचञ्चलम् ।
नानित्यताशनेस्त्रस्यन्विविक्तं ब्रह्मणः पदम् ॥

६७ प्रमार्ष्टुमयशःपङ्कमिच्छेयं छद्मना कृतम् ।
वैधव्यतापितारातिवनितालोचनाम्बुभिः ॥

६८ अपहस्ये ऽथवा सद्धिः प्रमादो वास्तु मे धियः ।
अस्थानविहितायासः कामं जिह्रेतु वा भवान् ॥

६९ वंशलक्ष्मीमनुद्धृत्य समुच्छेदेन विद्विषाम् ।
निर्वाणमपि मन्ये ऽहमन्तरायं जयश्रियः ॥

७० अजन्मा पुरुषस्तावद्व्रतासुस्तृणमेव वा ।
यावन्नेषुभिरादत्ते विलुप्तमरिभिर्यशः ॥

A mountain, however high, and grown over with   63
    impenetrable forests, can still be scaled; but a man
    of great prowess, dignified with pride, can never be
    overcome.
It is such men, whose bright fame shames the moon's   64
    orb, who dignify their descendants with their name;
    through them the earth becomes fit to be called
    vasuṃdharā, she who bears riches.[7]
They are the examples used in benedictions, the foremost   65
    among men of self-respect, whose wrath strikes their
    enemies as a thunderbolt strikes a dead tree.
I do not crave the pleasures of sense, nor wealth,   66–67
    unsteady as the waves of the ocean; nor do I seek the
    sequestered haven of liberation, out of fear of that
    thunderbolt, the transience of human existence. I seek
    instead to wash away, with the tears of our enemy's
    grieving widows, the mud of disgrace that treachery
    has heaped upon us!
I do not care if I become the butt of ridicule for good men   68
    or if this undertaking is an error of judgment on my
    part. So do not feel too chagrined at having aimed
    your efforts at persuasion at an unsuitable target!
Until I exterminate my enemies and restore the reputation   69
    of my family, I shall think of liberation itself as an
    obstacle to victory!
So long as a man has not regained through his arrows the   70
    fame seized by his enemies, he is as good as if he had
    not been born, as if he were dead, as if he were a mere
    blade of grass.

७१ अनिर्जयेन द्विषतां यस्यामर्षः प्रशाम्यति ।
पुरुषोक्तिः कथं तस्मिन्ब्रूहि त्वं हि तपोधन ॥

७२ कृतं पुरुषशब्देन जातिमात्रावलम्बिना ।
यो ऽङ्गीकृतगुणैः श्लाघ्यः सविस्मयमुदाहृतः ॥

७३ ग्रसमानमिवौजांसि सदसा गौरवेरितम् ।
नाम यस्याभिनन्दन्ति द्विषो ऽपि स पुमान्पुमान् ॥

७४ यथाप्रतिज्ञं द्विषतां युधि प्रतिचिकीर्षया ।
ममैवाध्येति नृपतिस्तृष्यन्निव जलाञ्जलेः ॥

७५ स वंशस्यावदातस्य शशाङ्कस्येव लाञ्छनम् ।
कृच्छ्रेषु व्यर्थया यत्र भूयते भर्तुराज्ञया ॥

७६ कथं वादीयतामर्वाङर्जुनिता धर्मरोधिनी ।
आश्रमानुक्रमः पूर्वैः स्मर्यते न व्यतिक्रमः ॥

७७ आसक्ता धूरियं रूढा जननी दूरगा च मे ।
तिरस्करोति स्वातन्त्र्यं ज्यायांश्चाचारवान्नृपः ॥

७८ स्वधर्ममनुरुन्धन्ते नातिक्रममरातिभिः ।
पलायन्ते कृतध्वंसा नाहवान्मानशालिनः ॥

If a man's indignation can be stilled before he has defeated   71
his enemy, how can he still be called a man? Tell me,
sage, yourself!

Of what use is it to call him a man who is a man by mere   72-73
accident of birth? That man alone is worthy of being
called such who is spoken of with admiration by men
who treasure virtue, and whose name, uttered with
awe in the assembly of men, overpowers other men
and draws praise even from his enemies.

Seeking to fulfill his vow of taking revenge on his enemies   74
in war, the king has placed his hopes in me, like a
thirsty man in a handful of water.

That man is a blot on his noble family, like the spot on the   75
moon, who fails, when hard times come, to carry out
his master's command.

What is more, how can I take up renunciation before its   76
due time, a course that would interfere with the code
of conduct laid down for me? The ancient lawgivers
teach us to take the stages of life in order, and not to
violate their sequence.[8]

This tremendous yoke has fallen upon my shoulders; my   77
mother too is far away, my brother is my king, elder
to me and very pious—all these things constrain my
freedom to choose.

Self-respecting men stand by the code of conduct   78
appropriate for them and do not transgress it. Even
when crushed by the enemy, they do not flee from
battle.

७९ विच्छिन्नाभ्रविलायं वा विलीये नगमूर्धनि ।
आराध्य वा सहस्राक्षमयशःशल्यमुद्धरे ॥

८० इत्युक्तवन्तं परिरभ्य दोर्भ्यां तनूजमाविष्कृतदिव्यमूर्तिः ।
अघोपघातं मघवा विभूत्यै भवोद्भवाराधनमादिदेश ॥

८१ प्रीते पिनाकिनि मया सह लोकपालै-
र्लोकत्रये ऽपि विहिताप्रतिवार्यवीर्यः ।
लक्ष्मीं समुत्सुकयितासि भृशं परेषा-
मुच्चार्य वाचमिति तेन तिरोबभूवे ॥

I shall either propitiate Indra, god with the thousand eyes,   79
    and pluck out the thorn of dishonor, or perish upon
    this mountain peak, like a shattered cloud."⁹

When Arjuna fell silent, Indra the bounteous revealed   80
    his own divine form and gathered his son into his
    embrace. He then instructed the hero to propitiate
    Shiva, source of birth and death, by means of
    austerities that destroy evil, with the aim of winning
    supreme power.

"When you have pleased Shiva the archer with heroic   81
    deeds enabled by myself and the guardian gods of the
    worlds—deeds that will remain unmatched in all three
    worlds—you will win back royal fortune from your
    enemies." With this, the god vanished.

CHAPTER 12

Shiva's Noble Plan

१ अथ वासवस्य वचनेन रुचिरवदनस्त्रिलोचनम् ।
   क्लान्तिरहितमभिराधयितुं विधिवत्तपांसि विदधे धनंजयः ॥

२ अभिरश्मिमालि विमलस्य धृतजयधृतेरनाशुषः ।
   तस्य भुवि बहुतिथास्तिथयः प्रतिजग्मुरेकचरणं निषीदतः ॥

३ वपुरिन्द्रियोपतपनेषु सततमसुखेषु पाण्डवः ।
   व्याप नगपतिरिव स्थिरतां महतां हि धैर्यमविभाव्यवैभवम् ॥

४ न पपात संनिहितपक्तिसुरभिषु फलेषु मानसम् ।
   तस्य शुचिनि शिशिरे च पयस्यमृतायते हि सुतपः सुकर्मणाम् ॥

५ न विसिस्मिये न विषसाद मुहुरलसतां न चाददे ।
   सत्त्वमुरुधृति रजस्तमसी न हतः स्म तस्य हतशक्तिपेलवे ॥

६ तपसा कृशं वपुरुवाह स विजितजगत्त्रयोदयम् ।
   त्रासजननमपि तत्त्वविदां किमिवास्ति यत्र सुकरं मनस्विभिः ॥

७ ज्वलतो ऽनलादनुनिशीथमधिकरुचिरम्भसां निधेः ।
   धैर्यगुणमवजयन्निजयी ददृशे समुन्नततरः स शैलतः ॥

८ जपतः सदा जपमुपांशु वदनमभितो विसारिभिः ।
   तस्य दशनकिरणैः शुशुभे परिवेषभीषणमिवार्कमण्डलम् ॥

At Indra's command, the handsome hero Arjuna   1
    rigorously practiced the observances of austerity, to
    please Shiva, god with three eyes.[1]
His heart set on victory over the Pandavas' enemies,   2
    and pure of mind and body, he fasted for many days,
    standing with one leg planted on the ground, face
    turned toward the sun.[2]
Constantly subjecting body and senses to harsh   3
    austerities, the Pandava prince grew firm as Himalaya,
    king of mountains. The fortitude of great men beggars
    the imagination.[3]
He did not crave the ripe, fragrant fruit that hung within   4
    reach, nor water, cool and pure. Noble austerity is
    ambrosia itself for men of good conduct.
He neither exulted nor despaired over his austerities,   5
    nor slackened his effort. Rendered quite powerless,
    neither passion nor dark inertia could destroy his
    boundless, enduring lucidity of mind.[4]
His body wasted by austerity, he yet surpassed the powers   6
    of the three worlds, and even wise men were seized by
    fear. There is nothing in the world a courageous man
    cannot accomplish.
Arjuna the conqueror appeared taller than a mountain,   7
    excelled the ocean's depths in tranquility, and shone
    brighter than a blazing fire at midnight.[5]
Encircled by the light flashing from his teeth as he   8
    constantly chanted secret mantras, his face shone like
    the sun's orb surrounded by a fierce halo.

९ कवचं स बिभ्रदुपवीतपदनिहितसज्यकार्मुकः ।
शैलपतिरिव महेन्द्रधनुःपरिवीतभीमगहनो विदिद्युते ॥

१० प्रविवेश गामिव कृशस्य नियमसवनाय गच्छतः ।
तस्य पदविनमितो हिमवानगुरुतां नयन्ति हि गुणा न संहतिः ॥

११ परिकीर्णमुद्यतभुजस्य भुवनविवरे दुरासदम् ।
ज्योतिरुपरि शिरसो विततं जगृहे निजान्मुनिदिवौकसां पथः ॥

१२ रजनीषु राजतनयस्य बहुलसमये ऽपि धामभिः ।
भिन्नतिमिरनिकरं न जहे शशिरश्मिसंगमयुजा नभः श्रिया ॥

१३ महता मयूखनिचयेन शमितरुचि जिष्णुजन्मना ।
ह्रीतमिव नभसि वीतमले न विराजते स्म वपुरंशुमालिनः ॥

१४ तमुदीरितारुणजटांशुमधिगुणशरासनं जनाः ।
रुद्रमनुदितललाटदृशं दद‍शुर्मिमन्थिषुमिवासुरीः पुरीः ॥

Wearing a suit of armor, his strung bow serving as the   9
warrior's sacred thread, he shone like Himalaya,
lord of mountains, its perilous forests wreathed by a
rainbow.[6]

When, an emaciated ascetic, he walked to the river for his   10
ritual bath, the Himalaya seemed to sink to the earth,
crushed by his steps. Virtue, not physical bulk, lends
substance to a man's character.

At night, as Arjuna stood with arms raised, a blinding light   11
rose above his head, spread over space, and blocked
the celestial paths of gods and sages.

Even in the nights of the dark fortnight,* the brilliant   12
light emanating from the prince dispersed the massed
darkness, brightening the sky with the lovely light of
the moon.[7]

Eclipsed by the multitude of rays of light streaming from   13
Arjuna, the sun stopped shining even in a clear sky, as
if put to shame.

With matted red hair piled high on his head and carrying   14
a strung bow, Arjuna seemed to the mountain's
inhabitants like Rudra† without the forehead eye
and poised to annihilate the three flying cities of the
demons.[8]

---

* When the moon is waning.
† Shiva.

233

१५ मरुतां पतिः स्विदहिमांशुरुत पृथुशिखः शिखी तपः ।
तप्तुमसुकरमुपक्रमते न जनो ऽयमित्यवयये स तापसैः ॥

१६ न ददाह भूरुहवनानि हरितनयधाम दूरगम् ।
न स्म नयति परिशोषमपः सुसहं बभूव न च सिद्धतापसैः ॥

१७ विनयं गुणा इव विवेकमपनयभिदं नया इव ।
न्यायमवधय इवाशरणाः शरणं ययुः शिवमथो महर्षयः ॥

१८ परिवीतमंशुभिरुदस्तदिनकरमयूखमण्डलैः ।
शंभुमुपहततृशः सहसा न च ते निचायितुमभिप्रसेहिरे ॥

The ascetics who lived there wondered, "Could this be   15
Indra himself, or the blazing sun, or the god of fire,
with leaping flames, who is practicing such fierce
austerity? This is no ordinary man!"[9]
Indra's son's far-reaching, fiery radiance did not burn the   16
forests on the mountain or dry up the lakes. And yet
the ascetics and demigods who lived on the mountain
found that fire impossible to bear.[10]
Then, like virtues in need of cultivation, like policies   17
in need of discriminating intelligence, the nemesis
of bad strategy, like contracts in need of proper
observance, the helpless sages sought refuge in
Shiva.[11]
For a moment, blinded by the rays of light emanating from   18
Shambhu, more dazzling than the rays of the sun, they
could not see the god.

१९ अथ भूतभव्यभवदीशमभिमुखयितुं कृतस्तवाः ।
तत्र महसि दृदृशुः पुरुषं कमनीयविग्रहमयुग्मलोचनम् ॥

२० ककुदे वृषस्य कृतबाहुमकृशपरिणाहशालिनि ।
स्पर्शसुखमनुभवन्तमुमाकुचयुग्ममण्डल इवार्द्रचन्दने ॥

२१ स्थितमुन्नते तुहिनशैलशिरसि भुवनातिवर्तिना ।
साद्रिजलधिजलवाहपथं सदिगश्वानमिव विश्वमोजसा ॥

२२ अनुजानुमध्यमवसक्तविततवपुषा महाहिना ।
लोकमखिलमिव भूमिभृता रवितेजसामवधिनाधिवेष्टितम् ॥

२३ परिणाहिना तुहिनराशिविशदमुपवीतसूत्रताम् ।
नीतमुरगमनुरञ्जयता शितिना गलेन विलसन्मरीचिना ॥

२४ प्लुतमालतीसितकपालकुमुदमवरुद्धमूर्धजम् ।
शेषमिव सुरसरित्पयसां शिरसा विसारि शशिधाम बिभ्रतम् ॥

२५ मुनयस्ततो ऽभिमुखमेत्य नयनविनिमेषनोदिताः ।
पाण्डुतनयतपसा जनितं जगतामशर्म भृशमाचचक्षिरे ॥

Then, in that blaze of light they could make out the   19-24
    handsome god with the three eyes, and they sang
    hymns of praise to please the lord who commands
    the past, present, and future. He sat on the summit of
    Himalaya, mountain of snow, resting his hand on his
    bull's broad hump, savoring the touch as if caressing
    the goddess Uma's breasts moist with sandalwood
    cream. He radiated an extraordinarily powerful
    brilliance that enveloped the mountains, oceans, and
    sky, covering the entire universe in every direction.
    Crossed legs bound by a winding snake that served as
    a yoga band stretched across his knees, he looked like
    the earth world itself, wrapped by the mountain range
    where the sun rises and sets.* Shimmering light from
    his blue-black throat colored the stout snake, white as
    massed snow, that served him for a sacred thread. The
    broad rays of the moon on his head, like waters left
    behind by the Ganga, river of the gods, engulfed his
    hair and bathed the skull that was like a lotus adorning
    it, white as jasmine.[12]

Then the sages stepped forward and, spurred to speech   25
    by a blink of the god's eye, described at length the
    suffering Pandu's son had inflicted on the worlds with
    his austerities.

---

* The mountain range *lokāloka*.

२६ तरसैव को ऽपि भुवनैकपुरुष पुरुषस्तपस्यति ।
ज्योतिरमलवपुषो ऽपि रवेरभिभूय वृत्र इव भीमविग्रहः ॥

२७ स धनुर्महेषुधि बिभर्ति कवचमसिमुत्तमं जटाः ।
वल्कमजिनमिति चित्रमिदं मुनितराविरोधि न च नास्य राजते ॥

२८ चलने ऽवनिश्चलति तस्य करणनियमे सदिङ्मुखम् ।
स्तम्भमनुभवति शान्तमरुद्ग्रहतारकागणयुतं नभस्तलम् ॥

२९ स तदोजसा विजितसारममरदितिजोपसंहितम् ।
विश्वमिदमपिदधाति पुरा किमिवास्ति यन्न तपसामदुष्करम् ॥

३० विजिगीषते यदि जगन्ति युगपदथ संजिहीर्षति ।
प्राप्तुमभवमभिवाञ्छति वा वयमस्य नो विषहितुं क्षमा रुचः ॥

३१ किमुपेक्षसे कथय नाथ न तव विदितं न किंचन ।
त्रातुमलमभयदार्हसि नस्त्वयि मा स्म शासति भवत्पराभवः ॥

३२ इति गां विधाय विरतेषु मुनिषु वचनं समाददे ।
भिन्नजलधिजलनादगुरु ध्वनयन्दिशां विवरमन्धकान्तकः ॥

"Supreme lord of the universe! A man is practicing   26
violent austerity on our mountain, terrible as the
demon Vritra, outshining the sun itself with his fiery
brilliance.

Clad in a suit of armor, he carries a bow with two mighty   27
quivers, and a great sword. He wears his hair in
matted locks, and he is dressed in deerskin and bark.
This strange attire goes against the rules for ascetics,
and yet he shines in it!

When he moves, the whole earth moves with him; when   28
he restrains his senses in states of contemplation,
space stands still in every direction, with unmoving
wind, planets, and stars.

He will soon conquer the entire universe, subduing gods   29
and demons with his power. After all, no goal is
beyond reach when austerity is the means.[13]

Whether he wants to conquer the worlds or to annihilate   30
them, or whether he desires liberation from birth and
death, we cannot bear his austerity's brilliant fire.

Tell us, lord, what is your will? There is nothing you do not   31
know. Savior, you must rescue us! With you for our
master, how can we be crushed?"

When the sages ended their speech, Shiva, slayer of the   32
demon Andhaka, spoke, and his voice, rumbling
deeply like the roar of the ocean's turbulent waves,
echoed in all the regions of space.

३३ बदरीतपोवननिवासनिरतमवगात मान्यथा ।
धातुरुदयनिधने जगतां नरमंशमादिपुरुषस्य गां गतम् ॥

३४ द्विषतः परासिसिषुरेष सकलभुवनाभितापिनः ।
क्रान्तकुलिशकरवीर्यबलान्मदुपासनं विहितवान्महत्तपः ॥

३५ अयमच्युतश्च वचनेन सरसिरुहजन्मनः प्रजाः ।
पातुमसुरनिधनेन विभू भुवमभ्युपेत्य मनुजेषु तिष्ठतः ॥

३६ सुरकृत्यमेतदवगम्य निपुणमिति मूकदानवः ।
हन्तुमभिपतति पाण्डुसुतं त्वरया तदत्र सह गम्यतां मया ॥

३७ विवरे ऽपि नैनमनिगूढमभिभवितुमेष पारयन् ।
पापनिरतिरविशङ्कितया विजयं व्यवस्यति वराहमायया ॥

३८ निहते विडम्बितकिरातनृपतिवपुषा रिपौ मया ।
मुक्तनिशितविशिखः प्रसभं मृगयाविवादमयमाचरिष्यति ॥

३९ तपसा निपीडितकृशस्य विरहितसहायसंपदः ।
सत्त्वविहितमतुलं भुजयोर्बलमस्य पश्यत मृधे ऽधिकुप्यतः ॥

"Know that this person is no ordinary man, but a sage   33
   descended to earth from his celestial abode in the
   Badari hermitage—Nara, who is a portion of the
   divine essence of Vishnu Narayana, the primal Person
   who creates and destroys the universe.[14]
Seeking to destroy enemies who have overthrown Indra   34
   himself, wielder of the thunderbolt, and who are
   oppressing the entire universe, this man is worshiping
   me with his fierce austerity.
At the command of lotus-born Brahma,[15] this hero and   35
   Krishna have come to earth and live among mortals to
   protect humankind from oppressive demons.
Shrewdly guessing this turn of events to be the work of the   36
   gods, a demon named Muka will attack Pandu's son
   with intent to kill. Come with me now, let us quickly
   go to Arjuna's hermitage!
Knowing that he cannot overcome the prince even though   37
   alone and vulnerable to attack, this demon, who is
   addicted to vile deeds, will turn himself into a magic
   boar, engineering his own victory through deception.
Disguised as a hunter chief, I will kill the boar. Then   38
   Arjuna, having shot his own keen arrow at his
   assailant, will argue vehemently with me over his
   claim to the prey.
And you shall witness the matchless feats of arms the   39
   hero, drawing on his innate strength, will perform
   when, wasted by harsh austerities and lacking allies,
   he plunges into combat with me in righteous anger."

४० इति तानुदारमनुनीय विषमहरिचन्दनालिना ।
घर्मजनितपुलकेन लसद्ध्वजमौक्तिकावलिगुणेन वक्षसा ॥

४१ वदनेन पुष्पितलतान्तनियमितविलम्बिमौलिना ।
बिभ्रदरुणनयनेन रुचं शिखिपिच्छलाञ्छितकपोलभित्तिना ॥

४२ बृहदुद्ध्वहज्जलदनादि धनुरुपहितैकमार्गणम् ।
मेघनिचय इव संववृते रुचिरः किरातपृतनापतिः शिवः ॥

४३ अनुकूलमस्य च विचिन्त्य गणपतिभिरात्तविग्रहैः ।
शूलपरशुशरचापभृतैर्महती वनेचरचमूर्विनिर्ममे ॥

४४ विरचय्य काननविभागमनुगिरमथेश्वराज्ञया ।
भीमनिनदपिहितोरुभुवः परितो ऽपदिश्य मृगयां प्रतस्थिरे ॥

४५ क्षुभिताभिनिःसृतविभिन्नशकुनिमृगयूथनिःस्वनैः ।
पूर्णपृथुवनगुहाविवरः सहसा भयादिव ररास भूधरः ॥

४६ न विरोधिनी रुषमियाय पथि मृगविहंगसंहतिः ।
घ्नन्ति सहजमपि भूरिभियः सममागताः सपदि वैरमापदः ॥

४७ चमरीगणैर्गणबलस्य बलवति भये ऽप्युपस्थिते ।
वंशवितितिषु विषक्तपृथुप्रियबालवालधिभिराददे धृतिः ॥

४८ हरसैनिकाः प्रतिभये ऽपि गजमदसुगन्धिकेसरैः ।
स्वस्थमभिदद्दृशिरे सहसा प्रतिबोधजृम्भमुखैर्मृगाधिपैः ॥

४९ बिभरांबभूवुरपवृत्तजठरशफरीकुलाकुलाः ।
पङ्कविषमिततटाः सरितः करिरुग्णचन्दनरसारुणं पयः ॥

५० महिषक्षतागुरुतमालनलदसुरभिः सदागतिः ।
व्यस्तशुकनिभशिलाकुसुमः प्रणुदन्ववौ वनसदां परिश्रमम् ॥

५१ मथिताम्भसो रयविकीर्णमृदितकदलीगवेधुकाः ।
क्लान्तजलरुहलताः सरसीर्विदधे निदाघ इव सत्त्वसंप्लवः ॥

५२ इति चालयन्नचलसानुवनगहनजानुमापतिः ।
प्राप मुदितहरिणीदशनक्षतवीरुधं वसतिमैन्द्रसूनवीम् ॥

५३ स तमाससाद घननीलमभिमुखमुपस्थितं मुनेः ।
पोत्रनिकषणविभिन्नभुवं दनुजं दधानमथ सौकरं वपुः ॥

Having thus instructed them in the details of his noble
plan, Shiva transformed himself into the handsome
chief of a hunter tribe. His chest, glistening with
drops of perspiration and raised gooseflesh, was
streaked with sandalwood cream and draped with
a string of lustrous pearls from great elephants'
temples. His long, swaying locks of hair were bound
with tendrils of flowering creepers, and his face shone
brightly, with slightly reddened eyes and cheeks
decorated with pendant peacock feathers. Carrying
an enormous bow with a thunderous twang, nocked
with a single arrow, he looked like a mass of clouds
harboring a lightning bolt.

Eager to please their master, the leaders among Shiva's 4
spirit attendants transformed themselves into
hunters, forming a great army of troops equipped with
bows and arrows, tridents and axes.

At their lord's command, dividing up the forest regions 44
among themselves, they set out for a hunt on the
mountain and spread out over its vast tracts with
deafening roars.

All of a sudden the mountain seemed to cry out in fear, 45
when its caves and forests rang with the cries of
the birds and beasts driven from their dwellings,
separated from their flocks and herds, and scattered
widely.

The fleeing birds and animals forgot former hostilities. 46
Shared calamities posing great danger destroy natural
enmity.

Having thus instructed them in the details of his noble   40–42
plan, Shiva transformed himself into the handsome
chief of a hunter tribe. His chest, glistening with
drops of perspiration and raised gooseflesh, was
streaked with sandalwood cream and draped with
a string of lustrous pearls from great elephants'
temples. His long, swaying locks of hair were bound
with tendrils of flowering creepers, and his face shone
brightly, with slightly reddened eyes and cheeks
decorated with pendant peacock feathers. Carrying
an enormous bow with a thunderous twang, nocked
with a single arrow, he looked like a mass of clouds
harboring a lightning bolt.

Eager to please their master, the leaders among Shiva's   43
spirit attendants transformed themselves into
hunters, forming a great army of troops equipped with
bows and arrows, tridents and axes.

At their lord's command, dividing up the forest regions   44
among themselves, they set out for a hunt on the
mountain and spread out over its vast tracts with
deafening roars.

All of a sudden the mountain seemed to cry out in fear,   45
when its caves and forests rang with the cries of
the birds and beasts driven from their dwellings,
separated from their flocks and herds, and scattered
widely.

The fleeing birds and animals forgot former hostilities.   46
Shared calamities posing great danger destroy natural
enmity.

४७ चमरीगणैर्गणबलस्य बलवति भये ऽप्युपस्थिते ।
वंशविततिषु विषक्तपृथुप्रियबालवालधिभिराददे धृतिः ॥

४८ हरसैनिकाः प्रतिभये ऽपि गजमदसुगन्धिकेसरैः ।
स्वस्थमभिदद्दृशिरे सहसा प्रतिबोधजृम्भमुखैर्मृगाधिपैः ॥

४९ बिभरांबभूवुरपवृत्तजठरशफरीकुलाकुलाः ।
पङ्कविषमिततटाः सरितः करिरुग्णचन्दनरसारुणं पयः ॥

५० महिषक्षतागुरुतमालनलदसुरभिः सदागतिः ।
व्यस्तशुकनिभशिलाकुसुमः प्रणुदन्ववौ वनसदां परिश्रमम् ॥

५१ मथिताम्भसो रयविकीर्णमृदितकदलीगवेधुकाः ।
क्रान्तजलरुहलताः सरसीर्विदधे निदाघ इव सत्त्वसंप्लवः ॥

५२ इति चालयन्नचलसानुवनगहनजानुमापतिः ।
प्राप मुदितहरिणीदशनक्षतवीरुधं वसतिमैन्द्रसूनवीम् ॥

५३ स तमाससाद घननीलमभिमुखमुपस्थितं मुनेः ।
पोत्रनिकषणविभिन्नभुवं दनुजं दधानमथ सौकरं वपुः ॥

Although frightened by Shiva's spirit troops, herds of yaks   47
    forgot their fear and stood their ground with firm
    resolve when the precious hair on their broad tails got
    entangled in bamboo thickets.[16]

Yawning from being suddenly awakened, sleepy lions,   48
    their manes smelling of elephant ichor,[17] lay calmly
    watching the terrifying advance of Shiva's men.

Reddened by the sap of sandalwood trees broken by   49
    elephants, and swarming with dead fish floating with
    upturned bellies, river waters rushed past banks piled
    high with mud.

Scented with fragrant aloe, *tamāla,* and spikenard roots   50
    and twigs crushed by buffaloes, and scattering bits of
    parrot-green lichen,[18] a rising wind brought cooling
    relief to the oppressed inhabitants of the forest.

With their water churned up and lotus plants uprooted,   51
    with plantain trees and wild rice trampled and
    scattered by fleeing creatures, the mountain lakes
    were left devastated by the tumult of the beasts, as if
    by the coming of summer.

In this way, driving forward the creatures of the   52
    mountain's forests and thickets, Uma's husband,
    Shiva, reached the hermitage of Indra's son, where
    deer peacefully cropped the foliage on the trees and
    shrubs.

There he caught sight of the demon, now transformed into   53
    a boar, cloud-black and tearing up the earth with his
    snout, and about to confront the ascetic.

५४ कच्छान्ते सुरसरितो निधाय सेना-
मन्वीतः स कतिपयैः किरातवर्यैः ।
प्रच्छन्नस्तरुगहनैः सगुल्मजालै-
र्लक्ष्मीवाननुपदमस्य संप्रतस्थे ॥

Stationing his army along the bank of Ganga, river of the   54
gods, the majestic hunter chief took along a few of
his best hunter soldiers and, hiding in forest thickets
webbed with creepers, he began to track the beast.

CHAPTER 13

The Boar's Attack
and the Hunter's Claim

१ वपुषा परमेण भूधराणामथ संभाव्यपराक्रमं विभेदे ।
मृगमाशु विलोकयांचकार स्थिरदंष्ट्रोग्रमुखं महेन्द्रसूनुः ॥

२ स्फुटबद्धसटोन्नतिः स दूरादभिधावन्नवधीरितान्यकृत्यः ।
जयमिच्छति तस्य जातशङ्कें मनसीमं मुहुराददे वितर्कम् ॥

३ घनपोत्रविदीर्णशालमूलो निबिडस्कन्धनिकाषरुग्णवप्रः ।
अयमेकचरो ऽभिवर्तते मां समरायेव समाजुहूषमाणः ॥

४ इह वीतभयास्तपोऽनुभावाज्जहति व्यालमृगाः परेषु वृत्तिम् ।
मयि तां सुतरामयं विधत्ते विकृतिः किं नु भवेदियं नु माया ॥

५ अथ वैष कृतज्ञयेव पूर्वं भृशमासेवितया रुषा न मुक्तः ।
अवधूय विरोधिनीः किमारान्मृगजातीरभियाति मां जवेन ॥

६ न मृगः खलु को ऽप्ययं जिघांसुः स्खलति ह्यत्र तथा भृशं मनो मे ।
विमलं कलुषीभवच्च चेतः कथयत्येव हितैषिणं रिपुं वा ॥

७ मुनिरस्मि निरागसः कुतो मे भयमित्येष न भूतये ऽभिमानः ।
परवृद्धिषु बद्धमत्सराणां किमिव ह्यस्ति दुरात्मनामलङ्घ्यम् ॥

All of a sudden Indra's son saw a boar with solid tusks   1
protruding from a ferocious snout, and a massive
torso capable of uprooting mountains.

Arjuna, practicing austerities to gain victory over his   2
enemies, saw the beast racing straight toward him
with stiff, raised bristles. Perturbed, he began to
ponder the reasons for the boar's assault.

"Uprooting giant *śāla* trees with his thick snout,   3
tearing up the mountain slopes with thrusts of his
massive shoulders, my solitary assailant seems to be
challenging me to combat!

With their fear of one another dispelled by the influence   4
of my austerity, wild beasts no longer prey on each
other in this place. Strange that this creature should
single me out as his prey. Surely this is some sort of
sorcery.

Or is he driven by the memory of some intense hatred   5
conceived in a past life, that he attacks me alone with
such ferocity, ignoring the many hostile beasts in his
path?

Surely this is no mere animal, but a being determined to   6
kill me. Otherwise my mind would not be so troubled.
A calm heart signals a friend; an agitated one marks
out an enemy.

It would be unwise to remain complacent, thinking,   7
'I am a hermit. Who would want to harm me?' What
can deter a malicious person who cannot bear to see
others prosper?

८ दनुजः स्विदयं क्षपाचरो वा वनजे नेति बलं बतास्ति सत्त्वे ।
अभिभूय तथा हि मेघनीलः सकलं कम्पयतीव शैलराजम् ॥

९ अयमेव मृगव्यसत्रकामः प्रहरिष्यन्मयि मायया शमस्थे ।
पृथुभिर्ध्वजिनीरवैरकार्षीच्चकितोद्भ्रान्तमृगाणि काननानि ॥

१० बहुशः कृतसत्कृतेर्विधातुं प्रियमिच्छन्नथवा सुयोधनस्य ।
क्षुभितं वनगोचराभियोगाद्रणमाशिश्रियदाकुलं तिरश्चाम् ॥

११ अवलीढसनाभिरश्वसेनः प्रसभं खाण्डवजातवेदसा वा ।
प्रतिकर्तुमुपागतः समन्युः कृतमन्युर्यदि वा वृकोदरेण ॥

१२ बलशालितया यथा तथा वा धियमुच्छेदपरामयं दधानः ।
नियमेन मया निबर्हणीयः परमं लाभमरातिभङ्गमाहुः ॥

१३ कुरु तात तपांस्यमार्गदायी विजयायेत्यलमन्वशान्मुनिर्माम् ।
बलिनश्च वधाद्दते ऽस्य शक्यं व्रतसंरक्षणमन्यथा न कर्तुम् ॥

He must be a *dānava* demon, or one of the *rākṣasa*   8
ogres. No ordinary forest animal could possess such
strength. That is why this boar, dark as a cloud, has
been able to storm the king of mountains and shake
him up.

Claiming this forest as his hunting preserve, this creature   9
wants to use magic tricks to attack me, a peaceful
ascetic. That is why he has stirred up a great tumult
in these woods, with the din of armies, and beasts
running about in confusion.

Or is he some friend of Duryodhana's who, wishing   10
to repay favors done in the past, has mingled with
the multitude of frightened beasts agitated by the
hunters' attack on themselves and their forest habitat?

Could it be that Ashvasena, prince of snakes, has followed   11
me here out of anger, to avenge kinsmen horribly
burned to death in the fire that consumed Khandava
forest? Or is it someone who bears a grudge against
Bhima?¹

Whoever he may be, since he is attacking me with intent to   12
kill, with the arrogance of force, the creature deserves
to die by my hand. They say that destroying an enemy
is a hero's highest reward.

The sage's instruction was clear: 'Son,' he said, 'practice   13
austerity for the sake of victory, and do not yield to
anyone who opposes you!' I cannot keep my vow of
ascetic practice unless I kill this formidable assailant."

१४ इति तेन विचिन्त्य चापनाम प्रथमं पौरुषचिह्नमाललम्बे ।
उपलब्धगुणः परस्य भेदे सचिवः शुद्ध इवाददे च बाणः ॥

१५ अनुभाववता गुरु स्थिरत्वादविसंवादि धनुर्धनंजयेन ।
स्वबलव्यसने ऽपि पीड्यमानं गुणवन्मित्रमिवानतिं प्रपेदे ॥

१६ प्रविकर्षनिनादभिन्नरन्ध्रः पदविष्टम्भनिपीडितस्तदानीम् ।
अधिरोहति गाण्डिवं महेषौ सकलः संशयमारुरोह शैलः ॥

१७ दद‍ृशे ऽथ सविस्मयं शिवेन स्थिरपूर्णायतचापमण्डलस्थः ।
रचितस्तिसृणां पुरां विधातुं वधमात्मेव भयानकः परेषाम् ॥

१८ विचकर्ष च संहितेषुरुच्चैश्चरणास्कन्दननामिताचलेन्द्रः ।
धनुरायतभोगवासुकिज्यावदनग्रन्थिविमुक्तवह्नि शम्भुः ॥

१९ स भवस्य भवक्षयैकहेतोः सितसम्पेश्च विधास्यतोः सहार्थम् ।
रिपुराप पराभवाय मध्यं प्रकृतिप्रत्यययोरिवानुबन्धः ॥

Reflecting thus, he took up that foremost symbol of heroic 14
manhood, the bow. He strung it and fitted on a clean
arrow that was like an honest counselor who knows
the enemy's strengths and weaknesses and helps his
king to break his defenses.[2]

Fully spanned by Dhanamjaya with determination, even 15
though he was weakened by the exertion of ascetic
practice, the great, strung bow bent readily, though
it was so hard as to be inflexible, like a magnanimous
friend, a man of integrity, responding at once when an
ruined man appeals to him for help.[3]

When Arjuna fitted the Gandiva bow with a formidable 16
arrow, the mountain nearly collapsed under the
weight of his step, its caves crumbling with the echo of
the bowstring's twang.

Shiva beheld the hero with wonder, as he stood with bow 17
firmly drawn and stretched to the utmost, as though
looking at his own self, terrifying his demon enemies
as he stood poised to destroy their three flying cities.[4]

Shiva, too, placed his arrow and, depressing the mountain 18
with a leap, drew his bow, with the great snake Vasuki
stretched across it as the string, knotted by the snake's
mouth breathing fire.

Destined for destruction, like a coded syllable placed 19
between a grammatical base and ending when they
come together to make a word,[5] the beast was caught
between Shiva, sole cause of the destruction of the
universe, and Arjuna, warrior with the white horse, as
they contended for the prize.

२० अथ दीपितवारिवाहवर्त्मा रववित्रासितवारणादवार्यः ।
निपपात जवादिषुः पिनाकान्महतो ऽभ्रादिव वैद्युतः कृशानुः ॥

२१ व्रजतो ऽस्य बृहत्पतत्त्वजन्मा कृतताक्ष्योपनिपातवेगशङ्कः ।
प्रतिनादमहान्महोरगाणां हृदयश्रोत्रभिदुत्पपात नादः ॥

२२ नयनादिव शूलिनः प्रवृत्तैर्मनसो ऽप्याशुतरं यतः पिशङ्गैः ।
विदधे विलसत्तडिल्लताभैः किरणैर्व्योमनि मार्गणस्य मार्गः ॥

२३ अपयन्धनुषः शिवान्तिकस्थैर्विवरेसद्भिरभिख्यया जिहानः ।
युगपद्दृशो विशन्वराहं तदुपोढैश्च नभश्वरैः पृषत्कः ॥

२४ स तमालनिभे रिपौ सुराणां घननीहार इवाविष्क्तवेगः ।
भयविप्लुतमीक्षितो नभःस्थैर्जगतीं ग्राह इवापगां जगाहे ॥

२५ सपदि प्रियरूपपवरेखः सितलोहाग्रनखः खमाससाद ।
कुपितान्तकतर्जनाङ्गुलिश्रीर्व्यथयन्प्राणभृतः कपिध्वजेषु ॥

२६ परमास्त्रपरिग्रहोरुतेजः स्फुरदुल्काकृति विक्षिपन्वनेषु ।
स जवेन पतन्परःशतानां पततां व्रात इवारवं वितेने ॥

Then from Shiva's bow, Pinaka, whose twang terrified   20
elephants, an invincible arrow flew out, lighting up the
sky like a bolt of lightning from a huge cloud.

As the arrow whizzed by, the loud echoing whir of its   21
wide feathers pierced the ears and hearts of the great
snakes, with the terrifying prospect of a sudden attack
from the eagle Garuda, king of birds.[6]

As it tore through the sky, swifter than thought, the arrow   22
left a trail of red-gold rays, shimmering like streaks of
lightning or flames from Shiva's eye of fire.[7]

The celestials accompanying Shiva, those inhabiting   23
the sky, and those who stood near the boar,
simultaneously saw that shining arrow as it flew from
Shiva's bow and entered the beast's body.

Looking down from the sky, the terrified celestial beings   24
saw the arrow pass unchecked, as if through snow,
through the body of the enemy of the gods, dark
as *tamāla* wood, and plunge into the earth like a
crocodile diving into a river.

At the same moment, Arjuna's arrow, fitted with   25
beautifully decorated knots, tore through the sky.
Tipped as if with a nail by white steel, with lovely lines
at the joints, it resembled the menacing index finger of
the angry god of death that terrifies all creatures.

With the intense power of a celestial weapon, it blazed a   26
trail of pulsating light as it flew through the forest like
a comet, making a sound like the wings of countless
birds flapping.

२७ अविभावितनिष्क्रमप्रयाणः शमितायाम इवातिरंहसा सः ।
सह पूर्वतरं नु चित्तवृत्तेरपतित्वा नु चकार लक्ष्यभेदम् ॥

२८ स वृषध्वजसायकावभिन्नं जयहेतुः प्रतिकायमेषणीयम् ।
लघु साधयितुं शरः प्रसेहे विधिनेवार्थमुदीरितं प्रयत्नः ॥

२९ अविवेकवृथाश्रमाविवार्थं क्षयलोभाविव संश्रितानुरागम् ।
विजिगीषुमिवानयप्रमादाववसादं विशिखौ विनिन्यतुस्तम् ॥

३० अथ दीर्घतमं तमः प्रवेक्ष्यन्सहसा रुग्णरयः स संभ्रमेण ।
निपतन्तमिवोष्णरश्मिमुर्व्यां वलयीभूततरुं धरां च मेने ॥

३१ स गतः क्षितिमुष्णशोणितार्द्रः खुरदंष्ट्राग्रनिपातदारिताश्मा ।
असुभिः क्षणमीक्षितेन्द्रसूनुर्विहितामर्षगुरुध्वनिर्निरासे ॥

३२ स्फुटपौरुषमापपात पार्थस्तमथ प्राज्यशरः शरं जिघृक्षुः ।
न तथा कृतवेदिनां करिष्यन्नियतामेति यथा कृतावदानः ॥

The arrow flew so swiftly that no one could tell exactly 27
when it had left the bow, or how long it stayed in the
air. Did it strike its target with the speed of thought,
or even before thought arose in the mind, or perhaps
without ever leaving the bow?

That arrow, destined to achieve victory, easily penetrated 28
the enemy, the target pierced by Shiva's arrow,
succeeding in its task like ritual actions undertaken
according to the injunctions of scripture.

Like ignorance and useless effort ruining a worthy 29
undertaking, like greed and loss of fortune eroding the
affection of a rich man's friends, like misguided policy
and lack of vigilance bringing down a man who seeks
supreme power, those two arrows simultaneously
felled the beast.

Suddenly stopped in his tracks, poised on the brink of 30
the abiding darkness of death, senses whirling, the
boar saw the sun plummeting to earth and the trees
spinning.

Bathed in his own warm blood, he fell to the ground, 31
tearing up rocks as he clawed at the earth with tusk
and hoof. With a roar of rage, he glared at Arjuna for a
moment, and fell dead.

Despite his great store of arrows, Partha ran toward 32
the boar to recover the arrow that had displayed its
abilities. One who has accomplished his task is dearer
to a grateful man than one who merely holds out the
promise of future deeds.

३३ उपकार इवासति प्रयुक्तः स्थितिमप्राप्य मृगे गतः प्रणाशम् ।
कृतशक्तिरवाङ्कुरखो गुरुत्वाज्जनितव्रीड इवात्मपौरुषेण ॥

३४ स समुद्धरता विचिन्त्य तेन स्वरुचं कीर्तिमिवोत्तमां दधानः ।
अनुयुक्त इव स्ववार्त्तमुच्चैः परिरेभे नु भृशं विलोचनाभ्याम् ॥

३५ तत्र कार्मुकभृतं महाभुजः पश्यति स्म सहसा वनेचरम् ।
संनिकाशयितुमग्रतः स्थितं शासनं कुसुमचापविद्विषः ॥

३६ स प्रयुज्य तनये महीपतेरात्मजातिसदृशीं किलानतिम् ।
सान्त्वपूर्वमभिनीतिहेतुकं वक्तुमित्थमुपचक्रमे वचः ॥

३७ शान्तता विनययोगि मानसं भूरिधाम विमलं तपः श्रुतम् ।
प्राह ते नु सदृशी दिवौकसामन्ववायमवदातमाकृतिः ॥

३८ दीपितस्त्वमनुभावसंपदा गौरवेण लघयन्महीभृतः ।
राजसे मुनिरपीह कारयन्नाधिपत्यमिव शातमन्यवम् ॥

३९ तापसो ऽपि विभुतामुपेयिवानानास्पदं त्वमसि सर्वसंपदाम् ।
दृश्यते हि भवतो विना जनैरन्वितस्य सचिवैरिव द्युतिः ॥

Like a favor done to a villain, the arrow did not find a   33-34
foothold in the beast's carcass but vanished into it.
Having demonstrated its ability, that solid arrow
nobly faced downward as though such a display of
valor were an embarrassment, and it carried its luster
like a peerless reputation. As Arjuna stood there,
carefully drawing the arrow out, was he anxiously
asking after its welfare or clasping it in his eyes' warm
embrace?

Suddenly a hunter armed with a bow appeared before the   35
strong hero to convey a message from Shiva, slayer of
the god of love.[8]

The hunter bowed to the prince in the manner of his   36
tribe, and began to make a courteous and conciliatory
speech.

"Your tranquility bespeaks a courteous nature, the   37
dazzling brilliance of your ascetic power indicates
flawless learning in the scriptures, and your godlike
figure proclaims your pure lineage.

Blazing with spiritual power, you put kings to shame with   38
your majesty. Although you are an ascetic, it is clear
that Indra himself has appointed you to rule this
mountain on his behalf.

Although you practice austerities, you have achieved   39
dominion and command every attribute of
sovereignty. Living all alone, you shine with the
brilliance of a king surrounded by ministers.

४० विस्मयः क इव वा जयश्रिया नैव मुक्तिरपि ते दवीयसी ।
ईप्सितस्य न भवेदुपाश्रयः कस्य निर्जितरजस्तमोगुणः ॥

४१ ह्रेपयन्नहिमतेजसं त्विषा स त्वमित्थमुपपन्नपौरुषः ।
हर्तुमर्हसि वराहभेदिनं नैनमस्मदधिपस्य सायकम् ॥

४२ स्मर्यते तनुभृतां सनातनं न्याय्यमाचरितमुत्तमैर्नृभिः ।
ध्वंसते यदि भवादृशस्ततः कः प्रयातु वद तेन वर्त्मना ॥

४३ आकुमारमुपदेष्टुमिच्छवः संनिवृत्तिमपथान्महापदः ।
योगशक्तिजितजन्ममृत्यवः शीलयन्ति यतयः सुशीलताम् ॥

४४ तिष्ठतां तपसि पुण्यमासजन्संपदो ऽनुगुणयन्सुखैषिणाम् ।
योगिनां परिणमन्विमुक्तये केन नास्तु विनयः सतां प्रियः ॥

४५ नूनमत्रभवतः शराकृतिं सर्वथायमनुयाति सायकः ।
सो ऽयमित्यनुपपन्नसंशयः कारितस्त्वमपथे पदं यया ॥

४६ अन्यदीयविशिखे न केवलं निःस्पृहस्य भवितव्यमाहृते ।
निघ्नतः परनिबर्हितं मृगं व्रीडितव्यमपि ते सचेतसः ॥

But then, it is not surprising you have a conqueror's air,   40
for liberation itself is within your reach. What desire
of a man can remain unfulfilled when he has subdued
ignorance and passion?

And so, since you put the sun to shame with your powerful   41
brilliance, and your martial prowess is self-evident,
you ought not to seize the arrow with which my lord
killed the boar.

The great lawgivers teach that men should always act   42
justly. If men like you should swerve from the path of
right conduct, tell me, who would follow it?

Having overcome birth and death through the power of   43
yoga, world-renouncing ascetics constantly practice
gentle conduct, for they wish to instruct all men,
down to little boys, to eschew the disastrous path of
wrongdoing.

Small wonder that all good men treasure disciplined   44
conduct, for it confers merit on those who practice
austerity, makes fortune smile on those who seek the
pleasures of life, and brings yogis closer to liberation.

To be sure, this arrow resembles yours in every way, and   45
it was the resemblance that led you to err, never
doubting that the arrow was yours.

You appear to be a man of detachment; if that is true,   46
you ought not to claim another man's arrow. But
what's more, as a man of conscience, you ought to be
ashamed of shooting an animal that was already killed
by another.

४७ संततं निशमयन्त उत्सुका यैः प्रयान्ति मुदमस्य सूरयः ।
कीर्तितानि हसिते ऽपि तानि यं व्रीडयन्ति चरितानि मानिनम् ॥

४८ अन्यदोषमिव स स्वकं गुणं ख्यापयेत्कथमधृष्टताजडः ।
उच्यते स खलु कार्यवत्तया धिग्विभिन्नबुधसेतुमर्थिताम् ॥

४९ दुर्वचं तदथ मा स्म भून्मृगस्त्वय्यसौ यदकरिष्यदोजसा ।
नैनमाशु यदि वाहिनीपतिः प्रत्यपत्स्यत शितेन पत्रिणा ॥

५० को न्विमं हरितुरंगमायुधस्थेयसीं दधतमङ्गसंहतिम् ।
वेगवत्तरमृते चमूपतेर्हन्तुमर्हति शरेण दंष्ट्रिणम् ॥

५१ मित्रमिष्टमुपकारि संशये मेदिनीपतिरयं तथा च ते ।
तं विरोध्य भवता निरासि मा सज्जनैकवसतिः कृतज्ञता ॥

५२ लभ्यमेकसुकृतेन दुर्लभा रक्षितारमसुरक्ष्यभूतयः ।
स्वन्तमन्तविरसा जिगीषतां मित्रलाभमनु लाभसंपदः ॥

Although wise men take endless delight in listening 47
to accounts of his deeds, my master is a person of
self-respect, embarrassed to have his achievements
praised even in jest.

So how would he, a warrior not given to boasting, speak of 48
his own merits, any more than of other men's faults?
You see, I speak of his character only out of necessity.
A curse on supplication, which violates the modesty of
the wise!

May that unspeakable fate never befall you, the fate to 49
which that beast would most certainly have brought
you with his attack, had not our commander swiftly
shot a sharp arrow at him!

Who, other than my commander, could so speedily kill 50
with a single arrow this boar with fierce tusks, his
body hard as Indra's thunderbolt?

Furthermore, my king has been a good friend and 51
benefactor to you in your need. Do not antagonize
him and thereby cast to the winds gratitude, whose
sole abode is good men!

Warriors who seek conquest ought to value alliance with 52
a good man above wealth. Such an alliance—which is
easily won with even a single good deed, safeguards
one's interests, and confers welfare—is far superior to
wealth, which is difficult to acquire and even harder to
keep and enjoy, and when lost, as it invariably must be,
leads to nothing but grief.[9]

५३ चञ्चलं वसु नितान्तमुन्नता मेदिनीमपि हरन्त्यरातयः ।
भूधरस्थिरमुपेयमागतं मावमंस्त सुहृदं महीपतिम् ॥

५४ जेतुमेव भवता तपस्यते नायुधानि दधते मुमुक्षवः ।
प्राप्स्यते च सकलं महीभृता संगतेन तपसः फलं त्वया ॥

५५ वाजिभूमिरिभराजकाननं सन्ति रत्ननिचयाश्च भूरिशः ।
काञ्चनेन किमिवास्य पत्त्रिणा केवलं न सहते विलङ्घनम् ॥

५६ सावलेपमुपलिप्सिते पैररभ्युपैति विकृतिं रजस्यपि ।
अर्थितस्तु न महान्समीहते जीवितं किमु धनं धनायितुम् ॥

५७ तत्तदीयविशिखातिसर्जनादस्तु वां गुरु यदृच्छयागतम् ।
राघवप्लवगराजयोरिव प्रेम युक्तिमितरेतराश्रयम् ॥

५८ नाभियोक्तुमनृतं त्वमिष्यते कस्तपस्विविशिखेषु चादरः ।
सन्ति भूभृति शरा हि नः परे ये पराक्रमवसूनि वज्रिणः ॥

५९ मार्गणैरथ तव प्रयोजनं नाथसे किमु पतिं न भूभृतः ।
त्वद्विधं सुहृदमेत्य सोऽर्थिनं किं न यच्छति विजित्य मेदिनीम् ॥

Enemies grown powerful invariably rob a man of transient   53
wealth, and land—everything he owns. When this is
so, no warrior ought to insult a king who, solid as a
mountain, comes to help him of his own accord, when
in fact it is he who should be approached for aid.

Conquering your enemies is surely the goal of your ascetic   54
practice! Men who seek liberation do not bear arms.
But if only you will associate with our king, you will
gain the fruit of your austerity in full measure.

He owns vast fields of horses, a whole forest of elephants,   55
and many heaps of gems; what would he want with a
single golden arrow? It is just that he will not tolerate
an insult from anyone.

A great man takes offense if others try to take even his   56
dust, should they take it with arrogance; but if a man
approaches him in supplication, he does not hold his
own life dear, let alone his wealth.

Therefore, give up my master's arrow, and let a close and   57
mutual friendship arise between the two of you, a
friendship that is worthy, although it might have come
about by chance, like that of Rama of the Raghu line
and Sugriva, king of monkeys.[10]

We have no desire to lie to you. How could we possibly   58
care for a poor ascetic's arrows? On our mountain we
have plenty of other arrows that Indra himself would
gladly fight for.

If it is arrows that you need, why don't you ask our chief,   59
the lord of the mountain, for them? In return for
gaining such a friend as yourself, he would give the
whole world, taken in conquest.

६० तेन सूरिरुपकारिताधनः कर्तुमिच्छति न याचितं वृथा ।
सीदतामनुभवन्निवार्थिनां वेद यत्प्रणयभङ्गवेदनाम् ॥

६१ शक्तिरर्थपतिषु स्वयंग्रहं प्रेम कारयति वा निरत्ययम् ।
कारणद्वयमिदं निरस्यतः प्रार्थनाधिकबले विपत्फला ॥

६२ अस्त्रवेदमधिगम्य तत्त्वतः कस्य चेह भुजवीर्यशालिनः ।
जामदग्न्यमपहाय गीयते तापसेषु चरितार्थमायुधम् ॥

६३ अभ्यघानि मुनिचापलात्त्वया यन्मृगः क्षितिपतेः परिग्रहः ।
अक्षमिष्ट तदयं प्रमाद्यतां संवृणोति खलु दोषमज्ञता ॥

६४ जन्मवेषतपसां विरोधिनीं मा कृथाः पुनरमूमपक्रियाम् ।
आपदेत्युभयलोकदूषणी वर्तमानमपथे हि दुर्मतिम् ॥

६५ यष्टुमिच्छसि पितॄन्न सांप्रतं संवृतो ऽर्चिचयिषुर्दिवौकसः ।
दातुमेव पदवीमपि क्षमः किं मृगे ऽङ्ग विशिखं न्यवीविशः ॥

६६ सज्जनो ऽसि विजहीहि चापलं सर्वदा क इव वा सहिष्यते ।
वारिधीनिव युगान्तवायवः क्षोभयन्त्यनिभृता गुरूनपि ॥

This wise man, who holds charity as his sole wealth, would   60
    never reject your request, for he knows, as though he
    had himself felt it, the pain of a plea rejected, what
    men who become suppliants in their need experience.

Strength alone, or unreserved mutual affection, permits   61
    one to take a rich man's wealth for one's own. A man
    who lacks both these resources will be ruined if he
    covets the property of one stronger than himself.

Moreover, other than Parashurama, son of Jamadagni,   62
    who among ascetics has mastered the science of
    arms, to become an eminent warrior renowned for his
    expertise in wielding weapons?[11]

Rashness characteristic of ascetics led you to shoot an   63
    arrow at a beast that is our king's rightful property;
    and that is why he pardons you, for ignorance palliates
    the faults of reckless men.

Never again commit such an offense, one that contradicts   64
    your birth, garb, and vows, for ruin, destroying both
    this world and the world beyond, comes to the man of
    evil mind, who travels on wrong paths.

It is unlikely you intend to sacrifice to your ancestors   65
    at this time, for you have secluded yourself on this
    mountain in order to worship the gods. Why, then, did
    you shoot your arrow at the beast, when it would have
    been proper for you to avoid its path?

You are a good man—give up this rash behavior! For how   66
    long can a man be tolerant? Reckless people irritate
    even magnanimous men; the cyclones of universal
    dissolution roil the very oceans.

६७ अस्त्रवेदविदयं महीपतिः पर्वतीय इति मावजीगणः ।
गोपितुं भुवमिमां मरुत्वता शैलवासमनुनीय लम्भितः ॥

६८ तत्तितिक्षितमिदं मया मुनेरित्यवोचत वचश्चमूपतिः ।
बाणमत्रभवते निजं दिशन्नापृहि त्वमपि सर्वसंपदः ॥

६९ आत्मनीनमुपतिष्ठते गुणाः संभवन्ति विरमन्ति चापदः ।
इत्यनेकफलभाजि मा स्म भूदर्थिता कथमिवार्यसंगमे ॥

७० दृश्यतामयमनोकहान्तरे तिग्महेतिपृतनाभिरन्वितः ।
साहिवीचिरिव सिन्धुरुद्धतो भूपतिः समयसेतुवारितः ॥

७१ सज्यं धनुर्वहति यो ऽहिपतिस्थवीयः
स्थेयाञ्जयन्हरितुरंगमकेतुलक्ष्मीम् ।
अस्यानुकूलय मतिं मतिमन्ननेन
सख्या सुखं समभियास्यसि चिन्तितानि ॥

Our king is an expert in the science of weapons. Do not   67
    underestimate him, thinking him a mere mountain
    man! Indra himself asked him to live here on this
    mountain, in order to protect the world.

My commander says, "I have forgiven this offense on the   68
    part of the ascetic." Hand over the arrow that belongs
    to him and in return obtain welfare and riches of every
    kind!

Virtues and benefits accrue and misfortunes end for a   69
    man who makes friends with one who is good. So why
    should you not wish to gain the friendship of a noble
    man who offers such manifold rewards?

Look, there among those trees stands our proud king,   70
    surrounded by troops equipped with sharp weapons,
    and he is restrained only by consideration for the rules
    of good conduct, like the ocean at high tide, its waves
    full of snakes, held back only by a dike.

Carrying a strung bow stouter than Shesha, king of snakes,   71
    my formidable master outshines with his steadiness
    the pole of Indra's banner.* Win his favor, wise man,
    for with him as your friend you shall easily fulfill all
    your wishes!"

---

* A pole honoring Indra at the god's festival.

CHAPTER 14

Arjuna Defeats Shiva's Army of Spirits

१ ततः किरातस्य वचोभिरुद्धतैः पराहतः शैल इवार्णवाम्बुभिः ।
जहौ न धैर्यं कुपितो ऽपि पाण्डवः सुदुर्ग्रहान्तःकरणा हि
साधवः ॥

२ सलेशमुल्लङ्घितशात्रवेङ्गितः कृती गिरां विस्तरतत्त्वसंग्रहे ।
अयं प्रमाणीकृतकालसाधनः प्रशान्तसंरम्भ इवाददे वचः ॥

३ विविक्तवर्णाभरणा सुखश्रुतिः प्रसादयन्ती हृदयान्यपि द्विषाम् ।
प्रवर्तते नाकृतपुण्यकर्मणां प्रसन्नगम्भीरपदा सरस्वती ॥

४ भवन्ति ते सभ्यतमा विपश्चितां मनोगतं वाचि निवेशयन्ति ये ।
नयन्ति तेष्वप्युपपन्ननैपुणा गभीरमर्थं कतिचित्प्रकाशताम् ॥

५ स्तुवन्ति गुर्वीमभिधेयसंपदं विशुद्धिमुक्तेरपरे विपश्चितः ।
इति स्थितायां प्रतिपूरुषं रुचौ सुदुर्लभाः सर्वमनोरमा गिरः ॥

६ समस्य संपादयता गुणैरिमां त्वया समारोपितभार भारतीम् ।
प्रगल्भमात्मा धुरि धुर्य वाग्मिनां वनेचरेणापि सताधिरोपितः ॥

७ प्रयुज्य सामाचरितं विलोभनं भयं विभेदाय धियः प्रदर्शितम् ।
तथाभियुक्तं च शिलीमुखार्थिना यथेतरन्यायमिवावभासते ॥

274

Assaulted by the hunter's insolent words, like a mountain 1
lashed by the ocean's waves, the Pandava was roused
to anger, but he did not lose his composure. The
hearts of good men are very hard to disturb.

Fully understanding his opponent's hidden motives and 2
in a manner suited to the occasion and context, the
hero, who was expert in conveying the matter of a long
speech in a few words, spoke as though quite calm.

"Speech endowed with words clear and rich in thought, 3
adorned with distinct enunciation, sweet sounding,
and pleasing even the hearts of enemies does not
come forth from men who are without the merit of
good deeds in their past.[1]

Most accomplished among wise men are those able to 4
express their thoughts in precise words; and even
among such men, few command the extraordinary gift
of articulating some very deep thought.

Some learned men praise depth of meaning; others, a 5
faultless style. When men have such varied tastes,
speech that pleases everybody is rare.

Emissary entrusted with great responsibilities, you have 6
brought together in your speech all the excellences I
have spoken of, and you have delivered it most boldly.
With this achievement, although you are a mere
forester, you have elevated yourself to the ranks of the
best orators.

८ विरोधि सिद्धेरिति कर्तुमुद्यतः स वारितः किं भवता न भूपतिः ।
हिते नियोज्यः खलु भूतिमिच्छता सहार्थनाशेन नृपो ऽनुजीविना ॥

९ ध्रुवं प्रणाशः प्रहितस्य पत्त्रिणः शिलोच्चये तस्य विमार्गणं नयः ।
न युक्तमत्रार्यजनातिलङ्घनं दिशत्यपायं हि सतामतिक्रमः ॥

१० अतीतसंख्या विहिता ममाग्निना शिलीमुखाः खाण्डवमत्तुमिच्छता ।
अनाहृतस्यामरसायकेष्वपि स्थिता कथं शैलजनाशुगे धृतिः ॥

११ यदि प्रमाणीकृतमार्यचेष्टितं किमित्यदोषेण तिरस्कृता वयम् ।
अयातपूर्वा परिवादगोचरं सतां हि वाणी गुणमेव भाषते ॥

१२ गुणापवादेन तदन्यरोपणाद्दृशाधिरूढस्य समञ्जसं जनम् ।
द्विधेव कृत्वा हृदयं निगूहतः स्फुरन्नसाधोर्विवृणोति वागसिः ॥

१३ वनाश्रयाः कस्य मृगाः परिग्रहाः शृणाति यस्तान्प्रसभेन तस्य ते ।
प्रहीयतामत्र नृपेण मानिता न मानिता चास्ति भवन्ति च श्रियः ॥

You have used flattery, and then bribery, and employed   7
threats to break my resolve.[2] And your statement
about your master's claim to the arrow, namely that it
is a just claim, is itself unjust.

Why did you not restrain your king when he tried   8
to do something that you knew was bound to be
unsuccessful? A servant mindful of his own welfare
should guide his king in the right direction, since his
own fortunes are bound to his master's.

Once an arrow has been shot, it is sure to disappear.   9
The right thing to do then is to look for it on the
mountain. Under the circumstances, you ought not to
insult a noble man. Nothing but trouble results from
antagonizing good men.

The god of fire, who wanted to consume the Khandava   10
forest, gave me arrows past counting.[3] When I scorn
the arrows of the gods themselves, why should I care
anything for the arrow of a mountaineer?

If you hold up the conduct of the virtuous as your   11
standard, why have I, innocent as I am, been insulted
with false accusations? Good men speak only of the
virtues of others, and are not given to slandering
them.

When an assailant abuses a good man by denying his   12
virtues and ascribing faults to him, the flashing sword
of the abuser's speech rips open and reveals his heart,
no matter how hard he tries to conceal it.

१४ न वर्त्म कस्मैचिदपि प्रदीयतामिति व्रतं मे विहितं महर्षिणा ।
जिघांसुरस्मान्निहतो मया मृगो व्रताभिरक्षा हि सतामलंक्रिया ॥

१५ मृगान्विनिघ्नन्मृगयुः स्वहेतुना कृतोपकारः कथमिच्छतां तपः ।
कृपेति चेदस्तु मृगः क्षतः क्षणादनेन पूर्वं न मयेति का गतिः ॥

१६ अनायुधे सत्त्वजिघांसिते मुनौ कृपेति वृत्तिर्महतामकृत्रिमा ।
शरासनं बिभ्रति सज्यसायकं कृतानुकम्पः स कथं प्रतीयते ॥

१७ अथो शरस्तेन मदर्थमुज्झितः फलं च तस्य प्रतिकायसाधनम् ।
अविक्षते तत्र मयात्मसात्कृते कृतार्थता नन्वधिका चमूपतेः ॥

१८ यदात्थ कामं भवता स याच्यतामिति क्षमं नैतदनल्पचेतसाम् ।
कथं प्रसह्याहरणैषिणां प्रियाः परावनत्या मलिनीकृताः श्रियः ॥

१९ अभूतमासज्य विरुद्धमीहितं बलादलभ्यं तव लिप्सते नृपः ।
विजानतो ऽपि ह्यनयस्य रौद्रतां भवत्यपाये परिमोहिनी मतिः ॥

Whose property are the animals of the forest? They   13
belong to whoever is strong enough to kill them. Tell
your king to give up his proud claim to this beast—
ownership does not follow simply from arrogance.

'Do not yield to anyone': this is the vow the sage Vyasa   14
enjoined upon me. The boar tried to kill me, and I
killed him, for a good man is duty bound to keep his
vows.

How can a hunter who kills animals for his livelihood be   15
supposed to have killed the boar in order to serve an
ascetic? You say he did it out of compassion? If you
insist. But when the animal was hit by both of us at
once, how can you say he struck it before I did?

If a great man shows compassion for an unarmed ascetic   16
about to be killed by an animal, such a gesture is
sincere; but how can one suppose he acted out of such
compassion toward a man holding a bow with arrow
poised?

Suppose he shot the arrow for my sake, and the result was   17
the death of the boar who attacked me. Would your
commander's purpose not be all the better secured if
I got the full benefit of this result?

As for your suggestion that I should bow to him as a   18
suppliant, that is impossible for anyone but a fool.
How can a warrior, who normally acquires things by
force, take joy in wealth sullied by his obeisance?

Your king seeks to fulfill a contrary and impossible wish by 19
making false claims. It seems that when a man's ruin is
imminent, his mind grows confused, even though he
knows well the terrible nature of unjust acts.

२० असिः शरा वर्म धनुश्च नोच्चकैर्विविच्य किं प्रार्थितमीश्वरेण ते ।
अथास्ति शक्तिः कृतमेव याञ्चया न दूषितः शक्तिमतां स्वयंग्रहः ॥

२१ सखा स युक्तः कथितः कथं त्वया यदृच्छयासूयति यस्तपस्यते ।
गुणार्जनोच्छायविरुद्धबुद्धयः प्रकृत्यमित्रा हि सतामसाधवः ॥

२२ वयं क्व वर्णाश्रमरक्षणोचिताः क्व जातिहीना मृगजीवितच्छिदः ।
सहापकृष्टैर्महतां न संगतं भवन्ति गोमायुसखा न दन्तिनः ॥

२३ परो ऽवजानाति यदज्ञताजडस्तदुन्नतानां न विहन्ति धीरताम् ।
समानवीर्यान्वयपौरुषेषु यः करोत्यतिक्रान्तिमसौ तिरस्क्रिया ॥

२४ यदा विगृह्णाति हतं तदा यशः करोति मैत्रीमथ दूषिता गुणाः ।
स्थितिं समीक्ष्योभयथा परीक्षकः करोत्यवज्ञोपहतं पृथग्जनम् ॥

२५ मया मृगान्हन्तुरनेन हेतुना विरुद्धमाक्षेपवचस्तितिक्षितम् ।
शरार्थमेष्यत्यथ लप्स्यते गतिं शिरोमणिं दृष्टिविषाज्जिघृक्षतः ॥

Why does your lord not straightaway ask for each of my   20
weapons—sword, arrows, armor, and unique bow?
Or, if he has the strength, what need is there for
supplication? When strong men seize things by force,
their conduct is not censured.

How can you say he is a suitable friend for me, when he,   21
for no reason at all, abuses an ascetic? Wicked men
are born enemies of the good, because they hate the
nobility of the pursuit of virtue.

What connection can there be between me, a warrior   22
whose nature and duty are to preserve the social
orders and life stages, and a low-caste hunter? Great
men do not associate with outcastes—elephants do
not form friendship with jackals!

When a common fool insults a distinguished warrior, the   23
warrior does not lose his composure. It is only when a
man of equal strength, lineage, and heroism treats one
with insolence that the act becomes a real insult.

If a high-minded person quarrels with a dishonorable   24
man, his reputation is lost; if, on the other hand,
he befriends him, his virtue is sullied. A man of
judgment, considering both sides, destroys his ignoble
enemy simply by ignoring him.

For this reason I have tolerated the false accusations of   25
this hunter. Now, if he should still try to seize the
arrow, he shall meet the fate of one who tries to seize
the jewel from a cobra's hood!"

२६ इतीरिताकूतमनीलवाजिनं जयाय दूतः प्रतितर्ज्य तेजसा ।
यथौ समीपं ध्वजिनीमुपेयुषः प्रसन्नरूपस्य विरूपचक्षुषः ॥

२७ ततो ऽपवादेन पताकिनीपतेश्चचाल निर्ह्रादवती महाचमूः ।
युगान्तवाताभिहतेव कुर्वती निनादमम्भोनिधिवीचिसंहतिः ॥

२८ रणाय जैत्रः प्रदिशन्निव त्वरां तरङ्गितालम्बितकेतुसंततिः ।
पुरो बलानां सघनाम्बुशीकरः शनैः प्रतस्थे सुरभिः समीरणः ॥

२९ जयारवक्षवेडितनादमूर्च्छितः शरासनज्यातलवारणध्वनिः ।
असंभवन्भूधरराजकुक्षिषु प्रकम्पयन्नागमवतस्तरे दिशः ॥

३० निशातरौद्रेषु विकासतां गतैः प्रदीपयद्भिः ककुभामिवान्तरम् ।
वनेसदां हेतिषु भिन्नविग्रहैर्विपुस्फुरे रश्मिमतो मरीचिभिः ॥

३१ उद्दूढवक्षःस्थगितैकदिङ्मुखो विकृष्टविस्फारितचापमण्डलः ।
वितत्य पक्षद्वयमायतं बभौ विभुर्गणानामुपरीव⁹ मध्यगः ॥

३२ सुगेषु दुर्गेषु च तुल्यविक्रमैर्जवादहंपूर्विकया यियासुभिः ।
गणैरविच्छेदनिरुद्धमाबभौ वनं निरुच्छ्वासमिवाकुलाकुलम् ॥

When Arjuna had spoken his mind, the hunter chief's 26
emissary threatened the hero with bravado, promising
his imminent defeat, and returned to Shiva, who
had joined his army, highly pleased with Arjuna's
response.

Then, at a signal from the general, Shiva's huge army 27
charged forward, making a great din and roaring like
the ocean's waves lashed by the storm winds of the
dissolution of the worlds.

Making the army's rows of banners flutter, a favorable, 28
scented breeze, laden with drops of water, slowly
began to blow before the troops, urging them forward
to battle.

Echoing off the mountain's caves and making the earth 29
quake, the twanging of bowstrings and the clang
of the soldiers' steel arm guards, mingled with the
army's thundering war cries, spread out over the
regions of space.

Refracted by the surfaces of the forester troops' sharp, 30
menacing axes, the sun's rays flashed with a pulsating
light, illuminating the regions of space.

Chest held high and torso expanded, Shiva stood twanging 31
his bow drawn to the fullest, covering an entire region
of space and looking as if floating above the troops,
even though he was in their midst.

Overwhelmed by Shiva's soldiers, their courage equal to 32
the greatest challenge as they vied with each other to
lead the charge into battle, the forest seemed to hold
its breath in terror even before the attack was fully
under way.

३३ तिरोहितश्वभ्रनिकुञ्जरोधसः समश्नुवानाः सहसातिरिक्ताम् ।
    किरातसैन्यैरपिधाय रेचिता भुवः क्षणं निम्नतयेव भेजिरे ॥

३४ पृथूरुपर्यस्तबृहल्लतातितर्जवानिलाघूर्णितशालचन्दना ।
    गणाधिपानां परितः प्रसारिणी वनान्यवाञ्छीव चकार संहितिः ॥

३५ ततः सदर्पं प्रतनुं तपस्यया मदस्रुतिक्षाममिवैकवारणम् ।
    परिज्वलन्तं निधनाय भूभृतां दहन्तमाशा इव जातवेदसम् ॥

३६ अनादरोपात्तधृतैकसायकं जये ऽनुकूले सुहृदीव सस्पृहम् ।
    शनैरपूर्णप्रतिकारपेलवे निवेशयन्तं नयने बलोदधौ ॥

३७ निषण्णमापत्प्रतिकारकारणे शरासने धैर्य इवानपायिनि ।
    अलङ्घनीयं प्रकृतावपि स्थितं निवातनिष्कम्पमिवापगापतिम् ॥

३८ उपेयुषीं बिभ्रतमन्तकद्युतिं वधाद्दूरे पतितस्य दंष्ट्रिणः ।
    पुरः समावेशितसत्पशुं द्विजैः पतिं पशूनामिव हूतमध्वरे ॥

३९ निजेन नीतं विजितान्यगौरवं गभीरतां धैर्यगुणेन भूयसा ।
    वनोदयेनेव घनोरुवीरुधा समन्धकारीकृतमुत्तमाचलम् ॥

४० महर्षभस्कन्धमनूनकंधरं बृहच्छिलावप्रघनेन वक्षसा ।
    समुज्जिहीर्षुं जगतीं महाभरां महावराहं महतो ऽर्णवादिव ॥

With hunter troops massed among the mountain's 33
 hollows and thickets, the slopes suddenly appeared to
 expand to unaccustomed height and breadth, and to
 sink low again the moment the soldiers left them.
Widely scattering masses of large torn-up creepers 34
 and raising a strong wind that rocked giant *śāla*
 and sandalwood trees, the army of Shiva's spirits,
 advancing from every direction, turned the forest
 upside down.
At last Shiva's troops reached Arjuna, hero with the 35–42
 white horse, like water-laden clouds converging
 on a mountain at the end of the summer. Wasted
 by austerity, the proud hero looked like a solitary
 wild elephant emaciated by the flow of ichor. He
 was like a blazing fire burning the regions of space
 to annihilate kings. Counting on victory as if on a
 trusted friend, he disdainfully drew a single arrow
 from his quiver. He directed an unhurried gaze at that
 vast ocean of an army, looking down on it because it
 had not accomplished its mission of retaliation. He
 stood leaning on his bow, the means for overcoming
 his enemies, as if on his inflexible courage, keeping
 to his own calm nature and yet invincible, like the
 ocean unmoving without a breath of wind. Imbued
 with the splendor of Yama, god of death, with the
 boar he had killed lying at his feet, Arjuna looked
 like Pashupati, lord of the beasts,* standing over the

---

* Shiva.

४१ हरिन्मणिश्याममुदग्रविग्रहं प्रकाशमानं परिभूय देहिनः ।
मनुष्यभावे पुरुषं पुरातनं स्थितं जलादर्श इवांशुमालिनम् ॥

४२ गुरुक्रियारम्भफलैरलंकृतं गतिं प्रतापस्य जगत्प्रमाथिनः ।
गणाः समासेदुरनीलवाजिनं तपात्यये तोयघना घना इव ॥

४३ यथास्वमाशंसितविक्रमाः पुरा मुनिप्रभावक्षततेजसः परे ।
ययुः क्षणादप्रतिपत्तिमूढतां महानुभावः प्रतिहन्ति पौरुषम् ॥

४४ ततः प्रजह्ने सममेव तत्र तैरपेक्षितान्योन्यबलोपपत्तिभिः ।
महोदयानामपि संघवृत्तितां सहायसाध्याः प्रदिशन्ति सिद्धयः ॥

286

victim placed before him by priests who have invited
him to the sacrifice. He surpassed other warriors with
an invincible dignity, heightened by inborn courage,
like an extraordinarily high mountain enveloped by
the impenetrable darkness of dense forests overgrown
with creepers. Broad-necked, with the shoulders of
a mighty bull and a chest massive as a stone wall, he
looked like the great primeval boar about to lift up
the overburdened earth from the vast ocean.[4] Darkly
shining like an emerald, with a noble figure and a
majesty surpassing all creation, Arjuna was Purusha,
the highest Person, manifest in human form, like the
sun mirrored in water.[5] Dignified by the successful
outcomes of momentous undertakings, he was the
fount of feats of arms capable of conquering the
universe.

The feats of war performed by the enemy soldiers, who　　43
competed with each other to be the one to defeat the
hero, were overshadowed by the ascetic's prowess,
and the troops were quickly thrown into confused
indecision. A hero of extraordinary capability
overturns the actions of common men.

Then Shiva's warriors, relying on each other's strength for　　44
support, mounted a united assault on Arjuna. Tasks
whose successful completion depends on collective
action prompt even the most capable men to work
together.

४५ किरातसैन्यादुरुचापनोदिताः समं समुत्पेतुरुपात्तरंहसः ।
महावनादुन्मनसः खगा इव प्रवृत्तपत्रध्वनयः शिलीमुखाः ॥

४६ गभीररन्ध्रेषु भृशं महीभृतः प्रतिस्वनैरुन्नमितेन सानुषु ।
धनुर्निनादेन जवादुपेयुषा विभिद्यमाना इव दध्वनुर्दिशः ॥

४७ विधूनयन्ती गहनानि भूरुहां तिरोहितोपान्तनभोदिगन्तरा ।
महीयसी वृष्टिरिवानिलेरिता रवं वितेने गणमार्गणावलिः ॥

४८ त्रयीमृतूनामनिलाशिनः सतः प्रयाति पोषं वपुषि प्रहृष्यतः ।
रणाय जिष्णोर्विदुषेव सत्वरं घनत्वमीये शिथिलेन वर्मणा ॥

४९ पतत्सु शस्त्रेषु वितत्य रोदसी समन्ततस्तस्य धनुर्दुधूषतः ।
सरोषमुल्केव पपात भीषणा बलेषु दृष्टिर्विनिपातशंसिनी ॥

५० दिशः समूहन्निव विक्षिपन्निव प्रभां रवेराकुलयन्निवानिलम् ।
मुनिश्चचाल क्षयकालदारुणः क्षितिं सशैलां चलयन्निवेषुभिः ॥

Shot from the great bows of the forester troops, the 45
feathers whirring as they gained speed, arrows flew in
every direction like excited birds flying from a dense
forest, their wings flapping.

The regions of space resounded as if split asunder by the 46
twanging of bows, instantly reverberating on the
mountain's peaks with echoes produced in its deep
caves.

Rocking the mountain's forests and completely covering 47
the sky and the regions of space, the volley of arrows
shot by the troops sounded like a heavy downpour
whipped on by a strong wind.

As Arjuna the victor grew eager for the combat that lay 48
ahead, his body, grown emaciated from three seasons
of fasting and living on nothing but air, began to
regain its bulk. As if aware, the armor that had hung
loose began instantly to tighten around his frame.

As arrows flew all around him, pervading the earth and 49
sky, Arjuna twanged his bow and shook it in anger, and
cast a look terrifying as a fiery meteor on the enemy
troops, portending death and destruction.

Terrible as the dissolution of the universe, as if wishing 50
to uproot the entire earth, with all its mountains, the
ascetic shot arrows that squeezed together the regions
of space, dispersed the light of the sun, and whirled
about the wind itself.

५१ विमुक्तमाशंसितशत्रुनिर्जयैरनेकमेकावसरं वनेचरैः ।
स निर्जघानायुधमन्तरा शरैः क्रियाफलं काल इवातिपातितः ॥

५२ गतैः परेषामविभावनीयतां निवारयद्भिर्विपदं विदूरगैः ।
भृशं बभूवोपचितो बृहत्फलैः शरैरुपायैरिव पाण्डुनन्दनः ॥

५३ दिवः पृथिव्याः ककुभां नु मण्डलात्पतन्ति बिम्बादुत तिग्मतेजसः ।
सकृद्विकृष्टादथ कार्मुकान्मुनेः शराः शरीरादिति ते ऽभिमेनिरे ॥

५४ गणाधिपानामविधाय निर्गतैः परासुतां मर्मविदारणैरपि ।
जवादतीये हिमवानधोमुखैः कृतापराधैरिव तस्य पत्रिभिः ॥

५५ द्विषां क्षतीर्याः प्रथमे शिलीमुखा विभिद्य देहावरणानि चक्रिरे ।
न तासु पेते विशिखैः पुनर्मुनेररुंतुदत्वं महतां ह्यगोचरः ॥

५६ समुज्झिता यावदराति निर्यती सहैव चापान्मुनिबाणसंहितः ।
प्रभा हिमांशोरिव पङ्कजावलिं निनाय संकोचमुमापतेश्चमूम् ॥

When the foresters, in their anxiety to defeat the enemy,   51
all at once directed a barrage of weapons at him, the
hero struck them down with his arrows—like the
outcome of actions ruined by delayed performance.

Pandu's son gained much advantage with the power of his   52
supremely effective arrows equipped with elongated
heads, as with battle strategies; both defied the
enemy's efforts to gain information about them or to
gauge their power, both were successful in warding
off misfortune, and both penetrated deep into enemy
territory.[6]

Shiva's troops were puzzled: "Are these arrows coming   53
from the sky or earth, from the regions of space or
the sun's orb, from the bow drawn just once or the
ascetic's own body?"

Although the ascetic's arrows pierced the leaders of   54
Shiva's army in their vitals, they failed to kill them.[7]
With downcast faces, as if overcome with guilt for
their failure, the arrows quickly passed beyond the
Himalaya mountain's side and went into hiding.

The ascetic did not aim his arrows at wounds inflicted on   55
the enemy by arrows he had shot earlier, piercing the
soldiers' armor. Honorable warriors do not strike at
the same spot twice.

Released from the bow in numbers that matched the   56
number of enemy troops, the ascetic's barrage of
arrows shrank Shiva's army, like the sun forcing a row
of lotuses to close their petals.

५७ अजिह्ममोजिष्ठममोघमक्रमं क्रियासु बह्वीषु पृथङ्नियोजितम् ।
प्रसेहिरे सादयितुं न सादिताः शरौघमुत्साहमिवास्य विद्विषः ॥

५८ शिवध्वजिन्यः प्रतियोधमग्रतः स्फुरन्तमुग्रेषुमयूखमालिनम् ।
तमेकदेशस्थमनेकदेशगा निदध्युरर्कं युगपत्रजा इव ॥

५९ मुनेः शरौघेण तदुग्ररंहसा बलं प्रकोपादिव विष्वगायता ।
विधूनितं भ्रान्तिमियाय सङ्गिनीं महानिलेनेव निदाघजं रजः ॥

६० तपोबलेनैष विधाय भूयसीस्तनूरदृश्याः स्विदिषूनिरस्यति ।
अमुष्य मायाविहतं निहन्ति नः प्रतीपमागत्य किमु स्वमायुधम् ॥

६१ हता गुणैरस्य भयेन वा मुनेस्तिरोहिताः स्वित्प्रहरन्ति देवताः ।
कथं न्वमी संततमस्य सायका भवन्त्यनेके जलधेरिवोर्मयः ॥

६२ जयेन कच्चिद्विरमेदयं रणाद्ध्रुवेदपि स्वस्ति चराचराय वा ।
तताप कीर्णा नृपसूनुमार्गणैरिति प्रतर्काकुलिता पताकिनी ॥

Under assault, the enemy soldiers could not withstand   57
    Arjuna's volley of arrows any more than they could
    his determination—both were unerring, supremely
    powerful, and unwearied, and skillfully achieved a
    wide array of feats.[8]

As he whirled about the battlefield, fighting each warrior   58
    face to face, haloed by arrows that flashed like rays of
    light, to Shiva's warriors the hero seemed to inhabit
    many places even while remaining in one place,
    as the sun appears to people in different regions
    simultaneously looking.

Assaulted by the barrage of arrows furiously converging   59
    on them from every direction at an alarming speed,
    Shiva's army was thrown into total confusion, like
    dust whirled about by a high wind in summer.

"Can he have created, by his austerity's magical power,   60-62
    countless invisible bodies to shoot arrows for him?
    Could our own weapons be striking us, turned on us
    by his sorcery? Are the gods attacking us, having made
    themselves invisible, for love of the ascetic's virtues
    or out of fear of him? How can he continually produce
    arrows countless as the ocean's waves? We can only
    hope he will stop fighting once he has gained victory,
    and that well-being will be restored to the universe,
    moving and still." Engulfed by the prince's arrows and
    tormented by doubts such as these, Shiva's army fell
    into despair.

६३ अमर्षिणा कृत्यमिव क्षमाश्रयं मदोद्धतेनेव हितं प्रियं वचः ।
बलीयसा तद्विधिनेव पौरुषं बलं निरस्तं न रराज जिष्णुना ॥

६४ प्रतिदिशं प्लवगाधिपलक्ष्मणा विशिखसंहतितापितमूर्तिभिः ।
रविकरग्लपितैरिव वारिभिः शिवबलैः परिमण्डलता दधे ॥

६५ प्रविततशरजालच्छन्नविश्रान्तराले
विधुवति धनुराविर्मण्डलं पाण्डुसूनौ ।
कथमपि जयलक्ष्मीर्भीतभीता विहातुं
विषमनयनसेनापक्षपातं विषेहे ॥

294

Like a good deed rejected by an angry man, like beneficent   63
counsel refused by one drunk with pride, like
courageous effort crushed by powerful fate, the army
of hunters, repulsed by Arjuna, became a thing to
pity.[9]

Wounded and tormented by the arrows shot in every   64
direction by Arjuna, hero with the monkey banner,
Shiva's troops were dispersed like so much water
dried up by the sun's hot rays.

With the web of arrows shot by the Pandava prince filling   65
the whole of space, and Arjuna still brandishing his
fully spanned bow, the frightened goddess of victory
very reluctantly made up her mind to give up the
allegiance she had owed to Shiva, god with three eyes.

CHAPTER 15

Arjuna's Combat with Shiva

१ अथ भूतानि वार्त्रघ्नशरेभ्यस्तत्र तत्रसुः ।
भेजे दिशः परित्यक्तमहेष्वासा च सा चमूः ॥

२ अपश्यद्धिरिवेशानं रणान्निववृते गणैः ।
मुह्यत्येव हि कृच्छ्रेषु संभ्रमज्ज्वलितं मनः ॥

३ खण्डिताशंसया तेषां पराङ्मुखतया तया ।
आविवेश कृपा केतौ कृतोच्छ्रैर्वानरं नरम् ॥

४ आस्थामालम्ब्य नीतेषु वशं क्षुद्रेष्वरातिषु ।
व्यक्तिमायाति महतां माहात्म्यमनुकम्पया ॥

५ स सासिः सासुसूः सासो येयायेयाययाययः ।
ललौ लीलां ललो ऽलोलः शशीशशिशुशीः शशन् ॥

६ त्रासजिह्मं यतश्चैतान्मन्दमेवान्वियाय सः ।
नातिपीडयितुं भग्नानिच्छन्ति हि महौजसः ॥

७ अथाग्रे हसता साचिस्थितेन स्थिरकीर्तिना ।
सेनान्या ते जगदिरे किंचिदायस्तचेतसा ॥

Terrified by the arrows shot by Indra's son in that battle,   1
Shiva's spirit troops scattered in all directions,
dropping their great bows.[1]
The warriors fled from the battlefield as though they had   2
lost sight of Shiva, their master. A mind inflamed with
anxiety in a crisis is easily deluded.
At the sight of the soldiers fleeing, their hopes for   3
victory crushed, Arjuna, warrior with the noble
monkey Hanuman on his banner, was overcome with
compassion.
The magnanimity of noble heroes becomes clearly   4
manifest in the compassion they show to enemies, no
matter how contemptible, whom they vanquish only
with effort.
Then the hero of unwavering determination looked   5
splendid as he sported on the battlefield, leaping
about with his bow, arrows, and sword, attacking
Skanda, the son of the moon-crested god, and he
shone with the auspicious signs of a winner of wealth
of both kinds, sought and unsought.[2]
He pursued those troops at a leisurely pace as they fled   6
in terror. Warriors of true courage do not unduly
torment enemies who are already broken.
Then Skanda, general of Shiva's army, warrior of unsullied   7
reputation, stood before the troops, blocking their
path. Laughing at their cowardice, although he was a
bit despondent, he began to address his men.[3]

८ मा विहासिष्ट समरं समरन्तव्यसंयतः ।
क्षतं क्षुण्णासुरगणैरगणैरिव किं यशः ॥

९ विवस्वदंशुसंश्लेषद्विगुणीकृततेजसः ।
अमी वो मोघमुद्धूर्णा हसन्तीव महासयः ॥

१० वने ऽवने वनसदां मार्गं मार्गमुपेयुषाम् ।
वाणैर्बाणैः समासक्तं शङ्के ऽशं केन शाम्यति ॥

११ पातितोत्तुङ्गमाहात्म्यैः संहृतायतकीर्तिभिः ।
गुर्वीं कामापदं हन्तुं कृतमावृत्तिसाहसम् ॥

१२ नासुरो ऽयं न वा नागो धरसंस्थो न राक्षसः ।
ना सुखो ऽयं नवाभोगो धरणिस्थो हि राजसः ॥

१३ मन्दमस्यन्निषुलतां घृणया मुनिरेष वः ।
प्रणुदत्यागतावज्ञं जघनेषु पशूनिव ॥

"You there, who look on battle as sport, do not run   8
from combat! Why would you warriors, who once
annihilated the ranks of *asura* demons, destroy your
fame in this way, as though you were not Shiva's
attendants?⁴

Raised in vain, these great swords of yours, their flashing   9
brilliance doubled by the sun's rays, seem to be
laughing at you!

I wonder if there can be any remedy for the sorrow that   10
grips your clanging arrows as you run along the tracks
of wild animals in a forest ruled by hunters?⁵

What danger could be so great that you would seek to   11
counter it so rashly, by running away from battle,
degrading your lofty character, and diminishing your
considerable fame?

This man is no demon, nor *nāga* snake, nor *rākṣāsa* ogre   12
in the shape of a mountain. In fact, he is just an
ordinary man, an easy target, a novice in combat, an
earthdweller driven by the passions.⁶

Shooting arrows soft as vines out of compassion for you   13
and prodding you in the flanks, as though you were
cattle, this ascetic is insulting you.

१४ न नोननुन्नो नुन्नोनो नाना नानानना ननु ।
नुन्नो ऽनुन्नो ननुन्नेनो नानेना नुन्ननुन्ननुत् ॥

१५ वरं कृतध्वस्तगुणादत्यन्तमगुणः पुमान् ।
प्रकृत्या ह्यमणिः श्रेयान्नालंकारश्च्युतोपलः ॥

१६ स्यन्दना नो चतुरगाः सुरेभा वाविपत्तयः ।
स्यन्दना नो च तुरगाः सुरेभावा विपत्तयः ॥

१७ भवद्भिरधुनारातिपरिहापितपौरुषैः ।
ह्रदैरिवार्कनिष्पीतैः प्राप्तः पङ्को दुरुत्तरः१० ॥

१८ वेत्रशाककुजे शैले ऽलेशैजे ऽकुकशात्रवे ।
यात किं विदिशो जेतुं तुञ्ज्ञेशो दिवि किंतया ॥

१९ अयं वः क्लैब्यमापन्नान्दृष्टपृष्ठानरातिना ।
इच्छतीशश्च्युताचारान्दारानिव निगोपितुम् ॥

302

You *gaṇa* troops with your various faces,[7] one who is   14
wounded by an inferior enemy is not a man. A man
by whom an inferior enemy is wounded—surely,
that man, too, is not a man. One whose master is not
wounded, even though he is himself wounded, is not
truly wounded—this truth applies to you. And a man
who wounds someone already heavily wounded is not
free of blame; but Arjuna is not that kind of man, so
you should not flee.[8]

A man without any virtues is better than one who has lost   15
the virtues that he had cultivated; an ornament with
no gems is better than one that has lost its gems.[9]

We possess smooth-running chariots, swift horses, loudly   16
trumpeting celestial elephants, and foot soldiers who
remain unscathed in battle.[10]

But at this time, stripped of courageous action by your   17
enemy, you are deeply mired in dishonor, like lakes
thickly caked with mud, their waters dried up by the
sun.

You, who once vanquished demons in the world of gods   18
but are now reduced to this pitiable state on this
unshakeable mountain, impossible for enemies to
penetrate, thickly covered with bamboo thickets and
teak trees—are you setting off on some campaign to
conquer the regions of space?[11]

Since you have failed in your duty by turning your back to   19
the enemy, and therefore have been emasculated, your
lord wants to shield you, the way a man shields his
unfaithful wives.

२० ननु हो मथना राघो घोरा नाथमहो नु न ।
तयदातवदा भीमा माभीदा बत दायत ॥

२१ किं त्यक्तापास्तदेवत्वमानुष्यकपरिग्रहैः ।
ज्वलितान्यगुणैर्गुर्वी स्थिता तेजसि मानिता११ ॥

२२ निशितासिरतो ऽभीको न्येजते ऽमरणा रुचा ।
सारतो न विरोधी नः स्वाभासो भरवानुत ॥

२३ तनुवारभसो भास्वानधीरो ऽविनतोरसा ।
चारुणा रमते जन्ये को ऽभीतो रसिताशिनि ॥

Warriors! Able soldiers, a torment to your enemies,   20
    devoted to your master, guardians, pure of character,
    eloquent, fierce, givers of protection from fear! Tell
    me, how could you not be men of integrity?[12]

O *gaṇa* troops, who are superior to gods and men, who   21
    brilliantly manifest extraordinary virtues, why have
    you abandoned the lofty pride of warriors, founded on
    manly energy?

Immortals! Wielding a sharp sword, fearless, handsome   22
    on account of his majesty, and fit for the challenge of
    combat, because of his strength our enemy does not
    tremble.[13]

Shining in a suit of armor, his handsome chest thrust   23
    forward, effulgent, who is this man who sports
    fearlessly and without pause in the heart of battle,
    whose very sound devours life?

२४ निर्भिन्नपातिताश्वीयनिरुद्धरथवर्त्मनि¹² ।
हतद्विपनगच्छ्यूतरुधिराम्बुनदाकुले ॥

२५ देवाकानिनि कावादे वाहिकास्वस्वकाहि वा ।
काकारेभभरे काका निःस्वभव्यव्यभस्वनि ॥

२६ प्रनृत्तशववित्रस्तततुरगाक्षिप्तसारथौ ।
मारुतापूर्णतूणीरविक्रुष्टहतसादिनि ॥

२७ ससत्त्वरतिदे नित्यं सदरामर्षनाशिनि ।
त्वराधिककसन्नादे रमकत्वमकर्षति ॥

२८ आसुरे लोकवित्रासविधायिनि महाहवे ।
युष्माभिरुन्नतिं नीतं निरस्तमिह पौरुषम् ॥

२९ इति शासति सेनान्यां गच्छतस्ताननेकधा ।
निषिध्य हसता किंचित्तस्थे तत्रान्धकारिणा ॥

३० मुनीषुदहनात्माॅल्ज्जया निविवृत्सतः¹³ ।
शिवः प्रह्लादयामास तान्निषेधहिमाम्बुना ॥

३१ दूनास्ते ऽरिबलादूना निरेभा बहु मेनिरे ।
भीताः शितशराभीताः शंकरं तत्र शंकरम् ॥

Piles of carcasses of dismembered horses clogged the   24–28
    chariot paths; the ground was muddied by blood
    pouring from mountains of slain elephants. Full
    of altercations between the opponents, that battle
    filled the gods with the excited anticipation of
    victory. Warriors attacked their enemies with expert
    maneuvers, rutting elephants covered the battlefield,
    and combat engulfed both the brave and the cowardly.
    Startled by the involuntary dance of corpses, horses
    threw off charioteers, while the wind roared through
    the quivers of slain cavalrymen as their bodies were
    dragged about in the field. It delighted brave men, it
    disheartened cowards, it was filled with the excited
    cries of warriors, it increased their zest for battle.
    Despicable cowards! That was then; in *that* great
    battle with the demons, which terrified the universe,
    you took heroism to its acme, but you have thrown
    away that very valor today!"[14]

When Skanda the general had ended his exhortation to   29
    combat, Shiva, slayer of the demon Andhaka, stood
    before the troops who were running in all directions,
    blocking their path and laughing faintly.[15]

As the warriors tried to flee from battle, scorched by   30
    the ascetic's arrows and burning with shame, Shiva
    refreshed them with the cool water of his command to
    desist.

Distressed and weakened by the enemy's power,   31
    enveloped by sharp arrows and mute with fear, the
    soldiers were grateful to Shiva for soothing them with
    comforting words.[16]

३२ महेषुजलधौ शत्रोर्वर्तमाना दुरुत्तरे ।
प्राप्य पारमिवेशानमाशश्वास पताकिनी ॥

३३ स बभार रणापेतां चमूं पश्चादवस्थिताम् ।
पुरःसूर्यादपावृत्तां छायामिव महातरुः ॥

३४ मुञ्चतीशे शराञ्जिष्णौ पिनाकस्वनपूरितः ।
दध्वान ध्वनयन्नाशाः स्फुटन्निव धराधरः ॥

३५ तद्दृणा दृष्टशुर्भीमं चित्रसंस्था इवाचलाः ।
विस्मयेन तयोर्युद्धं चित्रसंस्था इवाचलाः ॥

३६ परिमोहयमाणेन शिक्षालाघवलीलया ।
जैष्णवी विशिखश्रेणी परिजह्रे पिनाकिना ॥

३७ अवद्यन्पत्रिणः शाम्भोः सायकैरवसायकैः ।
पाण्डवः परिचक्राम शिक्षया रणशिक्षया ॥

३८ चारुचुञ्चुश्चिरारेची चञ्चुच्छीररुचा रुचः ।
चचार रुचिरश्चारु चारैराचारचञ्चुरः ॥

३९ स्फुरत्पिशङ्गमौर्वीकं धुनानः स बृहद्धनुः ।
धृतोल्कानलयोगेन तुल्यमंशुमता बभौ ॥

Drowning in the powerful arrows discharged by the   32
  enemy, an ocean hard to cross, the army breathed in
  relief on reaching Shiva the Lord, as if he were the
  shore.

He led that army, which had turned away from battle,   33
  behind him, like a tall tree bearing its shadow turned
  away from the sun in front.

When the Lord began to shoot arrows at Arjuna the   34
  victor, the mountain, resounding with the twang of
  the Pinaka bow, roared as if exploding, making the
  directions echo.

Looking like mountains of various shapes, Shiva's spirit   35
  troops watched the combat between Shiva and Arjuna
  with wonder, standing motionless like mountains in a
  painting.[17]

With the ease of an expert archer skilled in outwitting   36
  the enemy, Shiva, the Pinaka bowman, successfully
  countered the stream of arrows shot by Arjuna the
  conqueror.

The Pandava, expert in combat and bent on defeating   37
  Shambhu, excitedly circled around his enemy,
  breaking the god's arrows with deadly ones of his
  own.[18]

The splendid hero, master of military maneuvers, skilled   38
  in relentless combat with enemies, and expert in the
  conduct of war, shone as he whirled about in exquisite
  combat moves, his bark garment glittering brightly.[19]

Shaking his mighty bow with its flashing golden-hued   39
  string, he shone like the sun aligned with a fiery
  comet.

४० पार्थबाणाः पशुपतेरावव्रुर्विशिखावलिम् ।
पयोमुच इवारन्ध्राः सावित्रीमंशुसंहतिम् ॥

४१ शरवृष्टिं विधूयोर्वीमुदस्तां सव्यसाचिना ।
रुरोध मार्गणैर्मार्गं तपनस्य त्रिलोचनः ॥

४२ तेन व्यातेनिरे भीमा भीमार्जनफलाननाः ।
न नानुकम्प्य विशिखाः शिखाधरजवाससः ॥

४३ द्युवियद्व्यामिनी तारसंरावविहतश्रुतिः ।
हैमीषुमाला शुशुभे विद्युतामिव संहतिः ॥

४४ विलङ्घ्य पत्त्रिणां पङ्क्तिं भिन्नः शिवशिलीमुखैः ।
ज्यायो वीर्यमुपाश्रित्य न चकम्पे कपिध्वजः ॥

Like a heavy bank of clouds covering the sun's rays, 40
Arjuna's arrows covered over the chain of arrows shot
by Shiva, lord of the beasts.

Repelling the thick shower of arrows shot by Savyasachin, 41
the ambidextrous archer,* the three-eyed god
obstructed the sun's path with arrows.

It was out of compassion, not from lack of pity, that Shiva 42
discharged arrows fletched with peacock feathers,
terrifying arrows yet fitted with tips that were
destined to dispel fear.[20]

Pervading earth and sky and piercing the ear with a high- 43
pitched whine, the volley of golden shafts shot by
Shiva shone like a barrage of lightning flashes.[21]

Although pierced by Shiva's arrows, which subdued his 44
own string of shafts, the hero with the monkey banner
was not shaken; instead, he manifested even greater
courage.

That man, Arjuna who was the sage Nara, was splendid 45a
like Himalaya, king of mountains. The hero was
handsome like a lion, dark complexioned, a royal
protector and munificent giver, engaged in combat
with Shiva and determined to win; the Himalaya was
shining white as shell lime, a protector of the world,
loved by the lions for whom he was a refuge, and the
repository of faith for demons, sages, and the god of
love.[22]

---

* Arjuna.

४५ जगतीशरणे युक्तो हरिकान्तः सुधासितः ।
दानवर्षी कृताशंसो नागराज इवाबभौ ॥

४६ विफलीकृतयत्नस्य क्षतबाणस्य शंभुना ।
गाण्डीवधन्वनः खेभ्यो निश्चक्राम हुताशनः ॥

४७ स पिशङ्गजटावलिः किरन्नुरुतेजः परमेण मन्युना ।
ज्वलितौषधिजातवेदसा हिमशैलेन समं विदिद्युते ॥

४८ शतशो विशिखानवघ्नते भृशमस्मै रणवेगशालिने ।
प्रथयन्ननिवार्यवीर्यतां प्रजिगायेषुमघातुकं शिवः ॥

४९ शंभोर्धनुर्मण्डलतः प्रवृत्तं तं मण्डलादंशुमिवांशुभर्तुः ।
निवारयिष्यन्निवदधे सिताश्वः शिलीमुखच्छायवृतां धरित्रीम् ॥

Arjuna was splendid like Airavata, the god Indra's 45b
elephant. Both were expert in battling demons and
capable of great conquests; the hero was pure as
ambrosia with his great virtues, and was a giver of
great gifts; Airavata was white as ambrosia, and flowed
with ichor.

Arjuna was splendid like Shesha, king of snakes and 45c
Vishnu's couch. Both were appointed to support
the earth and loved by Vishnu. The hero was a great
donor, the serpent was fond of ambrosia; and both
were praised by demons, seers, and Lakshmi, goddess
of fortune.

When Shambhu had broken the strength of his arrows and 46
defeated his efforts, fire shot out of every orifice in the
body of the wielder of the Gandiva bow.

With tawny matted hair piled up on his head and blazing 47
brightly with his mighty rage for combat, he shone like
the Himalaya mountain, burning with its luminous
herbs and forest fires.[23]

Eager fully to manifest the irresistible courage of the hero 48
who cut down enemy arrows by the hundreds, driven
by battle fury, Shiva shot an arrow calculated to hit the
mark, but not to kill.

To fend off an arrow that emerged from Shambhu's bow 49
drawn full circle, like a ray issuing from the orb of the
sun, the hero with the white horse canopied the earth
with the shade of his arrows.[24]

५०	घनं विदार्यार्जुनबाणपूगं ससारवाणो ऽयुगलोचनस्य ।
घनं विदार्यार्जुनबाणपूगं ससार बाणो ऽयुगलोचनस्य ॥

५१	रुजन्महेषून्बहुधाशुपातिनो[१४] मुहुः शरौघैरपवारयन्दिशः ।
चलाचलो ऽनेक इव क्रियावशान्महर्षिसंघैर्बुबुधे धनंजयः ॥

५२	विकाशमीयुर्जगतीशमार्गणा विकाशमीयुर्जगतीशमार्गणाः ।
विकाशमीयुर्जगतीशमार्गणा विकाशमीयुर्जगतीशमार्गणाः ॥

५३	संपश्यतामिति शिवेन वितायमानं
लक्ष्मीवतः क्षितिपतेस्तनयस्य वीर्यम् ।
अज्ञान्यभिन्नमपि तत्त्वविदां मुनीनां
रोमाञ्चमञ्चिततरं बिभराम्बभूवुः ॥

The god with three eyes, whom mortal vision cannot   50
apprehend, discharged a mighty arrow that broke the
arrows Arjuna had just shot and sailed into a forest of
arjuna, bāṇa, and areca trees.[25]

Blocking Shiva's great, swift-flying arrows with an array   51
of maneuvers, and at the same time covering the skies
with a rain of shafts, with his ever-changing motions,
the single Dhanamjaya appeared as many warriors to
the crowd of sages gathered on the mountain.

Arjuna's arrows gained the upper hand, and Shiva's arrows   52
fell to the ground, broken. Shiva's spirit troops, slayers
of demons, were delighted with the hero's feat, and
the celestial devotees of Shiva, lord of the universe,
assembled in the sky, eager to see him.[26]

As the sages witnessed the magnificent heroic deeds of   53
the prince, caused to be put on display in this manner
by Shiva, even though they were persons of true
understanding,[27] they felt every hair in their body
rising with a deep, sweet thrill.

CHAPTER 16

A Contest with Supernatural Weapons

१ ततः किराताधिपतेरलघ्वीमाजिक्रियां वीक्ष्य विवृद्धमन्युः ।
स तर्कयामास विविक्ततर्कश्चिरं विचिन्वन्निति कारणानि ॥

२ मदस्रुतिश्यामितगण्डलेखाः क्रामन्ति विक्रान्तनराधिरूढाः ।
सहिष्णवो नेह युधामभिज्ञा नागा नगोच्छायमिवाक्षिपन्तः ॥

३ विचित्रया चित्रयतेव भिन्नां रुचं रवेः केतनरत्नभासा ।
महारथौघेन न संनिरुद्धा पयोदमन्द्रध्वनिना धरित्री ॥

४ समुल्लसत्त्रासमहोर्मिमालं परिस्फुरच्चामरफेनपङ्क्ति ।
विभिन्नमर्यादमिहातनोति नाश्रीयमाशा जलधेरिवाम्भः ॥

५ हताहतेत्युद्धतभीमघोषैः समुज्झिता योद्धृभिरभ्यमित्रम् ।
न हेतयः प्राप्ततडित्त्विषः खे विवस्वदंशुज्ज्वलिताः पतन्ति ॥

६ अभ्यायतः संततधूमधूम्रं व्यापि प्रभाजालमिवान्तकस्य ।
रजः प्रतूर्णाश्वरथाङ्घ्रिनुन्नं तनोति न व्योम्नि मातरिश्वा ॥

७ भूरेणुना रासभधूसरेण तिरोहिते वर्त्मनि लोचनानाम् ।
नास्त्यत्र तेजस्विभिरुत्सुकानामहि प्रदोषः सुरसुन्दरीणाम् ॥

His battle fury inflamed by the hunter chief's magnificent   1
feats in combat, Arjuna, warrior of flawless judgment,
began to wonder about the reasons for the enemy's
unusual skills.

"In this battle I see no tough war elephants—seasoned   2
in combat, taller than mountains, cheeks stained
dark with streams of ichor—striding about on the
battlefield, mounted by men performing impressive
feats of war.[1]

The ground is not covered with throngs of chariots, rolling   3
with the deep rumble of thunderclouds and coloring
the sunlight with the rainbow glitter of the gems
decorating their many-colored banners.

Cavalry units do not press forward in every direction, an   4
ocean surging over the shore, with gleaming spears for
great waves, and rows of dazzling white flywhisk fans
for surf.

Axes, reflecting the sun's rays and flashing like bolts   5
of lightning, do not fly through the air, hurled by
warriors at enemy soldiers with loud, terrifying shouts
of 'Kill!' and 'Strike!'

The wind does not cloud the sky with the all-pervading   6
dust ceaselessly kicked up by chariots drawn by swift
horses—smoke-gray dust, darkly gleaming like the
god of death arrived at the battlefield to seize lives.

Blinded by dust gray as a donkey, kicked up on the   7
battlefield, celestial nymphs, eager to transport
intrepid heroes to the heavens, could not tell day from
night.

८ रथाङ्गसंक्रीडितमश्वहेषा बृहन्ति मत्तद्विपबृंहितानि ।
संघर्षयोगादिव मूर्छितानि ह्रादं निगृह्लन्ति न दुन्दुभीनाम् ॥

९ अस्मिन्यशःपौरुषलोलुपानामरातिभिः प्रत्युरसं क्षतानाम् ।
मूर्छान्तरायं मुहुरुच्छिनत्ति नासारशीतं करिशीकराम्भः ॥

१० असृङ्ग्दीनामुपचीयमानैर्विदारयद्भिः पदवीं ध्वजिन्याः ।
उच्छ्रायमायान्ति न शोणितौघैः पङ्कैरिवाश्यानघनैस्तटानि ॥

११ परिक्षते वक्षसि दन्तिदन्तैः प्रियाङ्कशीता नभसः पतन्ती ।
नेह प्रमोहं प्रियसाहसानां मन्दारमाला विरलीकरोति ॥

१२ निषादिसंनाहमणिप्रभौघे परीयमाणे करिशीकरेण ।
अर्कत्विषोन्मीलितमभ्युदेति न खण्डमाखण्डलकार्मुकस्य ॥

१३ महीभृता पक्षवतेव भिन्ना विगाह्य मध्यं परवारणेन ।
नावर्तमाना निनदन्ति भीममपां निधेराप इव ध्वजिन्यः ॥

१४ महारथानां प्रतिदन्त्यनीकमधिस्यदस्यन्दनमुत्थितानाम् ।
आमूललूनैरतिमन्युनेव मातङ्गहस्तैर्क्रियते न पन्थाः ॥

Here the din of war drums is not drowned out by the   8
    squealing of chariot wheels, the neighing of horses,
    and the trumpeting of mighty war elephants,
    amplified from mixing together.

In this battle, men hungry for fame as war heroes,   9
    wounded in the chest by enemy soldiers, are not
    constantly revived from fainting—a hindrance to feats
    of war—by cool water showered like steady rainfall
    from the trunks of elephants.

The banks of the rivers of blood flowing on this battlefield   10
    do not grow higher, as if from mud, from fresh
    infusions of half-congealed blood that obstruct the
    marching army.

In this battle, wounded heroes are not revived by garlands   11
    of heavenly coral flowers falling from the sky,[2] cool as
    a beloved girl's embrace, on chests gored by elephant
    tusks.

There is no chance for a chunk of Indra's bow, the   12
    rainbow, to form here, with sunlight refracting
    the flash of gems studding the elephant drivers'
    breastplates, mingled with drops of water sprayed
    from the trunks of elephants.

Scattering right and left when an enemy elephant plunges   13
    into their midst, these troops are not whirled about,
    roaring loudly, like the ocean's waters penetrated by a
    winged mountain.[3]

As great chariot warriors, seated in their swift cars,   14
    advance toward the enemy's elephant division,
    elephant trunks, severed at the root, do not leap up in
    a frenzy to obstruct their path.

१५ धृतोत्पलापीड इव प्रियायाः शिरोरुहाणां शिथिलः कलापः ।
न बर्हभारः पतितस्य शङ्क्रोर्निषादिवक्षःस्थलमातनोति ॥

१६ उज्झत्सु संहार इवास्तसंख्यमह्नाय तेजस्विषु जीवितानि ।
लोकत्रयास्वादनलोलजिह्वं न व्याददात्याननमत्र मृत्युः ॥

१७ इयं च दुर्वारमहारथानामाक्षिप्य वीर्यं महतां बलानाम् ।
शक्तिर्ममावस्यति हीनयुद्धे सौरीव ताराधिपधाम्नि दीप्तिः ॥

१८ माया स्विदेषा मतिविभ्रमो वा ध्वस्तं नु मे वीर्यमुताहमन्यः ।
गाण्डीवमुक्ता हि यथा पुरा मे पराक्रमन्ते न शराः किराते ॥

१९ पुंसः पदं मध्यममुत्तमस्य द्विधेव कुर्वन्धनुषः प्रणादैः ।
नूनं तथा नैष यथास्य वेषः प्रच्छन्नमप्यूहयते हि चेष्टा ॥

२० धनुः प्रबन्धध्वनितं रुषेव सकृद्द्विकृष्टा विततेव मौर्वी ।
संधानमुत्कर्षमिव व्युदस्य मुष्टेरसंभेद इवापवर्गे ॥

In this battle, the peacock feather crest of the lance buried   15
in the elephant rider's chest does not hang limp like
his beloved's loosened coiffure with its chaplet of blue
lotuses.

In this battle, as countless shining warriors lose their lives   16
in an instant, death's mouth does not gape wide with
tongue greedy to devour the three worlds, as it does at
the dissolution of the universe.

And my own strength, which once vanquished the might   17
of great armies of invincible warrior heroes, is
overpowered now, in a battle with inferior men,* like
sunshine by the light of the moon!

Is this magic, or just my mind's confused imaginings?   18
Has my heroic power failed me, or have I turned into
another person altogether? Unlike with enemies in the
past, the arrows shot from Gandiva seem to have no
impact on the hunter!

His bow twangs splitting space itself asunder, where the   19
primal Person placed his second step when measuring
the cosmos,[4] how could this man be a mere hunter,
although he is dressed like one? Actions are the best
clues to a person's true nature, even when it is hidden
from sight.

This hunter never stops fiercely twanging his bow, which   20
stays perpetually spanned. The arrow is fitted to the
bowstring with no perceptible movement of the hand,
and arrows fly without his ever making a fist.

―――

* Tribal hunters are low caste or outcaste.

२१ अंसाववष्टब्धनतौ समाधिः शिरोधराया रहितप्रयासः ।
धृता विकारांस्त्यजता मुखेन प्रसादलक्ष्मीः शशलाञ्छनस्य ॥

२२ प्रहीयते कार्यवशागतेषु स्थानेषु विष्टब्धतया न देहः ।
स्थितप्रयातेषु ससौष्ठवश्च लक्ष्येषु पातः सदृशः शराणाम् ॥

२३ परस्य भूयान्विवरे ऽभियोगः प्रसह्य संरक्षणमात्मरन्ध्रे ।
भीष्मे ऽप्यसंभाव्यमिदं गुरौ वा न संभवत्येव वनेचरेषु ॥

२४ अप्राकृतस्याहवदुर्मदस्य निवार्यमस्यास्तबलेन वीर्यम् ।
अल्पीयसो ऽप्यामयतुल्यवृत्तेर्महापकाराय रिपोर्विवृद्धिः ॥

२५ स संप्रधार्यैवमहार्यसारः सारं विनेष्यन्सगणस्य शत्रोः ।
प्रस्वापनास्त्रं द्रुतमाजहार ध्वान्तं घनानद्ध इवार्धरात्रः ॥

२६ प्रसक्तदावानलधूमधूम्रा निरुन्धती धाम सहस्ररश्मेः ।
महावनानीव महातमिस्रा छाया ततानेशबलानि काली ॥

His shoulders are straight, yet relaxed; neck and body are 21
aligned with effortless ease. Showing no strain at all,
his face shines with the serenity of the moon. The
archer's shifting stances never disturb the firm body's
poise.

Unerringly hitting the target every time, whether 22
moving or stationary, his arrows reveal his skillful
marksmanship.

Not even grandfather Bhishma, or our guru Drona, could 23
match the skill with which this hunter attacks the
enemy's weak spots, all the while protecting his own.
No mere hunter could command such expertise.

I must use magical missiles to counter the assault of this 24
extraordinary opponent, this person drunk with
war lust. Enemies are like diseases; even the ones
that seem insignificant soon grow to dangerous
proportions."

Having decided that this was the course of action he 25
needed to take in order to destroy the strength of
his opponent, along with his entire army, Arjuna,
hero with indomitable power, quickly bent his bow,
discharging the sleep-maker missile, like midnight,
thick with clouds, pouring out darkness.

Dark as the smoke rising from a raging forest fire, 26
obscuring the light of the sun, a vast black shadow
spread over Shiva's troops, like dense darkness
spreading over deep forests.

२७ आसादिता तत्प्रथमं प्रसह्य प्रगल्भतायाः पदवीं हरन्ती ।
सभेव भीमा विदधे गणानां निद्रा निरासां प्रतिभागुणस्य ॥

२८ गुरुस्थिराण्युत्तमवंशजत्वाद्विज्ञातसाराण्यनुशीलनेन ।
केचित्समाश्रित्य गुणान्वितानि सुहृत्कुलानीव धनूंषि तस्थुः ॥

२९ कृतान्तदुर्वृत्त इवापरेषां पुरः प्रतिद्वन्दिनि पाण्डवास्ते ।
अतर्कितं पाणितलान्निपेतुः क्रियाफलानीव तदायुधानि ॥

३० अंसस्थलैः केचिदभिन्नधैर्याः स्कन्धेषु संश्लेषवतां तरूणाम् ।
मदेन मीलन्नयनाः सलीलं नागा इव स्रस्तकरा निषेदुः ॥

३१ तिरोहितेन्दोरथ शंभुमूर्ध्नः प्रणम्यमानं तपसां निवासैः ।
सुमेरुशृङ्गादिव बिम्बमार्कं पिशङ्गमुच्चैरुदियाय तेजः ॥

३२ छायां विनिर्धूय तमोमयीं तां तत्त्वस्य संवित्तिरिवापविद्याम् ।
ययौ विकासं द्युतिरिन्दुमौलेरालोकमभ्यादिशती गणेभ्यः ॥

No sooner did darkness enveloped the *gaṇa* forces than   27
a terrible slumber overpowered them, forcibly
snatching away their boldness and undoing their wit,
as if it were an august assembly they were appearing
before.

Some warriors stood leaning on their spanned bows like   28
worthy comrades. Made of the best cane, the bows
were strong and solid; born in noble lineages, the
friends were powerful and reliable; both had proven
their substantive capability—the bows, from repeated
use, and the men, from devoted service.[5]

From the hands of other soldiers confronted by the   29
Pandava's hostile missile, the weapons slipped of their
own accord like the fruit of deeds snatched by a cruel
fate.

Yet others, their courage unbroken, sat with shoulders   30
resting against the trunks of nearby trees, eyes closed
and arms hanging down, like rutting elephants resting
in the midst of play, trunks hanging limp and eyes
closed in intoxication.

Then, like the sun rising from the crest of Mount Sumeru,   31
a brilliant, golden light arose from Shiva's head, where
the crescent moon was invisible,[6] and the Himalayan
sages bowed to the light.

Dispelling the dark shadow of sleep cast by Arjuna's   32
missile, like the realization of right knowledge
dispelling false cognition, the radiance beamed by the
moon-crested god fanned out, providing light to the
troops.

३३ त्विषां ततिः पाटलिताम्बुवाहा सा सर्वतः पूर्वसरीव संध्या ।
निनाय तेषां द्रुतमुल्लसन्ती विनिद्रतां लोचनपङ्कजानि ॥

३४ पृथग्विधान्यस्तविरामबुद्धाः शस्त्राणि भूयः प्रतिपेदिरे ते ।
मुक्ता वितानेन बलाहकानां ज्योतींषि रम्या इव दिग्विभागाः ॥

३५ द्यौरुन्नमामेव दिशः प्रसेदुः स्फुटं विसस्रे सवितुर्मयूखैः ।
क्षयं गतायामिव यामवत्यां पुनः समीयाय दिनं दिनश्रीः ॥

३६ महास्त्रदुर्गे शिथिलप्रयत्नं दिग्वारणेनेव परेण रुग्णे ।
भुजंगपाशान्भुजवीर्यशाली प्रबन्धनाय प्रजिघाय जिष्णुः ॥

३७ जिह्वाशतान्युल्लसयन्त्यजस्रं लसत्तडिल्लोलविषानलानि ।
त्रासान्निरस्तां भुजगेन्द्रसेना नभश्चरैस्तत्पदवीं विवव्रे ॥

३८ दिग्नागहस्ताकृतिमुद्वहद्भिर्भोगैः प्रशस्तासितरत्ननीलैः ।
रराज सर्पावलिरुल्लसन्ती तरङ्गमालेव नभोऽर्णवस्य ॥

३९ निःश्वासधूमैः स्थगितांशुजालं फणावतामुत्फणमण्डलानाम् ।
गच्छन्निवास्तं वपुरभ्युवाह विलोचनानां सुखमुष्णरश्मिः ॥

४० प्रतप्तचामीकरभासुरेण दिशः प्रकाशेन पिशङ्गयन्त्यः ।
निश्चक्रमुः प्राणहरेक्षणानां ज्वाला महोल्का इव लोचनेभ्यः ॥

Quickly spreading in every direction and reddening the   33
    clouds, that stream of light opened the warriors' eyes,
    like sunlight making lotuses bloom at dawn.

Awakened from sleep when freed from the power of   34
    Arjuna's missile, the men picked up their weapons
    once more, like the regions of space shining with stars
    when a veil of clouds has lifted.

As though night had ended and day had returned with   35
    its radiant beauty, the sky seemed to spring up, the
    regions of space became clear, and the sun's rays
    began to spread out freely.

When the mighty sleep-maker missile had been   36
    effortlessly broken by the enemy, like a fortress by
    a cosmic elephant who guards a region of space, the
    hero famed for his feats of strength discharged snake
    nooses to bind the enemy troops.

Incessantly flashing hundreds of lolling tongues of   37
    poisonous flames that dazzled like bolts of lightning,
    an army of mighty snakes engulfed the path in the sky
    abandoned by celestials as they fled in fright.

The glittering row of snakes, coils curved like the trunks of   38
    cosmic elephants and shimmering blue like rare dark
    sapphires, swelled like a line of waves in the ocean that
    was the sky.

Its rays obscured by the smoke breathed out by the snakes,   39
    with their hoods extended, the sun took on a lovely
    aspect as if on the verge of setting.

Flames darted from the snakes' eyes, like long firebrands,   40
    coloring the regions of space with a brilliant tawny
    light that shone like molten gold.

४१ आक्षिप्तसंपातमपेतशोभमुद्वद्धि धूमाकुलदिग्विभागम् ।
वृतं नभो भोगिकुलैरवस्थां परोपरुद्धस्य पुरस्य भेजे ॥

४२ तमाशु चक्षुःश्रवसां समूहं मन्त्रेण ताक्ष्योदयकारणेन ।
नेता नयेनेव परोपजापं निवारयामास पतिः पशूनाम् ॥

४३ प्रतिघ्नतीभिः कृतमीलितानि द्युलोकभाजामपि लोचनानि ।
गरुत्मतां संहतिभिर्विहायः क्षणप्रकाशाभिरिवावतेने ॥

४४ ततः सुपर्णव्रजपक्षजन्मा नानागतिर्मण्डलयञ्जवेन ।
जरत्तृणानीव वियन्निनाय वनस्पतीनां गहनानि वायुः ॥

४५ मनःशिलाभङ्गनिभेन पक्षान्निरुध्यमानं निकरेण भासाम् ।
व्यूढैरुरोभिश्च विनुद्यमानं नभः ससर्पेव पुरः खगानाम् ॥

४६ दरीमुखैरासवरागताम्रं विकासि रुक्मच्छदधाम पीत्वा ।
जवानिलाघूर्णितसानुजालो हिमाचलः क्षीब इवाचकम्पे ॥

४७ प्रवृत्तनक्तंदिवसंधिदीप्तैर्नभस्तलं गां च पिशङ्गयद्भिः ।
अन्तर्हितार्कैः परितः पतद्भिश्छायाः समाचिक्षिपिरे वनानाम् ॥

All movement was blocked, all beauty lost. Fires burned 41
everywhere, every direction engulfed in smoke.
Penned in by the battalion of snakes, the sky looked
like a city under siege.

Like a general using strategy to counter an enemy effort 42
to incite disloyalty among his troops, Shiva, lord of
the beasts, quickly countered the pack of snakes with
a mantra that conjured up Garuda, king of golden
eagles.

The sky was covered with a flock of birds that flashed like 43
lightning, and blinded by their brilliant light, even the
gods, who never blink, closed their eyes.

Then a fierce wind rose from the wings of the flock of 44
golden eagles. Blowing in every direction, it lifted up
entire forest groves in an instant and whirled them
about in the sky like dried-up blades of grass.

Blocked at the back by a mass of light that looked like a 45
chunk of red arsenic, the sky seemed to glide in front
of the birds, pushed forward by their powerful breasts.

Its peaks whipped about by the fierce wind, the Himalaya 46
mountain seemed to reel like a drunken man after
drinking with its cave mouths the tawny light, the
color of rum, radiating from the wings of the golden
eagles.

Those birds, which completely encircled space and 47
obscured the sun, reddened earth and sky with their
own brilliance and destroyed the shadows of the
forests, like the onset of twilight.

४८ स भोगिसंघः शममुग्रधाम्नां सैन्येन निन्ये विनतासुतानाम् ।
महाध्वरे विध्यपचारदोषः कर्मान्तरेणेव महोदयेन ॥

४९ साफल्यमस्ते रिपुपौरुषस्य कृत्वा गते भाग्य इवापवर्गम् ।
अनिन्धनस्य प्रसभं समन्युः समाददे ऽस्त्रं ज्वलनस्य जिष्णुः ॥

५० ऊर्ध्वं तिरश्चीनमधश्च कीर्णैर्ज्वालासटैर्लिङ्गितमेघपङ्क्तिः ।
आयस्तसिंहाकृतिरुत्पपात प्राण्यन्तमिच्छन्निव जातवेदाः ॥

५१ भित्त्वेव भाभिः सवितुर्मयूखाञ्ज्ज्वाल विष्वग्विसृतस्फुलिङ्गः ।
विदीर्यमाणाश्मनिनादधीरं ध्वनिं वितन्वन्नकृशः कृशानुः ॥

५२ चयानिवाद्रीनिव तुङ्गशृङ्गान्क्वचित्पुराणीव हिरण्मयानि ।
महावनानीव च किंशुकानां ततान वह्निः पवनानुवृत्त्या ॥

५३ मुहुश्चलत्पल्लवलोहिनीभिरुच्चैः शिखाभिः शिखिनो ऽवलीढाः ।
तलेषु मुक्ताविशदा बभूवुः सान्द्राञ्जनश्यामरुचः पयोदाः ॥

५४ लिलिक्षतीव क्षयकालरौद्रे लोकं विलोलार्चिषि रोहिताक्षे ।
पिनाकिना हूतमहाम्बुवाहमस्त्रं पुनः पाशभृतः प्रणिन्ये ॥

As a ritual error at a great sacrifice is corrected by   48
    performing an efficacious compensatory rite, so the
    pack of snakes was vanquished by the army of golden
    eagles, the powerful progeny of Vinata.

When the enemy's combat tactic had succeeded and   49
    the snake missile had perished like the hero's luck,
    Arjuna the conqueror, his pride stung, responded
    by deploying a missile that produced fire without
    kindling.

Fire leaped up as if to devour all living things, taking shape   50
    as a rampant lion, flying up, down, and in the middle
    of space, the flames that were the hairs of his mane
    rising above the clouds.

The immense fire burned, throwing sparks all around,   51
    eclipsing the sun's rays with its light, and blazing with
    deep crackling noises, like a rock splitting asunder.

Driven by the wind, the fire spread, blazing in some places   52
    in the shape of the ramparts of a fort, or mountains
    with high peaks, or elsewhere like cities with golden
    buildings or great forests of red-flowered flame trees.

Leaping restlessly, the flames, red as the young shoots of   53
    a tree, burned the clouds that shone like moist, blue-
    black mascara, till their lower parts were bleached
    white as pearls.

When he saw that a fire fierce as that of the apocalypse   54
    was about to devour the worlds with its leaping
    flames, Shiva the archer conjured up immense clouds
    by summoning a missile governed by Varuna, god of
    the waters.

५५ ततो धरित्रीधरतुल्यरोधसस्तडिल्लतालिङ्गितनीलमूर्तयः ।
अधोमुखाकाशसरिन्निपातिनीरपः प्रसक्तं मुमुचुः पयोमुचः ॥

५६ पराहतध्वस्तशिखे शिखावतो वपुष्यधिक्षिप्तसमिद्धतेजसि ।
कृतास्पदास्तम्र इवायसि ध्वनिं पयोनिपाताः प्रथमे वितेनिरे ॥

५७ महानले भिन्नसिताभ्रपातिभिः समेत्य सद्यः क्रथनेन फेनताम् ।
व्रजद्भिरार्द्रेन्धनवत्परिक्षयं जलैर्वितेने दिवि धूमसंततिः ॥

५८ स्वकेतुभिः पाण्डुरनीलपाटलैः समागताः शक्रधनुःप्रभाभिदः ।
असंस्थितामादधिरे विभावसोर्विचित्रचीनांशुकचारुतां त्विषः ॥

५९ जलौघसंमूर्छनमूर्छितस्वनः प्रसक्तविद्युल्लसितैधितद्युतिः ।
प्रशान्तिमेष्यन्धृतधूममण्डलो बभूव भूयानिव तत्र पावकः ॥

६० प्रवृद्धसिन्धूर्मिचयस्थवीयसां चयैर्विभिन्नाः पयसां प्रपेदिरे ।
उपात्तसंध्यारुचिभिः सरूपतां पयोदविच्छेदलवैः कृशानवः ॥

६१ उपैत्यनन्तद्युतिरप्यसंशयं विभिन्नमूलो ऽनुदयाय संक्षयम् ।
तथा हि तोयौघविभिन्नसंहतिः स हव्यवाहः प्रययौ पराभवम् ॥

Beautiful as mountains with their wide expanses and   55
   curving edges, their blue-black silhouettes embraced
   by flashes of lightning, the clouds showered down
   torrents that fell with the force of the celestial river
   Ganga descending from heaven to earth.[7]

Striking the fire, which briefly blazed up as its flames were   56
   repelled and quenched, the first showers hissed like
   water poured on heated iron.

Falling into the fire like wisps of white cloud, the streams   57
   of water at once began to boil and foam. As the water
   evaporated, a trail of smoke arose as if from wet logs
   and spread in the sky.

The fire's flames outshone the rainbow's colors with the   58
   pale blue and tawny tongues of smoke they raised like
   flags, and shimmered like a length of colorful Chinese
   silk.

Crackling louder from mixing with water, shining brighter   59
   from being steadily lit up by lightning, even though
   that fire was dying, engulfed in smoke, it seemed to
   blaze up with greater intensity.

Dissolved and scattered by torrents of water larger than   60
   the ocean's waves at high tide, the flames looked like
   fragments of broken clouds, tinted red by the twilight.

When he has lost his base of support, even a man of great   61
   abilities succumbs to decisive defeat, never to rise
   again. Just so was that fire completely overcome, its
   core extinguished by the torrents of water.

६२ अथ विहितविधेयैराशु मुक्ता वितानै-
रसितनगनितम्बश्यामभासां घनानाम् ।
विकसदमलधाम्नां प्राप नीलोत्पलानां
श्रियमधिकविशुद्धां वह्निदाहादिव द्यौः ॥

६३ इति विविधमुदासे सव्यसाची यदस्तं
बहुसमरनयज्ञः सादयिष्यन्नरातिम् ।
विधिरिव विपरीतः पौरुषं न्यायवृत्ते:
सपदि तदुपनिन्ये रिक्ततां नीलकण्ठः ॥

६४ वीतप्रभावतनुरप्यतनुप्रभावः
प्रत्याचकाङ्क्ष जयिनीं भुजवीर्यलक्ष्मीम् ।
अस्त्रेषु भूतपतिनापहृतेषु जिष्णु-
र्वर्षिष्यता दिनकृतेव जलेषु लोकः ॥

Their task accomplished, the masses of clouds, dark as   62
Mount Anjana, quickly vanished, and the sky, purified
by fire, shone with the pellucid beauty of freshly
bloomed blue lotuses.

In this way, like a contrary fate defeating the actions of a   63
man of righteous conduct, Shiva the blue-throated[8]
instantly counteracted every missile that Arjuna,
ambidextrous archer* and expert in the strategies
of combat, had deployed, wishing to vanquish his
opponent.

When the benevolent lord of spirits had overpowered   64
all his missiles, the hero's innate power was
undiminished, even though he was disadvantaged by
the loss of weapons. Arjuna the conqueror remained
confident, relying on his unparalleled energy and
physical strength to perform heroic deeds that were
sure to bring him victory. And he was like people
who need to rely on strength and labor to sustain
themselves when the sun has dried up the waters
before showering rain upon the earth.

---

* Savyasachin, an epithet of Arjuna.

CHAPTER 17

The Loss of Arjuna's Weapons

१ अथापदामुद्धरणक्षमेषु मित्रेष्विवास्त्रेषु तिरोहितेषु ।
धृतिं गुरुश्रीर्गुरुणाभिपुष्यन्स्वपौरुषेणेव शरासनेन ॥

२ भूरिप्रभावेण रणाभियोगात्प्रीतो विजिह्वश्च तदीयवृद्ध्या ।
स्पष्टोऽप्यविस्पष्टवपुःप्रकाशः सर्पन्महाधूम इवाद्रिवह्निः ॥

३ तेजः समाश्रित्य परैरहार्यं निजं महन्मित्रमिवोरुधैर्यम् ।
आसादयन्नस्खलितस्वभावं भीमे भुजालम्बमिवारिदुर्गे ॥

४ वंशोचितत्वादभिमानवत्या संप्राप्तया संप्रियतामसुभ्यः ।
समक्षमादित्सितया परेण वध्वेव कीर्त्या परितप्यमानः ॥

५ पतिं नगानामिव बद्धमूलमुन्मूलयिष्यंस्तरसा विपक्षम् ।
लघुप्रयत्नं निगृहीतवीर्यस्त्रिमार्गगावेग इवेश्वरेण ॥

६ संस्कारवत्त्वादद्रमयत्सु चेतः प्रयोगशिक्षागुणभूषणेषु ।
जयं यथार्थेषु शरेषु पार्थः शब्देषु भावार्थमिवाशशंसे ॥

Even though he had lost his powerful weapons, friends   1-6
to aid him in adversity, Arjuna grew all the more
powerful as he seized his great bow with redoubled
determination, as though reaching for his innate
heroic spirit.[1] Delighted to fight against a mighty
warrior, yet downcast at the enemy's success, he
looked like a fire on a mountain, its brilliance dimmed
by billowing smoke. Relying on his invincible heroism
as on a close and faithful friend, he summoned the
courage that never failed him, a supporting arm in the
terrible crises of combat. He was filled with anxiety
over his fame that was like a proud wife worthy of
his lineage—dearer to him than life, and about to be
snatched away by the enemy before his very eyes.
He wanted quickly to uproot his enemy, who stood
rooted before him like the Himalaya mountain—
Shiva himself, who had effortlessly resisted the
hero's spirited assaults as he had once stemmed the
torrential current of the Ganga, river with three
paths.[2] Partha trusted his arrows to be true to their
nature, and therefore to bring him victory. Like
words that yield the right meaning because they have
ancient, pleasing associations and are made beautiful
by appropriate usage and stylistic virtues, the arrows
were honed and ready, and primed for action by years
of practice and application.[3]

७ भूयः समाधानविवृद्धतेजा नैवं पुरा युद्धमिति व्यथावान् ।
स निर्ववामास्रममर्षनुन्नं विषं महानाग इवेक्षणाभ्याम् ॥

८ तस्याहवायासविलोलमौलेः संरम्भताम्रायतलोचनस्य ।
निर्वापयिष्यन्निव रोषतप्तं प्रस्नापयामास मुखं निदाघः ॥

९ क्रोधान्धकारान्तरितो रणाय भ्रूभेदरेखाः स बभार तिस्रः ।
घनोपरुद्धः प्रभवाय वृष्टेरूर्ध्वांशुराजीरिव तिग्मरश्मिः ॥

१० स प्रध्वनय्याम्बुदनादि चापं हस्तेन दिङ्गग इवाद्रिश्रृङ्गम् ।
बलानि शंभोरिषुभिस्तताप चेतांसि चिन्ताभिरिवाशरीरः ॥

११ सद्वादितेवाभिनिविष्टबुद्धौ गुणाभ्यसूयेव विपक्षपाते ।
अगोचरे वागिव चोपरेमे शक्तिः शराणां शितिकण्ठकाये ॥

१२ उमापतिं पाण्डुसुतप्रणुन्नाः शिलीमुखा न व्यथयांबभूवुः ।
अभ्युत्थितस्याद्रिपतेर्नितम्बमर्कस्य पादा इव हैमनस्य ॥

Distressed by the unfamiliar taste of defeat and resolved　　7
　　to continue fighting with renewed vigor, he shed
　　tears of impatient anger, like a great serpent spewing
　　poison from its eyes.
As if to cool him, perspiration bathed his face, heated up　　8
　　with war lust, with hair knot loosened from strenuous
　　fighting and wide eyes red from anger.
As he prepared for combat, his face dark with anger, and　　9
　　with three lines furrowing his brow, he looked like
　　the sun streaming rays of light from behind a bank of
　　clouds to signal a shower of rain.
Like a celestial elephant that guards a region of space*　　10
　　and causes mountain peaks to resound with his
　　trumpeting, he twanged his bow, making it thunder
　　like a raincloud, and tormented Shambhu's troops
　　with arrows, as the bodiless god of love torments men
　　with cravings.[4]
Like a reasoned argument meant to persuade an obstinate　　11
　　man, like envy directed against an impartial person,
　　like speech employed to describe the ineffable real,
　　the arrows became powerless against the body of the
　　dark-throated god.[5]
Like the winter sun's rays striking a slope of high　　12
　　Himalaya, king of mountains, the arrows Pandu's son
　　shot at Shiva did not even hurt him.

---

* Eight elephants guard the eight directions.

१३ संप्रीयमाणो ऽनुबभूव तीव्रं पराक्रमं तस्य पतिर्गणानाम् ।
विषाणभेदं हिमवानसह्यं वप्रानतस्येव सुरद्विपस्य ॥

१४ तस्मै हि भारोद्धरणे समर्थं प्रदास्यता बाहुमिव प्रतापम् ।
चिरं विषेहे ऽभिभवस्तदानीं स कारणानामपि कारणेन ॥

१५ प्रत्याहतौजाः कृतसत्त्ववेगः पराक्रमं ज्यायसि यस्तनोति ।
तेजांसि भानोरिव निष्पतन्ति यशांसि वीर्यज्वलितानि तस्य ॥

१६ दृष्ट्वावदानाद्व्यथते ऽरिलोकः प्रध्वंसमेति व्यथिताच्च तेजः ।
तेजोविहीनं विजहाति दर्पः शान्तार्चिषं दीपमिव प्रकाशः ॥

१७ ततः प्रयात्यस्तमदावलेपः स जय्यतायाः पदवीं जिगीषोः ।
गन्धेन जेतुः प्रमुखागतस्य प्रतिद्विपस्येव मतङ्गजौघः ॥

१८ एवं प्रतिद्वन्द्विषु तस्य कीर्तिं मौलीन्दुलेखाविशदां विधास्यन् ।
इयेष पर्यायजयावसादां रणक्रियां शंभुरनुक्रमेण ॥

१९ मुनेर्विचित्रैरिषुभिः स भूयान्निन्ये वशं भूतपतेर्बलौघः ।
सहात्मलाभेन समुत्पतद्भिर्जातिस्वभावैरिव जीवलोकः ॥

As the Himalaya welcomes the powerful thrusts of Indra's   13
elephant ramming his tusks against its slopes, Shiva,
lord of *gaṇa* spirits, experienced great delight at
Arjuna's supreme heroism.

The god, origin of all origins, long endured the assault of   14
the hero, as though wishing to extend to Arjuna, in
the form of heroic deeds, an arm fit for bearing his
burdens.

When a warrior who has suffered defeat redoubles his   15-17
heroic energy and valiantly confronts a superior
enemy, martial power radiates from him like rays from
the sun. Enemies fear a man who has proved himself
in action; men who are intimidated quickly lose their
power; pride abandons powerless men, as light leaves
a lamp whose flame is extinguished. Thereafter, with
their pride and spirit broken, they become an easy
target for the conquering hero, as a herd of rutting
elephants is subdued by the leader of the enemy herd,
who confronts and masters them with his scent.[6]

And so, wishing to create among Arjuna's enemies a   18
reputation for him bright as the crescent moon he
bore on his own head, Shambhu devised a pattern of
combat where the combatants would win and lose by
turns.

Like living beings, who are seized by the inherent   19
attributes of their species the moment they are born,
Shiva's multitude of troops was overpowered by the
hermit's variety of arrows.

२० वितन्वतस्तस्य शरान्धकारं त्रस्तानि सैन्यानि रवं निशेमुः ।
प्रवर्षतः संततवेपथूनि क्षपाघनस्येव गवां कुलानि ॥

२१ स सायकान्साध्वसविप्लुतानां क्षिपन्परेषामतिसौष्ठवेन ।
शशीव दोषावृतलोचनानां विभिद्यमानः पृथगाबभासे ॥

२२ क्षोभेण तेनाथ गणाधिपानां भेदं ययावाकृतिरीश्वरस्य ।
तरङ्गकम्पेन महाह्रदानां छायामयस्येव दिनस्य कर्तुः ॥

२३ प्रसेदिवांसं न तमाप कोपः कुतः परस्मिन्पुरुषे विकारः ।
आकारवैषम्यमिदं च भेजे दुर्लक्ष्यचिह्ना महतां हि वृत्तिः ॥

२४ विस्फार्यमाणस्य ततो भुजाभ्यां भूतानि भर्त्रा धनुरन्तकस्य ।
भिन्नाकृतिं ज्यां ददृशुः स्फुरन्तीं क्रुद्धस्य जिह्वामिव तक्षकस्य ॥

२५ सव्यापसव्यध्वनितोग्रचापं पार्थः किराताधिपमाशशङ्के ।
पर्यायसंपादितकर्णतालं यन्ता गजं व्यालमिवापराद्धः ॥

२६ निजघ्निरे तस्य हरेषुजालैः पतन्ति वृन्दानि शिलीमुखानाम् ।
ऊर्जस्विभिः सिन्धुमुखागतानि यादांसि यादोभिरिवाम्बुराशेः ॥

Arjuna's arrows darkened the sky in their flight, and at   20
    their whizzing sound the terrified soldiers trembled
    like herds of cows at thunderclaps on a rainy night.

As the single moon appears double to men suffering from   21
    glaucoma, the hero, skillfully shooting arrows, became
    not one but many men to his enemies overcome by
    fear and confusion.[7]

At the agitation of his generals, the Lord's countenance   22
    registered a change—but no more than the sun
    reflected in a great lake changes with the rippling
    waves.[8]

The Lord was pleased with the hero and not angry—how   23
    can there be any real change in the supreme Person?—
    and yet his expression altered. The actions of great
    men are beyond comprehension.[9]

Shiva's spirit hosts then saw their master spanning the god   24
    of death's bow, its bowstring seemingly split in two,
    and flashing like his forked tongue when Takshaka,
    king of snakes, is enraged.

Like a trainer who has lost control over a rogue elephant   25
    warily watching the beast flapping its ears one after
    another, Partha watched with apprehension as the
    hunter chief twanged his fierce bow alternately to the
    left and the right.

As freshwater creatures, helplessly carried to the ocean by   26
    river currents, are devoured by mighty sea monsters,
    Arjuna's shower of arrows was destroyed by Hara's
    shafts.

२७ विभेदमन्तः पदवीनिरोधं विध्वंसनं चाविदितप्रयोगः ।
नेतारिलोकेषु करोति यद्यत्तत्तच्चकारास्य शरेषु शम्भुः ॥

२८ सोढावगीतप्रथमायुधस्य क्रोधोज्झितैर्वेगितया पतद्भिः ।
छिन्नैरपि त्रासितवाहिनीकैः पेते कृतार्थैरिव तस्य बाणैः ॥

२९ अलंकृतानामृजुतागुणेन गुरूपदिष्टां गतिमास्थितानाम् ।
सतामिवापर्वणि मार्गणानां भङ्गः स जिष्णोर्धृतिमुन्ममाथ ॥

३० बाणच्छिदस्ते विशिखाः स्मरारेरवाङ्मुखीभूतफलाः पतन्तः ।
अखण्डितं पाण्डवसायकेभ्यः कृतस्य सद्यः प्रतिकारमापुः ॥

३१ चित्रीयमाणानतिलाघवेन प्रमाथिनस्तान्भवमार्गणानाम् ।
समाकुलाया निचखान दूरं बाणान्ध्वजिन्या हृदयेष्वराति ॥

३२ तस्यातियत्नादतिरिच्यमाने पराक्रमे ऽन्योन्यविशेषणेन ।
हन्ता पुरां भूरि पृषत्कवर्षं निरास नैदाघ इवाम्बु मेघः ॥

Shambhu countered the hero's arrows as a warrior   27
   counters his enemies: with secret strategies he
   broke their ranks, obstructed their maneuvers, and
   annihilated them.

Although Arjuna's best darts had been treated with   28
   contempt and overcome by his enemy, the fresh
   arrows shot in rapid succession by the enraged hero,
   even as they were broken, were amply rewarded by
   their success in terrifying Shiva's troops.

Arjuna the conqueror's spirit was shaken by the   29
   destruction of his unerring arrows—arrows that
   always sped on the track charted by the archer and
   that were now broken even where there were no
   joints—as by the untimely downfall of good men, men
   of moral integrity, who always follow the path shown
   by their teachers.[10]

Although they succeeded in breaking the Pandava's   30
   arrows, Shiva's arrows failed in their mission of
   defeating Arjuna; instead, falling down with their
   heads broken, they reaped the full and immediate
   consequence for their misdeed.[11]

With consummate skill, Arjuna shot tricky arrows that   31
   destroyed Shiva's arrows and bored deep into the
   hearts of his confused troops.

Seeing Arjuna's feats of combat, reinforced by supreme   32
   effort, scaling new heights of excellence, Shiva,
   destroyer of the demons' cities, released a thick
   shower of arrows, like a cloudburst in the summer.

३३ अनामृशन्तः क्वचिदेव मर्म प्रियैषिणानुप्रहिताः शिवेन ।
सुहृत्प्रयुक्ता इव नर्मवादाः शरा मुनेः प्रीतिकरा बभूवुः ॥

३४ अस्त्रैः समानामतिरेकिणीं वा पश्यन्त्रिषूणामपि तस्य शक्तिम् ।
विषादवक्तव्यबलः प्रमाथी स्वमाललम्बे बलमिन्दुमौलिः ॥

३५ ततस्तपोवीर्यसमुद्धतस्य पारं यियासोः समराणॅवस्य ।
महेषुजालान्यखिलानि जिष्णोरर्कः पयांसीव समाचचाम ॥

३६ रिक्ते सविस्रम्भमथार्जुनस्य निषङ्गवक्त्रे निपतात् पाणिः ।
अन्यद्द्विपापीतजले सतर्षं मतङ्गजस्येव नगाश्मरन्ध्रे ॥

३७ च्युते स तस्मिन्निषुधौ शरार्थाद्दुस्तार्थसारे सहसेव बन्धौ ।
तत्कालमोघप्रणयः प्रपेदे निर्वाच्यताकाम इवाभिमुख्यम् ॥

३८ आघट्ट्यामास गतागताभ्यां सावेगमग्राङ्गुलिरस्य तूणौ ।
विधेयमार्गे मतिरुत्सुकस्य नयप्रयोगाविव गां जिगीषोः ॥

३९ बभार शून्याकृतिरर्जुनस्तौ महेषुधी वीतमहेषुजालौ ।
युगान्तसंशुष्कजलौ विजिह्वः पूर्वापरौ लोक इवाम्बुराशी ॥

The hermit found Shiva's shafts delightful, like pleasant 33
words spoken by a dear friend, for they were
dispatched with his welfare in mind and did not
wound him in any critical spot.

When he saw that the hero's powerful arrows matched 34
or surpassed his own weapons, and seeing his troops
crushed by despondency, the destroyer, the moon-
crested god, assumed his own divine powers.

Then, like the sun devouring the waters, he consumed the 35
entire store of arrows held by Jishnu, who strove to
cross the ocean of battle, energized by ascetic power
and heroic spirit.

Arjuna confidently put his hand inside the mouth of 36
his empty quiver, like a thirsty elephant inserting
its trunk into a rock cleft on a mountain that other
elephants have drunk dry.

Although it found the quiver empty of arrows, like a 37
kinsman who has suddenly lost his wealth, the hand
remained outstretched in supplication, like a man
reluctant to abandon his benefactor, in spite of the
certainty of immediate disappointment.

Like a warrior's mind investigating the science of 38
statecraft, eager to devise strategies for the conquest
of the world, Arjuna's index finger groped frantically
in the quiver.

Carrying the two great quivers emptied of their store 39
of arrows, the downcast hero looked pitiable, like
the ravaged world bearing the eastern and western
oceans when completely drained at the time of cosmic
dissolution.

४० तेनानिमित्तेन तथा न पार्थस्तयोर्यथा रिक्ततयानुतेपे ।
स्वामापदं प्रोज्झ्य विपत्तिमग्रं शोचन्ति सन्तो ह्युपकारिपक्षम् ॥

४१ प्रतिक्रियायै विधुरः स तस्मात्कृच्छ्रेण विश्लेषमियाय हस्तः ।
पराङ्मुखत्वे ऽपि कृतोपकारात्तूणीमुखान्मित्रकुलादिवार्यः ॥

४२ पश्चात्क्रिया तूणयुगस्य भर्तुर्जज्ञे तदानीमुपकारिणीव ।
संभावनायामधरीकृतायां पत्युः पुरः साहसमासितव्यम् ॥

४३ तं शंभुराक्षिप्तमहेषुजालं लौहैः शरैर्मर्मसु निस्तुतोद ।
हृतोत्तरं तत्त्वविचारमध्ये वक्तेव दोषैर्गुरुभिर्विपक्षम् ॥

४४ जहार चास्मादचिरेण वर्म ज्वलन्मणिद्योतितहैमलेखम् ।
चण्डः पतंगान्मरुदेकनीलं तडित्वतः खण्डमिवाम्बुदस्य ॥

४५ विकोशनिर्धौततनोर्महासेः फणावतश्च त्वचि विच्युतायाम् ।
प्रतिद्विपाबद्धरुषः समक्षं नागस्य चाक्षिप्तमुखच्छदस्य ॥

४६ विबोधितस्य ध्वनिना घनानां हरेरपेतस्य च शैलरन्ध्रात् ।
निरस्तधूमस्य च रात्रिवह्नेर्विना तनुत्रेण रुचिं स भेजे ॥

The empty quivers distressed Partha more than the bad   40
omen: ignoring their own troubles, good men grieve
over the misfortunes of their friends.

Although at a loss for a remedy, his hand parted   41
reluctantly from the quiver's mouth, like a loyal
person who finds it hard to leave a good friend who
has turned him away, for he has helped him in the
past.

At that moment it became clear that their master had   42
done the twin quivers a favor by placing them at his
back. It is impudence to stand before one's master,
having failed to fulfill one's appointed task.

Having destroyed the hero's vast store of arrows,   43
Shambhu pierced him with iron arrows in vulnerable
spots, like the speaker in a debate charging his
opponent with major fallacies, when the latter has
already lost the argument.

Swift as a strong wind ripping away from the sun a pure   44
black cloud, streaked with lightning, the god stripped
Arjuna of his suit of armor, chased in gold and
studded with gems.

Stripped of his armor, the hero looked like a great sword   45-46
unsheathed and blade gleaming; a snake that has
sloughed off its skin; a war elephant that has thrown
off its facecloth, enraged by an enemy elephant; a lion
who has emerged from his mountain cave, roused by
the rumble of rainclouds; a smokeless fire burning by
night.[12]

४७ अचित्ततायामपि नाम युक्तामनूर्ध्वतां प्राप्य तदीयकृच्छ्रे ।
महीं गतौ ताविषुधी तदानीं विवव्रतुश्चेतनयेव योगम् ॥

४८ स्थितं विशुद्धे नभसीव सत्त्वे धाम्ना तपोवीर्यमयेन युक्तम् ।
शास्त्राभिघातैस्तमजस्रमीशस्त्वष्टा विवस्वन्तमिवोल्लिलेख ॥

४९ संरम्भवेगोज्झितवेदनेषु गात्रेषु बाधिर्यमुपागतेषु ।
मुनेर्बभूवागणितेषुराशेर्लौहस्तिरस्कार इवात्ममन्युः ॥

५० ततो ऽनुपूर्वायतवृत्तबाहुः श्रीमान्क्षरल्लोहितदिग्धदेहः ।
आस्कन्द्य वेगेन विमुक्तनादः क्षितिं विधुन्वन्निव पार्ष्णिघातैः ॥

५१ साम्यं गतेनाशनिना मघोनः शशाङ्कखण्डाकृतिपाण्डुरेण ।
शम्भुं बिभित्सुर्धनुषा जघान स्तम्बं विषाणेन महानिवेभः ॥

५२ रयेण सा संनिदधे पतन्ती भवोद्भवेनात्मनि चापयष्टिः ।
समुद्धता सिन्धुरनेकमार्गा परे स्थितेनौजसि जह्नुनेव ॥

५३ विकार्मुकः कर्मसु शोचनीयः परिच्युतौदार्य इवोपचारः ।
विचिक्षिपे शूलभृता सलीलं स पत्रिभिर्दूरमदूरपातैः ॥

Although the quivers lying on the ground were manifestly   47
inanimate, in facing downward at the time of the
hero's distress they surely demonstrated they were
endowed with consciousness.[13]

As Arjuna stood steadfast in his courage like the sun in   48
a clear sky, joined with the twofold glory stemming
from asceticism and his own heroic nature, the Lord
wore him down with an incessant barrage of arrows,
just as Tvashta, smith of the gods, trimmed down the
sun with his lathe.

Heroic indignation became a suit of steel armor against   49
the opponent's countless arrows for the hermit, whose
limbs were rigid with battle fury and impervious to all
sensation.

Then, with a roar of anger, the hero, his arms long and   50
well formed, his splendid body streaming with blood,
leaped up with such force that the earth shook under
his feet.

And, like a mighty elephant ramming its hitching post   51
with its tusks, wishing to crush Shiva, he struck him
with his bow, bright and curved like the crescent
moon or Indra's thunderbolt.

Swiftly Shiva absorbed into himself the bow that flew at   52
him, just as the sage Jahnu, immersed in meditation
on the supreme light, consumed the turbulent streams
of the river Ganga.[14]

Bereft of his bow, and therefore pitiable in his deeds, like   53
hospitality lacking generosity, Arjuna was deeply
wounded by the relentless shower of arrows that
Shiva shot at him with playful ease.[15]

५४ उपोढकल्याणफलो ऽभिरक्षन्वीरव्रतं पुण्यरणाश्रमस्थः ।
जपोपवासैरिव संयतात्मा तेपे मुनिस्तैरिषुभिः शिवस्य ॥

५५ ततो ऽग्रभूमिं व्यवसायसिद्धेः सीमानमन्यैरतिदुस्तरं सः ।
तेजःश्रियामाश्रयमुत्तमासिं साक्षादहंकारमिवाललम्बे ॥

५६ शरानवद्यन्ननवद्यकर्मा चचार चित्रं प्रविचारमार्गैः ।
हस्तेन निस्त्रिंशभृता स दीप्तः साकार्ंशुना वारिधिरूर्मिणेव ॥

५७ यथा निजे वर्त्मनि भाति भाभिश्छायामयश्चाप्सु सहस्ररश्मिः ।
तथा नभस्याशु रणस्थलीषु स्पष्टद्विमूर्तिर्ददृशे स भूतैः ॥

५८ शिवप्रणुन्नेन शिलीमुखेन त्सरुप्रदेशादपवर्जिताङ्गः ।
ज्वलन्नसिस्तस्य पपात पाणेर्घनस्य वप्रादिव वैद्युतो ऽग्निः ॥

५९ आक्षिप्तचापावरणेषुजालश्छिन्नोत्तमासिः स मृधे ऽवधूतः ।
रिक्तः प्रकाशश्च बभूव भूमेरुत्सादितोद्यान इव प्रदेशः ॥

६० स खण्डनं प्राप्य परादमर्षवान्भुजद्वितीयो ऽपि विजेतुमिच्छया ।
ससर्ज वृष्टिं परिरुग्णपादपां द्रवेतरेषां पयसामिवाश्मनाम् ॥

His endeavor about to bear auspicious fruit, the sage in   54
the purifying hermitage of battle observed his vow of
heroic combat, mortifying himself with Shiva's arrows
instead of with mantras and fasting.

Then he grasped as his last resort the warrior's ultimate   55
means for achieving his goals, that which is invincible
by his enemies, the treasure house of war might, his
mighty sword, as though it were his pride incarnate.

Parrying Shiva's arrows, Arjuna, the perfect warrior,   56
skillfully made a swordsman's moves, saber blazing in
his hand, shining like the ocean with a sunlit wave.

As the sun shines with the brilliance of a thousand rays   57
both in his own realm and in his reflected image in
the water, to Shiva's hosts the swiftly moving hero
appeared to have two distinct forms, one in the sky,
and another on the battlefield.

Severed from its hilt by an arrow shot by Shiva, his   58
bright sword rolled from his hand, like a fiery bolt of
lightning from a cloudbank.

Deprived of bow and arrows and armor, his fine sword   59
broken, defeated in combat, he stood clean and bare,
like land stripped clean of vegetation.

Defeated by Shiva, yet determined to conquer him, the   60
proud hero, with nothing left but the strength of
his arms, pelted his opponent with a hail of rocks,
knocking down the forest trees.

६१ नीरन्ध्रं परिगमिते क्षयं पृषत्कै-
भूतानामधिपतिना शिलावितानेे ।
उच्छ्रायस्थगितनभोदिगन्तरालं
चिक्षेप क्षितिरुहजालमिन्द्रसूनुः ॥

६२ निःशेषं शकलितवल्कलाङ्गसारैः
कुर्वद्भिर्भुवमभितः कषायचित्राम् ।
ईशानः सकुसुमपल्लवैर्नगैस्तै-
रातेने बलिमिव रङ्गदेवताभ्यः ॥

६३ उन्मज्जन्मकर इवामरापगाया
वेगेन प्रतिमुखमेत्य बाणनद्धाः ।
गाण्डीवी कनकशिलानिभं भुजाभ्या-
माजघ्ने विषमविलोचनस्य वक्षः ॥

६४ अभिलषत उपायं विक्रमं कीर्तिलक्ष्यो-
रसुगममरिसैन्यैरङ्कमभ्यागतस्य ।
जनक इव शिशुत्वे सुप्रियस्यैकसूनो-
रविनयमपि सेहे पाण्डवस्य स्मरारिः ॥

When the lord of the *gaṇa* troops had completely   61-62
destroyed the shower of rocks with his arrows, Indra's
son threw at him a stream of uprooted trees that flew
up, covering the sky; but Shiva made a sacrificial
offering to the battlefield gods of those blossoming
trees with bark and marrow torn to bits and flowing
sap reddening the earth.

Like a crocodile surfacing from the river Ganga, Arjuna,   63
warrior with the Gandiva bow, shot up from the
stream of arrows, and throwing himself against the
three-eyed god, violently struck him with his fists on
his chest hard as a golden rock.

When his only son climbs into his lap seeking some treat,   64
a father will forgive any impoliteness, since it is just
a child. So did the slayer of the love god endure the
impertinence of the Pandava, who had come to him
seeking power of a kind his enemies with all their
troops could not hope to gain, the means to fame and
royal glory.

CHAPTER 18

Wrestling Match, Theophany, and Boon

१ तत उदग्र इव द्विरदे मुनौ रणमुपेयुषि भीमभुजायुधे ।
धनुरुपास्य सबाणधि शंकरः प्रतिजघान घनैरिव मुष्टिभिः ॥

२ हरपृथासुतयोर्ध्वनिरुत्पतन्नमृदुसंवलिताङ्गुलिपाणिजः ।
स्फुटदनल्पशिलारवदारुणः प्रतिननाद दरीषु दरीभृतः ॥

३ शिवभुजाहतिभिन्नपृथुक्षतीः सुखमिवानुबभूव कपिध्वजः ।
क इव नाम बृहन्मनसां भवेदनुकृतेरपि सत्त्ववतां क्षमः ॥

४ व्रणमुखच्युतशोणितशीकरस्थगितशैलतटाभभुजान्तरः ।
अभिनवौषसरागभृता बभौ जलधरेण समानमुमापतिः ॥

५ उरसि शूलभृतः प्रहिता मुहुः प्रतिहतिं ययुरर्जुनमुष्टयः ।
भृशरया इव सह्यमहीभृतः पृथुनि रोधसि सिन्धुमहोर्मयः ॥

६ निपतिते ऽधिशिरोधरमायते सममरन्ति युगे ऽयुगचक्षुषः ।
त्रिचतुरेषु पदेषु किरीटिना लुलितदृष्टि मदादिव चस्खले ॥

362

Then the ascetic began to fight with his formidable arms   1
as his only weapon, attacking Shiva with the fury of a
mighty fighting elephant.[1] At once Shiva threw aside
his own bow and quivers, and struck back at him with
fists like hammers.

The crackling sound that arose when Shiva and Arjuna's   2
fists forcefully struck each other echoed in the
mountain caves with loud reports, like the sound of a
huge rock splitting.

The hero with the monkey banner felt no pain from the   3
great wounds Shiva's fists inflicted on him. A man
of extraordinary courage is capable of incomparable
feats when provoked by an enemy.

His rock-hard chest covered with the blood streaming   4
from his wounds, Shiva shone like a cloud suffused
with the rosy glow of dawn.

Again and again Arjuna's fists struck the trident bearer's   5
chest, and glanced off, like the mighty waves of the
ocean rolling back after crashing against the broad
slope of the Sahya mountain.*

When the three-eyed god struck him on the neck with   6
both fists, Arjuna took a few staggering steps, eyes
rolling as if he were drunk.

---

* Sahyadri, a mountain range in southwest India.

७ अभिभवोदितमन्युविदीपितः समभिसृत्य भृशं जवमोजसा ।
भुजयुगेन विभज्य समाददे शशिकलाभरणस्य भुजद्वयम् ॥

८ प्रववृते ऽथ महाहवमलयोरचलसंचलनाहरणो रणः ।
करणशृङ्खलसंकलनागुरुर्गुरुभुजायुधगर्वितयोस्तयोः ॥

९ अयमसौ भगवानुत पाण्डवः स्थितमवाङ्मुनिना शशिमौलिना ।
समधिरूढमजेन नु जिष्णुना स्विदिति वेगवशान्मुमुहे गणैः ॥

१० प्रचलिते चलितं स्थितमास्थिते विनमिते नतमुन्नतमुन्नतौ ।
वृषकपिध्वजयोरसहिष्णुना मुहुरभावभयादिव भूभृता ॥

११ करणशृङ्खलनिःसृतयोस्तयोः कृतभुजध्वनि वल्गु विवल्गतोः ।
चरणपातनिपातितरोधसः प्रससृपुः सरितः परितः स्थलीः ॥

१२ वियति वेगपरिप्लुतमन्तरा समभिसृत्य रयेण कपिध्वजः ।
चरणयोश्चरणानमितक्षितिर्निजगृहे तिसृणां जयिनं पुराम् ॥

१३ विस्मितः सपदि तेन कर्मणा कर्मणां क्षयकरः परः पुमान् ।
क्षेतुकाममवनौ तमक्लमं निष्पिपेष परिरभ्य वक्षसा ॥

Enraged by defeat, he lunged forward with tremendous   7
force, and seizing the moon-crested god's arms with
his own, he forced them wide apart and held them
down.

Then those expert warriors, proud of having no weapons   8
but their mighty arms, their limbs locked together in
tricky wrestling grips, began a bout of fighting that
shook the mountain.

They moved so fast that Shiva's spirit troops were left   9
wondering: "Is this one over here the Lord, or is it the
Pandava? Is the ascetic lying under Shiva, or is the
moon-crowned god beneath him? Who is sitting on
top, Jishnu the conquering hero or the birthless god?"

Crushed by the weight of Arjuna and Shiva, and fearing to   10
be destroyed, the mountain moved when they moved,
stopped when they stopped, bent down when they
bent down, and straightened up when they stood up.

When the wrestlers released their grip around each   11
other's limbs and leaped gracefully about each other,
loudly striking their arms, the rivers, their banks
depressed by the wrestlers' steps, began to overflow.

Then Shiva, destroyer of the demons' three cities, took a   12
flying leap into the sky, and Arjuna, warrior with the
monkey banner, shot up after him, depressing the
earth with his feet, and seized the god's feet in midair.

Astonished by the deed, the supreme Person, the ender   13
of men's deeds, at once gathered into his arms
the peerless hero, who was about to throw him to
the ground, and pressed him to his chest in a tight
embrace.²

१४ तपसा तथा न मुदमस्य ययौ भगवान्यथा विपुलसत्त्वतया ।
गुणसंहतेः समतिरिक्तमहो निजमेव सत्त्वमुपकारि सताम् ॥

१५ अथ हिमशुचिभस्मभूषितं शिरसि विराजितमिन्दुलेखया ।
स्ववपुरतिमनोहरं हरं दधतमुदीक्ष्य ननाम पाण्डवः ॥

१६ सहशरधि निजं तथा कार्मुकं वपुरतनु तथैव संवर्मितम् ।
निहितमपि तथैव पश्यन्नसिं वृषभगतिरुपाययौ विस्मयम् ॥

१७ सिषिचुरवनिमम्बुवाहाः शनैः सुरकुसुममियाय चित्रं दिवः ।
विमलरुचि भृशं नभो दुन्दुभेर्ध्वनिरखिलमनाहतस्यानशे ॥

१८ आसेदुषां गोत्रभिदो ऽनुवृत्त्या गोपायकानां भुवनत्रयस्य ।
रोचिष्णुरत्नावलिभिर्विमानैर्द्यौराचिता तारकितेव रेजे ॥

१९ हंसा बृहन्तः सुरसद्मवाहाः संह्लादिकण्ठाभरणाः पतन्तः ।
चक्रुः प्रयत्नेन विकीर्यमाणैर्व्योम्नः परिष्वङ्गमिवाग्रपक्षैः ॥

२० मुदितमधुलिहो वितानीकृताः स्रज उपरि वितत्य सांतानिकीः ।
जलद इव निषेदिवांसं वृषे मरुदुपसुखयांबभूवेश्वरम् ॥

२१ कृतधृति परिवन्दितेनोच्चकैर्गणपतिभिरभिन्नरोमोद्गमैः ।
तपसि कृतफले फलज्यायसी स्तुतिरिति जगदे हरेः सूनुना ॥

366

The Lord was even more pleased by his boundless courage   14
than by his ascetic practices. To a man of right
conduct, how much more valuable is inborn courage
than a host of acquired virtues!

Then, beholding Shiva in his own splendid form, his body   15
covered with snow-white ash and his head crowned
with the crescent moon, the Pandava fell prostate
before him.

And the hero with the gait of a bull was amazed to find   16
himself as before, possessed once again of bow and
quivers, powerful frame clad in armor once again,
sword restored to its sheath.

Clouds showered the earth, a gentle rain of many-colored   17
celestial flowers fell from space, and the sound of
unstruck drums[3] filled a sky suddenly grown bright.

As the guardian gods of the three worlds, servants of   18
Indra, arrived in aerial chariots festooned with chains
of glittering jewels, the sky began to sparkle as if it
were studded with stars.

Celestial geese with tinkling bells around their necks flew   19
above, drawing the aerial cars of the gods, and the
birds' spreading wings seemed to embrace all of space.

Fashioning a canopy of garlands strung of celestial flowers   20
swarming with bees, the wind offered comfort to the
Lord, as he sat like a cloud on his bull.

Shiva's spirit attendants, the down on their bodies   21
rising with joy, sang in chorus, praising Indra's son.
Rejoicing at the fruit of his austerity, the hero praised
Shiva in a hymn that held the promise of the most
excellent outcome for his undertaking.[4]

२२ शरणं भवन्तमतिकारुणिकं भव भक्तिगम्यमधिगम्य जनाः ।
जितमृत्यवो ऽजित भवन्ति भये ससुरासुरस्य जगतः शरणम् ॥

२३ विपदेति तावदावसादकरी न च कामसंपदभिकामयते ।
न नमन्ति चैकपुरुषं पुरुषास्तव यावदीश न नतिः क्रियते ॥

२४ संसेवन्ते दानशीला विमुत्त्यै संपश्यन्तो जन्मदुःखं पुमांसः ।
यन्निःसङ्गस्त्वं फलस्यानतेभ्यस्तत्कारुण्यं केवलं न स्वकार्यम् ॥

२५ प्राप्यते यदिह दूरमगत्वा यत्फलत्यपरलोकगताय ।
तीर्थमस्ति न भवार्णवबाह्यं सार्वकामिकमृते भवतस्तत् ॥

२६ व्रजति शुचि पदं त्वयि प्रीतिमान्प्रतिहतमतिरेति घोरां गतिम् ।
इयमनघ निमित्तशक्तिः परा तव वरद न चित्तभेदः क्वचित् ॥

"O invincible Shiva, fount of compassion, gracious to   22
those who approach you with devotion! Men who take
refuge in you are certain of conquering death. Another
wonder: in time of peril, they themselves become
the refuge for the entire universe, encompassing the
worlds of gods and demons!

As long as a man does not honor you with worship, only so   23
long does he remain friendless and vulnerable, only
so long does crippling misfortune strike him, only so
long do his dearest wishes remain unfulfilled, only so
long do other men despise him.

Men who know the pain of birth and death worship you,   24
cultivating deeds of goodwill; they want to attain
liberation. But here is a wonder: you, whose nature
transcends all worldly attachments, fulfill your
devotees' desires out of pure compassion, with not a
tinge of self-interest!

A holy place that one need not travel far in this world to   25
reach; that offers its rewards without one traveling to
the other world; that transcends the ocean of birth
and death, and fulfills every desire: there is none such
apart from you.

Devoted to you, a man is sure to attain the perfect state   26
of liberation from existence, but those with minds
clouded by ignorance are destined for a horrible end.
Perfect Lord, giver of boons, such is the unfolding of
your supreme power as instrumental cause of action
in the cosmos, while your own will remains completely
disengaged.[5]

२७ दक्षिणां प्रणतदक्षिण मूर्तिं तत्त्वतः शिवकरीमविदित्वा ।
रागिणापि विहिता तव भक्त्या संस्मृतिर्भव भवत्यभवाय ॥

२८ दृष्ट्वा दृश्यान्याचरणीयानि विधाय
प्रेक्षाकारी याति पदं मुक्तमपायैः ।
सम्यग्दृष्टिस्तस्य परं पश्यति यस्त्वां
यश्चोपास्ते साधु विधेयं स विधत्ते ॥

२९ युक्ताः स्वशक्त्या मुनयः प्रजानां हितोपदेशैरुपकारवन्तः ।
समुच्छिनत्ति त्वमचिन्त्यधामा कर्माण्युपेतस्य दुरुत्तराणि ॥

३० संनिबद्धमपहर्तुमहार्यं भूरि दुर्गतिभयं भुवनानाम् ।
अद्भुताकृतिमिमामतिमायस्त्वं बिभर्षि करुणामय मायाम् ॥

370

Lord gracious to your devotees! Even if he is enmeshed   27
in worldly passions, even if he does not realize
the beneficent power of your embodiment as
Dakshinamurti, the teacher of wisdom, facing
southward,[6] just by learning to meditate on you with
devotion, a man is certain to be liberated from the
cycle of birth and death.

The man of intelligence and reflection can attain the safe   28
haven of liberation by cultivating right knowledge
and right action. But only that man achieves true
knowledge who achieves the vision of your supernal
form, as the supreme Person; only the man who
worships you is truly a man of right action.

Sages amass power through austerity, and they confer   29
good upon mankind with beneficent teaching. But
when a man gives himself over to *you* in devotion, O
god of immeasurable power, you destroy even the
insuperable consequences of his actions.

Beings in all the worlds live in constant dread of the states   30
of hell into which they are destined to be plunged by
the fetters of action and its consequences. Although
you exist beyond the material universe, maya, because
you wish to rescue them from fear, compassionate
Lord, you manifest yourself through your divine sport
in this marvelous embodied form.[7]

३१   न रागि चेतः परमा विलासिता वधूः शरीरे ऽस्ति न चास्ति
       मन्मथः ।
       नमस्क्रिया चोषसि धातुरित्यहो निसर्गदुर्बोधमिदं तवेहितम् ॥

३२   तवोत्तरीयं करिचर्म साङ्गजं ज्वलन्मणिः सारशनं महानहिः ।
       स्रगास्यपङ्क्तिः शवभस्म चन्दनं कला हिमांशोश्च समं चकासति ॥

३३   अविग्रहस्याप्यतुलेन हेतुना समेतभिन्नद्वयमूर्ति तिष्ठतः ।
       तवैव नान्यस्य जगत्सु दृश्यते विरुद्धवेषाभरणस्य कान्तता ॥

३४   आत्मलाभपरिणामनिरोधैर्भूतसंघ इव न त्वमुपेतः ।
       तेन सर्वभुवनातिग लोके नोपमानमसि नाप्युपेमयः ॥

३५   त्वमन्तकः स्थावरजङ्गमानां त्वया जगत्प्राणिति देव विश्वम् ।
       त्वं योगिनां हेतुफले रुणत्सि त्वं कारणं कारणकारणानाम् ॥

Yogi with a mind free of passion, you are master of the   31
   games of pleasure. Your wife shares your body, but
   you leave no room for desire, the god of love, whom
   you burned to ashes. Every day at dawn you worship
   the creator god, Brahma. Your paradoxes perfectly
   reflect your unfathomable character.
Your upper cloth is a raw, flayed elephant hide, your girdle   32
   a huge snake with a glittering jewel on its forehead. A
   garland of skulls decorates your chest; the crescent
   moon beautifies you, along with sandalwood cream
   and ashes of the dead.
Bodiless by nature, for some unfathomable reason you   33
   display yourself in two bodied forms, one uniting two
   bodies, the other standing alone. There are others in
   the worlds who cultivate odd and contrary dress and
   appearance, but you alone turn contradiction into
   extraordinary allure.
You, who are not born and do not age or die, are unlike   34
   any embodied being. And so, god who transcends the
   universe, how could we compare you with any other
   being, and how could any other being aspire to be
   compared with you?
You bring to an end all things moving and still. Through   35
   you, O god, the whole universe breathes. You stop
   karma and its result for practitioners of yoga. You are
   the cause of the causes of causes.[8]

३६ रक्षोभिः सुरमनुजैर्दिते: सुतैर्वा
यल्लोकेष्वविकलमाप्तमाधिपत्यम् ।
पाविन्याः शरणगतार्तिहारिणे त-
न्माहात्म्यं भव भवते नमस्क्रियायाः ॥

३७ तरसा भुवनानि यो बिभर्ति ध्वनति ब्रह्म यतः परं पवित्रम् ।
परितो दुरितानि यः पुनीते शिव तस्मै पवनात्मने नमस्ते ॥

३८ भवतः स्मरतां सदासने जयिनि ब्रह्ममये निषेदुषाम् ।
दहते भवबीजसंततिं शिखिने ऽनेकशिखाय ते नमः ॥

३९ आबाधामरणभयार्चिषा चिराय
प्लुष्टेभ्यो भव महता भवानलेन ।
निर्वाणं समुपगमेन यच्छते ते
बीजानां प्रभव नमो ऽस्तु जीवनाय ॥

४० यः सर्वेषामावरीता वरीयान्सर्वैर्भावैरनावृतो ऽनादिनिष्ठः ।
मार्गातीतायेन्द्रियाणां नमस्ते ऽविज्ञेयाय व्योमरूपाय तस्मै ॥

४१ अणीयसे विश्वविधारिणे नमो नमो ऽन्तिकस्थाय नमो दवीयसे ।
अतीत्य वाचां मनसां च गोचरं स्थिताय ते तत्पतये नमो नमः ॥

Lord who dispels suffering for your devotees! Whatever   36
sovereign dominion that *rākṣasas* and *dānavas*, gods
and human beings, have achieved in the worlds, all
that is made possible solely through the immensely
powerful act of worshiping you.

The manifestation that supports the worlds with its   37
power, the manifestation that is the source of mantra,
sacred sound embodied as syllable, the manifestation
that destroys every kind of sin, O Shiva, glory to your
manifestation as wind![9]

God who blazes with flames as fire! Glory to you, who   38
burn the seeds of the cycle of birth and death for
men who, seated in the supreme yoga posture that
embodies the transcendent condition of *brahma,*
focus their mind in meditation on you!

Source of all seeds! Glory to your manifestation as   39
water, giver of life, the manifestation in which you
extinguish, for those who worship you with devotion,
the fire of samsara that burns them with the flames of
spiritual anxiety and fear of death!

Glory to you in your manifestation as space, all pervasive,   40
enveloping all things, yourself untouched by any
object in the universe, without origin and end, beyond
the range of sense perception, glory to you, god
beyond all knowing!

Glory to you, god of most subtle form, who yet supports   41
the universe! Glory to you who are both far and near!
Glory, glory, to you who abide beyond the range of
thought and speech and yet rule over thought and
speech!

४२ असंविदानस्य ममेश संविदां तितिक्षितुं दुश्चरितं त्वमर्हसि ।
विरोध्य मोहात्पुनरभ्युपेयुषां गतिर्भवानेव दुरात्मनामपि ॥

४३ आस्तिक्यशुद्धमवतः प्रियधर्म धर्म
धर्मात्मजस्य विहितागसि शत्रुवर्गे ।
संप्राप्नुयां विजयमीश यया समृद्ध्या
तां भूतनाथ विभुतां वितराहवेषु ॥

४४ इति निगदितवन्तं सूनुमुच्चैर्मघोनः
प्रणतशिरसमीशः सादरं सान्त्वयित्वा ।
ज्वलदनलपरीतं रौद्रमस्त्रं दधानं
धनुरुपपदमस्मै वेदमभ्यादिदेश ॥

४५ स पिङ्गाक्षः श्रीमान्भुवनमहनीयेन महसा
तनुं भीमां बिभ्रत्त्रिगुणपरिवारप्रहरणः ।
परीत्येशानं त्रिः स्तुतिभिरुपगीतः सुरगणैः
सुतं पाण्डोर्वीरं जलदमिव भास्वानभिययौ ॥

४६ अथ शशधरमौलेरभ्यनुज्ञामवाप्य
त्रिदशपतिपुरोगाः पूर्णकामाय तस्मै ।
अवितथफलमाशीर्वादमारोपयन्तो
विजयि विविधमस्त्रं लोकपाला वितेरुः ॥

Lord of all knowledge, please forgive the misdeed I have   42
    committed in ignorance, for you are the sole refuge,
    even for wicked men who seek shelter in you and who
    opposed you in their delusion.[10]
Lord of living beings, who love dharma! Give me the   43
    power to gain victory in battle against the enemies
    who have wronged Yudhishthira, son of Dharma the
    god, king who upholds the infallible law laid down in
    Vedic scripture!"
When Indra's son finished his eloquent speech and stood   44
    with head bowed in reverence, the Lord lovingly put
    him at his ease, and transmitted to him the esoteric
    teaching called "The Bow," the mantra embodying the
    knowledge and practice of the Pashupata, the flaming
    weapon of Rudra.[11]
Tawny-eyed, auspicious, with terrifying body ablaze with   45
    an effulgence praised by all the worlds, carrying the
    trident as his weapon, and with gods singing hymns
    of praise for him, the deity that embodied the mantra
    thrice circumambulated Shiva. Then, like the sun
    entering a cloud, he entered the hero, Pandu's son.[12]
Then, to fulfill Arjuna's desire, the world-guardian gods   46
    led by Indra, at a sign from Shiva the moon-crested,
    gave the hero an array of weapons meant to bring
    victory in war, and blessed him with the certainty of
    success.

४७ असंहार्योत्साहं जयिनमुदयं प्राप्य तरसा
धुरं गुर्वीं वोढुं स्थितमनवसादाय जगतः ।
स्वधाम्ना लोकानां तमुपरि कृतस्थानममरा-
स्तपोलक्ष्म्या दीप्तं दिनकृतमिवोच्चैरुपजगुः ॥

४८ व्रज जय रिपुलोकं पादपद्मानतः स-
न्नादित इति शिवेन श्लाघितो देवसंघैः ।
निजगृहमथ गत्वा सादरं पाण्डुपुत्रो
धृतगुरुजयलक्ष्मीर्धर्मसूनुं ननाम ॥

The gods in chorus praised Arjuna, victor with   47
  indomitable energy, who had risen to preeminence
  with his power and stood bearing a heavy yoke for the
  preservation of the world, towering over all the worlds
  with the innate courage of a warrior and blazing with
  the fire of austerity.

When Shiva said, "Go forth and conquer your enemies!"   48
  Pandu's son bowed at the Lord's lotus feet. Then,
  praised by the hosts of gods and bearing the supreme
  majesty of victory, he returned home, and bowed
  before Dharma's son.

ABBREVIATIONS

Arjuna	*Arjuna and the Hunter,* the court epic poem *Kirātārjunīya of Bhāravi*
C	*Kirātārjunīya* Calcutta edition 1913
Ci	*Kirātārjunīya* 1918
C1	*Kirātārjunīya* 1934
G	*Kirātārjunīya* n.d. (2)
J	*Kirātārjunīya* 2008
Kir.	*Kirātārjunīya* of Bhāravi, Sanskrit text
KAŚ	*Arthaśāstra* of Kauṭilya
KĀ	*Kāvyādarśa* of Daṇḍin
KS	*Kāmasūtra* of Vātsyāyana Mallanāga
MBh	*Mahābhārata*
MS	*Manusmṛti*
N	*Kirātārjunīya* 1933
N1	*Kirātārjunīya* 1889
NŚ	*Nāṭyaśāstra* of Bharata
P	*Kirātārjunīya* ms. n.d. (1)
YS	*Yogasūtra* of Patañjali

NOTES TO THE TEXT

१ 1.25d
धियः] P, G; गिरः N, C.

२ 1.43c
रतिम्] परान् G, P, Ci.

३ 1.46b
शिथिलबलम्] P, G; शिथिलवसुम् N, C; शिथिलदशम् Ci.

४ 2.56b
आपदाम्] एनसाम् G, P, Ci.

५ 3.30d
आदेश] P, J, Ci; आदेशम् N, G, C.

६ 4.22b
अपङ्कृता महीम्] P, G; अपङ्कृतां मही N.

७ 8.48d
प्रियाङ्कसंश्लेषम्] P; प्रियाङ्कसंश्लेषम् N, G, C.

८ 9.6b
सायमण्डनम्] C, P; सायमण्डलम् N, G.

९ 14.31d
गणानाम्] C, P; गुणानाम् N, G.

१० 15.17.d
दुरुत्तरः] दुरुत्सहः G.

११ 15.21d
मानिता] मान्यता G.

१२ 15.24b
निर्भिन्न] P, G, J; विभिन्न N.

१३ 15.30b
निविवृत्सतः] G, C; निविवृत्स्यतः N.

१४ 15.51a
महेषून्] परेषून् G; खरेषून् P.

NOTES TO THE TRANSLATION

1. Queen Draupadi Calls for Action

1   Duryodhana, who rules the Kuru kingdom after exiling the Pandavas. Throughout the poem Bharavi also refers to Yudhishthira as "king," although he lives in exile.

2   Foresters and "crafty students" (i.e., a spy disguised as a religious student) are among the persons listed in Kautilya's *Arthaśāstra* (Treatise on Success; *KAŚ*) as suitable spies. See *KAŚ* 1.11.1–2 and 1.12.23. The Pandavas are spending a portion of their forest exile in a hermitage in Dvaitavana.

3   This verse contains an example of *arthāntaranyāsa,* "corroboration," a figure of speech in which a general statement corroborates a particular one; this is one of many instances of the figure appearing in the *Kirātārjunīya.*

4   Manu, first king and lawgiver, said to be the author of *Manusmṛti* (Law Code of Manu). Kautilya (*KAŚ* 1.6.1) names passion, anger, greed, pride, conceit, and excitement as the six passions constituting the set of six enemies of self-restraint for a king.

5   Three of the group of four aims of life that apply to the householder; liberation, the fourth, applies to the renouncer.

6   The figure of speech is *ekāvalī,* "a single row." The descriptor of a theme or object in the first clause or phrase becomes the object of description in the one that follows, and so on, forming a linked "row." Each following item becomes the qualifier of each preceding one.

7   "Seven-leaf": *saptacchada* or *saptapalāśa,* the Indian devil tree, bears clusters of six or seven leaves. Here Bharavi uses a poetic moniker, *ayugmacchada* ("with an odd number of leaves") for the seven-leaf tree.

8   In this verse Mallinatha ingeniously finds a complex example of *śleṣa,* "polysemy," a figure of speech in which words or phrases are used in double or multiple meanings, thus simultaneously applying to more than one object or phenomenon. He reads some words as having two different meanings, and splits others in two different ways to yield different meanings. To give a few examples: *ākhaṇḍalasūnu* is read as "Indra's son" (Arjuna) and

"Indra's younger brother" (the god Vishnu); *vikrama* is read as a single word meaning "heroic deeds" or a compound meaning "the tread (*krama*) of the feet of a bird (*vi*)," here referring to Vishnu's eagle Garuda, sworn enemy of snakes. I have chosen a more straightforward reading, adopted, for example, by the early commentator Prakashavarsha.

9   The word *hasta* is used in two meanings, "hand," and "(elephant's) trunk," enabling the figure of speech *śleṣa* (polysemy).

10 In Sanskrit literary convention royal fortune (*śrī*) is personified as a king's consort. The comparison between a man's wife and royal fortune in this verse is based on the polysemy of the words *kulajā* (born in a noble family, belonging to a royal lineage), *guṇa* (virtues, skill in political policy), and *para* (other men, enemies); the figure of speech is *śleṣa*, "polysemy." The comparison is particularly apt in the context of Draupadi's anger at her shaming in the assembly hall of the Kurus.

11 The wood of the *śamī*, a tree growing in arid regions of India, is quick to burn.

12 "Winner of wealth" (Dhanamjaya), one of Arjuna's epithets, refers to the wealth he won for the Pandavas in many expeditions. One of these was an expedition to Uttarakuru (the Northern Kuru land), a mythic country known for its fabulous riches in gold and silver (*Mbh.* 2.25.7–20).

13 An elaborate example of *śleṣa* (polysemy), involving a number of words, e.g., *jihma* (dim, weak); *vasu* (ray, prosperity), and *dīpti* (light, fighting spirit). The word *lakṣmī* denotes both radiance or glory and royal fortune, personified as the king's consort, and here, as the goddess Lakshmi, consort of the god Vishnu. Bharavi uses the word *lakṣmī* in the final verse in every one of the eighteen chapters, as a marker of propitious outcomes for Arjuna and the Pandavas. He also started a fashion for later poets, who adopted similar "signature" words in the final verses of the chapters in their works.

2. Yudhishthira and Bhima Debate Policy

1   The four knowledge systems are mentioned first in the *Arthaśāstra* (Treatise on Power; *KAŚ*) 1.2.1.

2   Bhima and Yudhisthira's debate over the proper course of action in this chapter revolves around interpretations of the teachings

in the *KAŚ*, Kautilya's manual on political theory. They discuss in particular the course of action of a would-be conqueror in relation to the "circle of kings" (*maṇḍala*) and the "six measures of foreign policy" (*ṣāḍguṇya*), explicated in books 6 and 7 of the *KAŚ*. Bhima's argument, for example, is based on but not identical with Kautilya's discussion of policy regarding an enemy in terms of relative decline and rise (*KAŚ* 7.13–19 and 23–41); verses 8 and 9 employ the technical terminology (e.g., *udaya*, "ascendancy") and Kautilya's elliptical style (e.g., *KAŚ* 7.26).

3   Royal fortune is personified as the consort of kings.

4   The comparison between the waxing moon and the king is enriched by the polysemic use of words, including *kṣaya* (waning/decline) and *svabhāvajaṃ dhāman* (innate light/energy).

5   Kautilya lists military power, energetic action, and counsel as the warrior-conqueror's three resources (*KAŚ* 6.2.33). The army and treasury are two of the seven constituent elements of the state. The following are listed in *KAŚ* 1.15.42 as the five points of deliberation in policy: allies, means for the accomplishment of objectives, determination of time and place, precaution against mishaps, and accomplishment of undertakings.

6   The figure of speech is *kāraṇamālā*, "garland of causes," in which several items are linked by the framework of each preceding item becoming the cause of the item that follows.

7   Celestial elephants hold up the sky in the eight cardinal directions.

8   The attributes of a good speech, some of which are described in vv. 26–28, are drawn from a range of disciplines treating words, sentences, meaning, and disputation, including grammar, hermeneutics, and logic (with its ancillary, science of argument). Verse 26 features the figure of speech *śleṣa* (polysemy), involving double meanings for several words, e.g., *śuci* (clean, pure/free of errors) and *viplava* (blemishes such as rust/violation of standards of proof). Looking in a mirror is believed to bring good luck.

9   The figure of speech in this verse is *arthāntaranyāsa*, "corroboration," where a general statement affirms the truth of a more particular one. This is one of the most famous verses in the *Kirātārjunīya*.

10   The figure here is *ekāvalī*, "single row," a sequence of qualifiers.

11   *Āgama* (science) here means political science (*arthaśāstra*).

12   Yudhisthira draws on *KAŚ* 1.6 and 1.7, where Kautilya discusses

mastery of the senses and control of the passions as elements in the moral training of a king. *Vijigīṣu*, "would-be conqueror," is a technical term.

13 *Śrutam* (science, *śāstra*): political science (*arthaśāstra*).

14 The Pandavas are cousins of the incarnation Krishna, who is a member of the Vrishni (Yadava) clan.

15 For example, the Panchalas (Draupadi's natal family). One related to a king through kinship on either the father's or the mother's side is "an ally by kinship, an innate ally" (*sahaja*), one of three kinds of allies in the circle of kings named in the *KAŚ* (6.2.20); the other two are the "natural ally" (by location) and the "contingent ally," the ally made on account of expediency. Mallinatha interprets the verse somewhat differently, to mean "the friends of the Vrishnis, both kinsmen and those who will not oppose their faction, put up with Dhritarashtra's son for their own interests only, their courtesy to him mere pretense."

16 The figure of speech is *kāraṇamālā*, "garland of causes."

17 "Domain," *maṇḍalam*, is not used here in its technical sense of "circle of kings," as in *KAŚ* book 6. Mallinatha explains, "outer, foreign (forces): kings who are allies, and others; inner: ministers, and others."

18 Living in forest exile, the Pandavas are dressed austerely, in bark cloth, such as that worn by ascetics.

3. Vyasa's Counsel

1 Pandu's wife Kunti conceived Yudhishthira as a gift of Dharma, god of law or justice, also identified as Yama Dharmaraja, god of death.

2 There is a play on the word *rajas*, which means both "dust" and "the quality of passion inherent in material nature."

3 A premarital son conceived by Pandu's wife Kunti as a gift of Surya, the sun god, Karna was brought up by a charioteer and his wife, Radha. Honored by Duryodhana when the Pandavas derided him for his low birth, Karna joined the Kauravas and fought on the Kaurava side in the Mahabharata war.

4 Parashurama ("Rama of the ax"), an incarnation of Vishnu, was born as the son of the Brahman sage Jamdagni. Through his devotion to Shiva, he became master of the martial arts and received an axe. When the king Kartaviryarjuna killed his father,

Parashurama avenged his death by annihilating the Kshatriya clans twenty-one times. A preceptor of the Kuru elders Bhishma and Drona, Parashurama was defeated by his pupil Bhishma, whom he challenged to combat during a dispute over Bhishma's treatment of Amba, a princess of Kashi (*Mbh.* 5.178.12–5.187.4).

5   Karna, born a Kshatriya, learned the science of weapons from Parashurama, who had sworn vengeance against Kshatriyas, by claiming he was a Brahman.

6   Mallinatha explains that this secret mantra (esoteric knowledge, *vidyā*) is presided over by the god Indra.

7   Arjuna's banner displayed an image of the monkey god Hanuman, the hero Rama's helper.

8   One of the goals of yogic contemplation, as explained in the Samkhya ("enumeration") and Yoga philosophical systems, is to be able to have direct and distinct realization of the twenty-four component elements (*tattva*) of the cosmos, discussed in the commentaries on Ishvarakrishna's *Sāṃkhyakārikā* (Verses on Samkhya) 1.3. Purusha, the unaffected self, is the twenty-fifth component.

9   Mallinatha identifies this mountain as "Indra's peak/staff" (*indrakīla*). Indra is known as breaker of mountains (*gotrabhid*), since he cut off the wings of mountains, who once had wings and flew about wreaking destruction in the cosmos.

10   In this simile, Bharavi displays his erudition. The word *ādeśa* is used in two senses: "instruction" and "substitute," a technical term in grammar. The *guhyaka* replaces the sage as a substitute replaces an original formal element (*sthānin*). According to Panini 1.1.56, a grammatical substitute behaves like the original (Abhyankar 1961: 54). Mallinatha misunderstands the verse, saying that the *guhyaka* appeared in the place where Arjuna stood.

11   The word *tamas* is used in two meanings: "darkness" and "grief."

12   The figure of speech is *arthāntaranyāsa*, "corroboration."

13   The *Mahābhārata* narrates Arjuna's acquisition of divine weapons from his preceptor Drona and from several gods. In an episode in which Arjuna and Krishna help Agni, the fire god, burn down the Khandava forest (*Mbh.* 1.214–225), Varuna, god of the waters, gifts Arjuna the great bow Gandiva, two inexhaustible quivers, gandharva horses, and a chariot with a monkey (identified as Hanuman, helper of the hero Rama) on its standard. See Katz 1989: 101, n. 5.

14 Since no enemy had ever seen Arjuna's back, they would not have seen the quivers.

15 A poetic reference to Arjuna's combat with Indra, with the god unable to counter Arjuna's arrows with his thunderbolt, described in the *Mahābhārata* episode of the burning of the Khandava forest (see note to v. 57 above).

16 One of the figures of speech occurring in this verse is *samāsokti*, "concise expression." A detailed description of a phenomenon simultaneously describes another.

4. Autumn Landscape

1 In this chapter Arjuna is portrayed as a sensitive connoisseur (*rasika*) of beauty and physical nature, an ideal of *kāvya* poetry.

2 *Bandhujīvaka* (also *bandhujīva*), a plant with a red flower opening at midday and withering away the next morning, and therefore known as the midday or afternoon flower.

3 In Sanskrit poetic convention peacocks dance in the rainy season.

4 The figure of speech is *arthāntaranyāsa*, "corroboration." Speech in which a person describes natural beauty to their friend or lover while at the scene is an old convention in *kāvya* and older epic poetry, associated with evoking the enjoyment of beauty and enhancing moods.

5 The figure of speech is *arthāntaranyāsa*, "corroboration."

6 The *kadamba* (also *nīpa*) is an evergreen tree with fragrant orange-colored blossoms.

7 Vedic hymns narrate the slaying of Vritra, a snake or dragon, by the god Indra.

8 Cows provide the milk and clarified butter required for the oblation in the Vedic fire-sacrifice to the gods.

9 The figure of speech is *samāsokti*, "concise expression."

10 Balarama is an incarnation of the cosmic serpent Shesha, born as the brother of Krishna, incarnation of Vishnu. Known for his love of wine, Balarama has a pale complexion that contrasts with Krishna's dark one, and the hero carries a plough.

5. The Magnificent Himalaya

1 The tone of this chapter is set in the long description of the Himalaya mountain with which it opens, suggesting the aesthetic emotion (*rasa*) of wonder (*adbhuta*). To facilitate and underscore

the wonder of the mountain, here Bharavi employs a variety of meters, colorful and fantastic imagery, and figures of speech based on play on sounds, words, and patterns. The syntactically connected description of the Himalaya in the first fifteen verses echoes Kalidasa's celebrated opening description of the mountain in his court epic poem *Kumārasaṃbhava* (The Birth of Kumara).

2   Shiva killed the demon elephant, Gajasura, and performed a dance of triumph, holding aloft the dark hide dripping with blood. Laughter is bright white by Sanskrit literary convention.

3   Earth, sky, and the world of the gods are the three principally inhabited worlds in the older set of "three worlds" in the Hindu cosmos.

4   This chapter is dotted with verses featuring figures of complex sound play and alliteration. In addition to alliteration, this verse employs the figure of speech *yamaka*, "meaningful repetition of sequences of syllables," a form of internal rhyme yielding multiple meanings. In *ākaribhiḥ karibhiḥ*, for example, the first instance of the sequence of sounds -*karibhiḥ* is part of a word (*ākaribhiḥ*) meaning "by (banks) that are the source (of gold and minerals)," while the second *karibhiḥ* means "by elephants" (*kari* is one of many words for elephant); likewise, *asamaiḥ*, "incomparable, matchless," is followed by *samaiḥ*, "level."

5   Another *yamaka* verse. The word *mānasa* is used in two senses: the name of the lake (Manasa), and "mind." Born as the daughter of the Himalaya mountain, the goddess Uma, also known as Parvati, wished to marry Shiva, who was immersed in yogic contemplation; she won Shiva's hand in marriage by performing arduous asceticism. As with the description of the Himalaya, in this chapter Bharavi frequently alludes to Kalidasa's description of the wedding of Shiva and Parvati in the *Kumārasaṃbhava* (chapter 7).

6   Deploying a cosmic bow and arrow, Shiva burned down three flying cities or citadels with which three demons played havoc on the universe.

7   Propitiated by the asceticism of King Bhagiratha, the celestial river Ganga descended to earth. Angered when she flooded his hermitage, the sage Jahnu drank her waters up, but released them at Bhagiratha's request.

8   Ganga is waving a flywhisk to serve Himalaya, king of mountains.

Once again the friendly yaksha becomes Arjuna's guide to the beauties of nature, and, in this case, to the mysterious and numinous Himalaya mountain, home of Kubera and his attendants. Kalidasa's lyric poem *Meghadūta* (The Messenger Cloud) concerns a message of love sent by an exiled yaksha to his beloved.

9   The figure of speech is *arthāntaranyāsa,* "corroboration."

10 The figure of speech is *atiśayokti,* "hyperbole."

11 Bhavani, "wife of Bhava (Shiva)," and Gauri, "fair one," are names of the goddess Parvati.

12 Mallinatha links the items cited in this verse as evidence of lovemaking to specific positions of sexual intercourse, such as "Elephant" or "Cat," described in the texts on erotics (*kāmaśāstra*), though these are mostly post-Bharavi.

13 The sweet-voiced koel (*kokila,* Indian black cuckoo) sings in the spring season. The figure of speech is *vibhāvanā,* "effect without cause."

14 The gods and demons churned the celestial milk ocean for ambrosia and other treasures, using Mount Mandara as the churning stick and the serpent Vasuki as the churning rope (*Mbh.* 1.16–18).

15 In addition to sound patterns created by *yamaka* (meaningful repetition of sequences of syllables), this verse features the figure of speech *samāsokti,* "concise expression." The personified bowers themselves instruct the young women to forget heaven.

16 The figure of speech is *bhāvika,* "vivid description," in which a past or future event is vividly described, affording the reader an unmediated apprehension of it. The event described here is the wedding of Shiva and Parvati, and the verse alludes to the goddess's asceticism.

17 See note to 5.27 above.

18 The figure of speech is *bhrāntimat,* "misperception."

19 Kalidasa (*Kumārasaṃbhava* 5.65–81; and 7.30–37) provides fine descriptions of the contrast between the contradictory, even ghoulish accouterments worn by Shiva, such as snakes and ash from the cremation ground, and the feminine and bridal decorations and ornaments worn by his wife, Parvati. On the figure of speech *bhāvika,* "vivid description," see note on 5.29 above.

20 "Thousand-rayed" (*sahasraraśmi*) is one of names of the sun. This is one of many verses in this chapter focusing on images of reflected and refracted light.

21 On Shiva's destruction of the three cities of demons see note on 5.14 above.

22 The figure of speech is *saṃdeha,* "doubt."

23 The figure of speech is *paryāyokti* (also *paryāyokta*), "periphrasis." Something relating to the object at hand is suggested by periphrasis, by describing another, similar object or phenomenon.

24 This lovely image earned Bharavi the soubriquet "Parasol Bharavi" (*ātapatrabhāravi*). The figure of speech is *nidarśanā,* "demonstration." Comparison between an object and a standard draws attention to (i.e., demonstrates) another, parallel comparison for the object.

25 This is an allusion to the Shiva's manifestation as "the lord who is half woman" (Ardhanarishvara). Shiva shares his body with the Goddess Parvati, god and goddess occupying the right and left halves, respectively.

26 The figures of speech are *saṃdeha,* "doubt," and *kāvyaliṅga,* "poetic cause."

27 Mallinatha names "Indrakila" (Indra's mountain) in his comment on this verse, although the name does not appear in the verse itself. "Yellow orpiment": *rocana,* a deep yellow-orange arsenic sulfide mineral. It was used for medicinal and cosmetic purposes.

28 The elaborate comparison of Arjuna's imminent heroic deeds with the Himalaya mountain is enabled by rich polysemy, in the figure of speech *śleṣa,* "polysemy." The verse foreshadows Arjuna's success in his undertaking.

6. Arjuna's Asceticism

1 The figure of speech is *nidarśanā,* "demonstration."

2 From verses 5 through 16, Arjuna continues to be portrayed as a connoisseur, *rasika,* imaginatively appreciating the variety and beauty of nature, gaining both pleasure and insight.

3 In Sanskrit *kāvya* poetry, shelldrake couples (*cakravāka*), doomed to be separated every night, are models of marital devotion. For variations on this theme, see *Kir.* 8.56, 9.13, 9.14, and 9.30.

4 The figure of speech is *arthāntaranyāsa,* "corroboration." Arjuna in his persona as Nara performed asceticism for thousands of years in the Badari hermitage with Narayana (the god Vishnu). The Nara-Narayana theme is reprised in chapter 12.

5 "Dark impurity": dark inertia (*tamas*) is one of the three innate

qualities of matter, the other two being lucidity (*sattva*) and energy or passion (*rajas*).

6   Mallinatha notes that Arjuna's practice involves mind, speech, and body, the three instruments of worship.

7   The idea is that a powerful ruler must not betray his emotions.

8   The figure of speech is *parikara*, "significant epithets."

9   There is a play on the word *rajas* (passion, dust).

10   The figure of speech is *arthāntaranyāsa*, "corroboration."

7. The Journey of the Apsarases and Gandharvas

1   Here the apsarases ride in celestial aerial cars (the gods' *vimānas*); these are imagined to be chariotlike, but the gandharvas accompany them in true chariots (*ratha*), forming part of an army.

2   The gandharvas' chariots are now described as "flying cars" (*vimāna*).

3   An allusion to a myth of winged mountains. When these mountains flew about wreaking havoc in the cosmos, Indra chased them and cut off their wings with his thunderbolt, but a few of them escaped by hiding in the ocean's bed. See *Kir.* 3.29.

4   Peacocks are said to dance in the rainy season.

5   The figure of speech is *parivṛtti*, "exchange." There is an exchange of attributes between the object at hand and another.

6   The roots of the madder plant (*māñjiṣṭha*) were used to produce a red dye.

7   On peacocks and rain, see note 4 on 5.22 above.

8. Playing in the Woods and the River Ganga

1   This refers to the "camp" that the gandharvas and apsarases set up when they landed on Indrakila, described in chapter 7. Nevertheless, it is described as an abiding (*sanātana*) city. Here they leave the camp to play in the woods. Note, however, that there is mention of mansions once again in chapter 9, in the sections on sunset and lovemaking. Bharavi's description of the erotic dalliance of the demigods in chapters 8 and 9 closely relates to the treatment of this theme in the treatises on erotics (*Kāmasūtra, KS*) and theater (Bharata's *Nāṭyaśāstra, NŚ*).

2   Literally, "each one with her partner" (*yathāyatham*).

3   The *aśoka* is a small evergreen tree with bright green leaves.

4   *Kalpalatā*, a fabulous creeper that can grant a person's wishes.

5 Mallinatha, wrongly, I think, places v. 7 in the voice of a lover speaking to his beloved, and v. 8 in the voice of the girlfriends. Following Prakashavarsha, I read the two verses together, as representing the girlfriends addressing a young woman, who is torn between desire and pride.

6 The figure of speech is *svabhāvokti,* "naturalistic description."

7 This is an abbreviated version of the conventional "toes to head" description of women.

8 A new descriptive topic, that of courtly lovers playing in the water (*jalakrīḍā*), begins with this verse.

9 The figure of speech is *saṃdeha,* "doubt."

10 Most women use mascara for beauty, but the apsarases had no need of it for that purpose, for the beauty remained even when the mascara was gone (i.e., the only reason they used it must have been to keep the redness down).

11 "Water-drenched bodies": that is, with decoration washed away. The figure of speech is *viṣama,* "incongruous" (here the incongruity lies in the wet bodies' ability to burn the rivals' eyes).

12 There are two figures of speech in this verse: *sāmānya* (identity, absence of distinction) and *yathāsaṃkhya* (relative order). *Gaura,* "fair," denotes a golden color, hence the comparison with saffron. In *yathāsaṃkhya* a number of objects are connected with an equal number of objects or attributes, named in respective order.

13 The figure of speech is *mīlana,* "concealment."

14 The night also (by literary convention) separates the male and female ducks and disturbs the ponds by forcing the lotuses to close.

9. The Lovemaking of the Apsarases and Gandharvas

1 The night revels of the lovers are portrayed in the conventional *kāvya* sequence of scenes of courtly love—sunset, nightfall, moonrise, the preparations for a night of lovemaking, messages, lover's quarrels, drinking sessions, and acts of love; the sequence ends with daybreak.

2 An elaborate example of the figure of speech *śleṣa,* "polysemy," this verse features a number of words used in two meanings and applied to the sun's enfeebled rays, on the one hand, and men who have lost their master, on the other.

3 *Kara,* the word used in this verse for the sun's rays, can also mean "hand." The "hands" have turned red from clutching at the trees—

to no avail, it seems, since the sun falls down.

4   The theme of devoted shelldrake couples, ordained to part at nightfall, is varied in several verses in this chapter in the context of descriptions of sunset and nightfall (9.13, 14, and 30). See also *Kir.* 6.8 and 8.56.

5   The figure of speech is *saṃdeha,* "doubt."

6   A reference to Shiva's dance after killing the elephant demon Gajasura. Smeared with ash, Shiva's body is white, in contrast to the dark elephant hide he holds up in his arms. See also *Kir.* 5.2.

7   In the third of his ten incarnations the god Vishnu manifested himself as a cosmic boar and retrieved the earth from the ocean, where it had been hidden by the demon who stole it.

8   By comparing the moon's color with the red-gold of saffron cream on a woman's breast, and the golden orb of the moon with a golden jar, Bharavi also hints at the conventional comparison of a woman's breast with a jar.

9   The figure of speech is *vibhāvanā,* "effect without cause."

10   For the myth of the gods and demons churning the milk ocean for ambrosia, see note to *Kir.* 5.27. *Mbh.* 1.16.21 describes trees flying off from Mount Mandara as the ocean is churned by the mountain.

11   Moods: the aesthetic emotions (*rasa*).

12   The texts on erotics, drama, and poetics list gooseflesh and perspiration among the involuntary signs of emotion (*sāttvikabhāva*) manifested by lovers. See *NŚ* 7.93–106.

13   The figure of speech is *saṃdeha,* "doubt."

14   Here, as in v. 9.38, the thrilling of the skin is a sign of involuntary emotion. *Ābhimukhya* is used in both literal and metaphorical senses: "facing another person" and "being favorable to someone."

15   The figure of speech is *sahokti,* "accompaniment"; an object or action is stated to be accompanied by another.

16   The nail marks and love bites left by the male lover are staples of erotic description in Sanskrit poetry. For a taxonomy of nail wounds and love bites, see *KS* 2.4.1.31; and 2.5.1–18.

17   In the sequence describing the drinking party of the gandharvas and apsarases (vv. 51–73), Bharavi uses a number of words for "wine" or "liquor," suggesting a variety of drinks without, however, being precise in his terminology. I have used the generic "wine" throughout.

18   *Cārutā,* the word used for "beauty" in this verse, is feminine in

gender, whereas *madhumada,* "drunkenness," is masculine.

19 That is, misplaced on the lovers' bodies because of drunkenness.

20 In literary convention, girlfriends comfort women, distressed at parting from their loves at the end of a night of lovemaking, by showing the nail wounds and other marks left on their bodies from love bouts.

10. A Failed Seduction

1 Velvety red mites (*indragopa*) cover grassy ground in the rainy season.

2 In Sanskrit *kāvya* poetry the call of the wild goose (*haṃsa*) is a standard comparison for the sound of a woman's anklet.

3 Two of the emblems of a universal emperor.

4 Mental and physical restraints (*yama*) and ritual observances (*niyama*) are the first two "limbs" of the eight steps of the practice of yoga (*aṣṭāṅgayoga*) (*YS* 2.29).

5 A considerable portion of the *Atharva Veda,* the fourth Veda, is devoted to mantras and rituals concerned with magic and healing; included are formulae concerning warfare, and charms and potions of various kinds.

6 The figure of speech is *ekāvalī,* "a single row."

7 The figure of speech is *virodha,* "contradiction." An object or phenomenon is said to combine conflicting attributes.

8 The six seasons of the Indian year are spring, summer, the rainy season, autumn, early winter, and late winter. Each of the seasons is associated with particular birds, flowers, and the like, but also with human emotions and activities, and phases of love.

9 The signs of the rainy season are described in vv. 19–23.

10 In this chapter Bharavi names varieties of jasmine appropriate to particular seasons. The *mālatī* jasmine blooms in the rainy season.

11 By poetic convention the rainy season is associated with longing and the suffering of lovers parted from each other. The figure of speech is *arthāntaranyāsa,* "corroboration."

12 *Kumuda* usually, but not always, indicates a red water lily species. Kalidasa describes the Goddess Uma holding an arrow in her hand at her wedding ceremony (*Kumārasaṃbhava* 7.8). The word *bāṇa* is used in two meanings: "arrow" and "*bāṇa* flower".

13 The figure of speech is *arthāntaranyāsa,* "corroboration." Joyful peacocks and blooming *kadamba* trees are associated with the

rains, while wild geese and blooming lotuses are attributes of the autumn season.

14 On red rain mites (*indragopa*) see note to 10.3. The flame-of-the-forest or flame tree is *kiṃśuka* (also *palāśa*).

15 The *phalinī* (also *priyaṅgu*) is a bush or creeper with purple and white flowers.

16 *Sinduvāra* or *nirguṇḍī*, a large aromatic tree with small purple or white flowers.

17 The figure of speech is *samāsokti*, "concise expression."

18 The figure of speech is *arthāntaranyāsa*, "corroboration."

19 The figure of speech is *viṣama*, "incongruous." *Viṣama* illuminates the incongruity between an object and its attributes.

20 In vv. 41–43 Bharavi invokes several aspects of Bharata's theory, in *NŚ*, of *abhinaya*, the representation of emotions (*bhāva*) through hand gestures (*hasta*), body movement, and expressions of the face and eyes in dance and drama, to culminate in the suggestion of aesthetic emotion (*rasa*). The point in this verse is that the dancers' hands fail to carry out the foremost ideal of *abhinaya*, cited by Mallinatha, namely: "Where the gesture points, the eye must follow."

21 The figure of speech is *bhrāntimat*, "misperception."

22 There is a pun on the word *rāga*, "desire, red color"; desire is red, like the designs of lac painted on the dancers' feet. The stage or ground is worshiped with flowers and other offerings in the ritual of *raṅgapūjā* (worship of the stage) at the beginning of a performance of dance or drama (*NŚ* 3).

23 The figure of speech is *paryāya*, "sequence," the description of the progression of an object in many locations, or of many objects appearing sequentially in a single location.

24 The figure of speech is *arthāntaranyāsa*, "corroboration."

25 The figure of speech is *arthāntaranyāsa*, "corroboration."

11. Indra Tests Arjuna

1 In this chapter Bharavi evokes the *Bhagavadgītā* in many ways: first, by his use of the *śloka* meter, the meter of the two old epics, including the *Bhagavadgītā*, embedded in the *Mahābhārata*. In the *Bhagavadgītā* Krishna teaches Arjuna, who is reluctant to fight against his cousins and kinsmen in the Mahabharata war, that he must fight. In *Kir.* chapter 11, the situation is reversed. Indra tries

to tempt Arjuna to give up his weapons and become an ascetic, but Arjuna strongly refuses, citing his duty to gain weapons from gods and fight in the war. In his exhortation to Arjuna to give up his weapons and commit himself to peaceful asceticism (11.10–36) Indra condemns sensual desire and attachment to wealth, using the language of Hindu and Buddhist ascetic texts, which are cast in the *śloka* meter.

2   "Father" is a common form of address for an old man, but here there is an intended irony as well, since Arjuna does not know that this man is in fact his father, Indra.

3   "Kinsmen": A *dāyāda* is literally a lineal kinsman who shares or competes with a person for inheritance rights. The figure of speech is *parikara*, "significant epithets."

4   Mallinatha explains *satyaṃkāra* as an amount of money or other goods paid in advance, either to secure the services of another or to pay in advance, as guarantee, a portion of the amount owed for a service.

5   Both because they cannot bear to do so and because Draupadi has turned away. The courtiers are the sun; Duhshasana the tree; Draupadi, whom he is dragging toward the assembly, the tree's shadow, which turns away from the tree under the gaze of the evening sun but cannot break loose. See *Kir.* 15.33.

6   This idea appears frequently in the *Kir.* See, for example, 11.72–73.

7   "Bright": *śubhra*, literally "white." In Sanskrit literary convention, fame (*yaśas*) is white in color, hence the frequent comparison between fame and the moon.

8   Arjuna refers to the sequence of the four stages of a man's life, the ways of life of a celibate student, householder, forest dweller, and renouncer.

9   The verse resonates with a verse in *Bhagavadgītā* 6.38, where Arjuna asks Krishna about the fate of the man who has neither faith nor discipline of action: "Doomed by this double failure, is he not like a cloud split apart (*chinnābhram iva*)?"

12. Shiva's Noble Plan

1   The description of Arjuna's austerities includes examples of the extreme or harsh practices enjoined for ascetics. See, for example, *MS* 6.22–28. The effects of the hero's *tapas* are of cosmic magnitude.

2 This is one of the many forms of self-mortification enjoined upon ascetics undertaking specific vows.

3 The figure is *arthāntaranyāsa*, "corroboration."

4 The yogi cultivates, first, the dominance of the quality of lucidity (*sattva*) over active passion (*rajas*) and inertia (*tamas*), the two other innate qualities of material nature (*prakṛti*), but absolute freedom from karma-samsara comes about only when "the lucidity of material nature and spirit are in pure equilibrium" (*YS* 3.55; "Spirit" is Purusha, the self as pure consciousness).

5 The figure of speech is *atiśayokti*, "hyperbole."

6 Men of the three upper social classes (Brahman, Kshatriya, and Vaishya) wear a sacred thread crosswise on the upper torso; they are invested with the thread at the ritual of initiation.

7 The figure of speech is *nidarśanā*, "demonstration."

8 The ascetic Shiva wears his hair in matted locks. On the three-eyed god's destruction of the three demon cities with a fiery arrow, see note to 5.14 above.

9 The figure of speech is *apahnava* (also known as *apahnuti*), "denial."

10 The figure of speech is *virodhābhāsa*, "apparent contradiction," a subtype of the figure "contradiction."

11 The figure of speech is *mālopamā*, "garland of similes." A comparison between an object and a standard is illuminated by two or more comparisons between other objects and standards, paralleling the one in question.

12 In v. 24, Bharavi imaginatively portrays interactions among three of the many objects Shiva wears on his matted hair—the white waters of the river Ganga, whose descent to earth he softened by catching its torrent in his spread-out hair; the crescent moon with its white light; and the skull, white as jasmine, but also compared to a white lotus (*puṇḍarīka*).

13 The figure of speech is *arthāntaranyāsa*, "corroboration." The epigram echoes *MS*. 240.

14 Vishnu is the primal Person, Purusha. In his form as Narayana he practiced asceticism in the Badari hermitage for thousands of years with the sage Nara ("Man"), a previous incarnation of Arjuna.

15 The creator god Brahma is seated on a lotus that grows out of Vishnu's navel when the god, as Narayana, lying in the cosmic ocean, stimulates a cycle of time with the creation of the universe.

16 Yaks were prized for their tail hairs, from which flywhisk fans were made.

17 In poetic convention lions and elephants are natural enemies.

18 Spikenard or nard (*nalada* or *jaṭāmāṃsī*) is a flowering plant whose stems are used for cosmetic and medicinal purposes. *Śilākusuma* usually indicates the storax plant or mountain balsam from whose bark a fragrant black resin is extracted. Mallinatha, however, identifies *śilākusuma* in this verse as *śaileya,* a word that can denote lichen or certain other plants. The description here, of bits of parrot-green *śilākusuma,* suggests that "lichen" is indeed the preferable reading. For *śaileya,* meaning "lichen," see Kalidasa, *Kumārasaṃbhava.* 1.55.

13. *The Boar's Attack and the Hunter's Claim*

1 Ashavasena and his father, Takshaka, king of snakes, lived in the Khandava forest, which was burned down by Arjuna, Krishna, and Agni.

2 The figure of speech is *śleṣa,* "polysemy." Several words are used in two senses. *Bheda:* breaking (physically) and destroying the enemy, by instigating dissension and the like; *śuddha:* clean (in the case of the arrow, without a poisoned tip) and honest; *guṇa:* bowstring and quality.

3 Another elaborate *śleṣa* verse, in which several words are used in two senses.

4 A reference to Shiva's destruction of the cities of the demons. See *Kir.* 5.14 and 12.14.

5 A simile from grammar; the phonemes used in the grammar of Panini and other Sanskrit grammarians as coded markers (*anubandha*) at the end of uninflected entities such as verb roots and noun bases are elided when an affix is added to the base.

6 Garuda, the eagle mount of the god Vishnu, is the proverbial enemy of great snakes (*nāgas*) who live in the underworld.

7 Shiva's forehead eye emits fire.

8 When Kama, god of love, disturbed his yogic meditation, Shiva burned him with fire emitted from his third eye, but later revived the god. From here on, Bharavi uses a new meter, marking the change in theme and scene.

9 The figure of speech in verses 52 and 53 is *vyatireka,* "superiority." The superiority of the object over the standard of comparison is asserted.

10 This is a reference to the alliance Rama, prince of Ayodhya and

hero of the Ramayana, made with Sugriva, king of the monkeys.
Rama helped Sugriva regain his kingdom (*Kishkindha*), by killing
his brother and rival Vali; Sugriva sent the monkeys to search for
Rama's abducted wife, Sita, and eventually to help him kill the
demon king Ravana in battle and regain Sita.

11 Parashurama, son of the Brahman ascetic Jamadagni, mastered the
science of weapons in order to avenge an insult done to his father
by warriors. See note to *Kir.* 3.18.

14. Arjuna Defeats Shiva's Army of Spirits

1 Such speech is nothing less than Sarasvati, the goddess who
presides over speech, pure and of dignified gait and lovely with a
bright face and ornaments. Several words used in two meanings,
beginning with *bhāratī,* "speech," and "Sarasvati, goddess of
speech," enable this comparison.

2 Flattery and bribery—more kindly referred to as "conciliation" and
"gifts"—are two of the four expedients of foreign policy advocated
in the *Arthaśāstra* (*KAŚ*) and other texts on politics. The remaining
two expedients are causing division and war.

3 Arjuna speaks of the *Mahābhārata* episode in which the hero and
Indra help Agni, the fire god, to burn the Khandava forest.

4 The reference is to Vishnu's incarnation as *varāha,* the primeval
boar. See *Kir.* 9.22.

5 The simile of the reflected sun is used in the Advaita Vedanta
philosophy to explain the relationship between the essential real
and the world appearance.

6 The figure of speech is *śleṣa,* "polysemy." Several words used in
two meanings enable detailed comparison between Arjuna's
battle fury and his volley of arrows. E.g., *vidūraga:* in the case of
arrows, "flying far," in the case of strategies, "deeply penetrating
the enemy's secrets and defenses"; *bṛhatphala:* in the case of the
arrows, "having elongated tips," in the case of strategies, "gaining
excellent results."

7 Shiva's spirit troops are immortal.

8 The *Nāṭyaśāstra* (7.21) names energy (*utsāha*), developing into
battle fury in the appropriate contexts, as the stable emotion that
gives rise to the heroic (*vīra*) aesthetic emotion.

9 The figure of speech is *mālopamā,* "garland of similes."

15. Arjuna's Combat with Shiva

1   In this chapter Bharavi alternates verses with figures of speech focusing on meaning (*arthālaṃkāra*), with verses featuring "pattern" (*citra*) figures, which feature visual and verbal patterns of various kinds, from simple repetitions of syllables to tours de force in geometric and mathematical symmetries.

2   This verse is framed on the pattern figure *ekākṣarapāda,* "variation on a single syllable in each verse quarter." A single consonant, joined with various vowels, is employed in each quarter of the verse. Here the consonants are (a) *s;* (b) *y;* (c) *l;* and (d) *ś.* Verses 1 and 3 contain instances of the figure of speech *yamaka,* "meaningful repetition of sequences of syllables."

3   This verse employs the pattern figure *nirauṣṭhya,* "without labial sounds"; consonants of the labial class *(p, ph, b, bh,* and *m)* are intentionally omitted.

4   This verse features instances of the figure *yamaka,* "meaningful repetition of sequences of syllables."

5   Another verse with *yamaka* sequences: e.g., *mārgaṃ mārgam;* the first word is an adjective, meaning "of animals (*mṛga*)," the second is a noun signifying "road," "trail," or "path."

6   The geometrical pattern figure featured in this verse is *gomūtrikā,* "cow piss," so called because the crisscross pattern formed by the collocation of syllables in the verse imitates the zigzag pattern of a cow's urination.

7   Shiva's *gaṇa* spirits are varied in appearance.

8   The pattern figure is *ekavyañjana,* "single consonant." As the name indicates, the verse exclusively uses a single consonant, here the consonant "n." Because of the complex rules of euphonic combination, the orthography of words thus linked can be ambiguous in Sanskrit. Mallinatha's reading of the verse is based on the specific way in which he splits the words, in their precombination forms: *na nā ūnanunnaḥ nunnonaḥ* (a) *nā anā nānānanāḥ nanu* (b) *nunnaḥ anunnaḥ nanunnenaḥ* (c) *nā anenāḥ nunnanunnanut* (d) (a,b, c, and d mark the ends of the verse quarters).

9   The figure of speech is *dṛṣṭānta,* "example" or "illustration." A statement made in one sentence in the verse is supported by a second statement, which also provides an example of the phenomenon.

10   Here we have the pattern figure *samudgaka,* "box" or "casket" (not mentioned by Mallinatha), as well as *yamaka* and the figure of speech *yathāsaṃkhya,* "relative order." In *samudgaka,* the first and second halves of the verse have the identical sequence of syllables, but the two halves mean different things, owing to the differing division of words or of differing meanings given to the words.

11   The pattern figure here is *pratilomānulomapāda,* "quarter-verse palindrome," in which each quarter verse can be read as a palindrome, that is, the sequence of syllables within each quarter verse is identical when read forward and backward.

12   The pattern figure is *pratilomānulomārdha,* "half-verse palindrome," in which each half verse can be read as a palindrome, that is, the sequence of syllables within each half verse is identical when read forward and backward.

13   Verses 22 and 23 together form the pattern figure *pratilomena ślokadvayam,* "inversions," a pair of verses that should be read as inversions of one another, the first verse reading forward and the second reading backward. Verse 23 thus provides a reversed image of v. 22.

14   Verse 25, *devākānini kāvāde,* features the pattern figure *sarvatobhadra,* "double palindrome," or "good from all sides, auspicious in all ways." This is a double palindrome, that is, a verse, "having the same number of lines as syllables, which can be read backwards and forwards both vertically and horizontally" (Gerow 1971: 189). As Mallinatha points out, the figure can be represented within a square of eight lines and sixty-four boxes, with a syllable occupying each box, and a quarter verse (eight syllables) forming a line. The verse is written twice, from beginning to end, from the top line of the square to the fourth line; and from end to beginning in the remainder of the square.

    de vā kā ni ni kā vā de
    vā hi kā sva sva kā hi vā
    kā kā re bha bha re kā kā
    ni sva bha vya vya bha sva ni

The figure *ardhabhramaka,* "half rotation" occurs in v. 27: "A type of word play in which a verse, each of whose four *pādas* (quarters) is written in a separate line, can be read either in the normal way or as a helix, from outer verticals inwards" (Gerow 1971: 178). Unlike the double palindrome the "half rotation" can only be read forward.

sa sa ttva ra ti de ni tyaṃ
sa da rā ma rṣa nā śi ni
tva rā dhi ka ka san nā de
ra ma ka tva ma ka rṣa ti

15 Like v. 7 above, an example of *nirauṣṭhya*, "without labial sounds."

16 This verse features *pādādyantayamaka*, "*yamaka* syllabic repetition at the beginning and end of a verse quarter," a variety of *yamaka* in which identical syllable sequences appear, with different meanings, at the beginning and end of each quarter (*pāda*) of the verse.

17 The figure is *dvicaturthayamaka*, "*yamaka* syllabic repetition of the second and fourth verse quarters"; the second and fourth quarters of the verse consist of identical syllable sequences.

18 A verse featuring *pādādyantayamaka*, "*yamaka* syllabic repetition at the beginning and end of a verse quarter," like v. 31 above.

19 Employing variations on syllabic sequences employing only the consonants *c* and *r* (and the palatal nasal *ñ*), this is an example of the figure *dvyakṣara*, "limited to two syllables (and consonant-vowel combinations)." Verses using this pattern figure consist of variations on syllabic sequences employing only two consonants.

20 Here we have *śṛṅkhalāyamaka*, "linking *yamaka*," in which the verse quarters are linked to each other by repeated syllable sequences.

21 In the figure *gūḍhacaturthapāda*, "hidden in the fourth quarter" selected syllables from the first three verse quarters appear in a scrambled pattern in the last quarter.

22 The pattern figure is *arthatrayavācin*, "to be read three ways." This verse can be read to yield three different meanings, by splitting "*nāgarāja ivābabhau*," the phrase forming the fourth quarter of the verse, in three different ways and in three senses, and by assigning different meanings to the remaining words in the verse. According to Mallinatha, in the first reading (45a), Arjuna is compared to the Himalaya, king of mountains: *nā agarāja iva ābabhau*. In the second (45b), he is compared to Airavata, Indra's white elephant: *nāgarāja iva ābabhau*, taking *nāgarāja* to mean "king of elephants (*nāga*)." In the third (45c), Arjuna is compared to Shesha, Vishnu's serpent couch. Here *nāgarāja* is read to mean "king of serpents (*nāga*)." Other commentators give other possible readings for the remainder of the verse.

23 Verses 47–48 are in the *vaitālīya* meter, with ten syllables in the first and third quarters and eleven in the second and fourth.
24 Verses 49–51 are in the *vaṃśastha* meter, with twelve syllables to the quarter verse.
25 This verse features the figure *ardhāvali*, "half repetition," a type of *yamaka* in which the sequence of syllables in the first half of the verse (quarters a and b) is identical with that in the second half of the verse, but yields a different meaning.
26 The figure is a *mahāyamaka*, "great syllabic repetition" or "grand *yamaka*," a pattern figure in which all four quarters of the verse feature an identical sequence of syllables, with each sequence yielding a different meaning.
27 That is, even though as men of true insight, they knew that Arjuna was a partial incarnation of Vishnu.

16. A Contest with Supernatural Weapons

1 In vv. 2–24 Arjuna comments on and speculates about the unusual nature of his battle with Shiva's troops, the extraordinary powers of his hunter opponent, and his own inability to counter him. The phrase "in this battle" is either explicitly used or should be understood in vv. 1–18.
2 The *mandāra* or coral tree is said to grow in Indra's paradise.
3 A reference to the myth of winged mountains. See *Kir.* 3.29 and 7.20.
4 Measuring the universe in three steps in his incarnation as the dwarf who turned into the cosmic strider, Vishnu placed his first step on earth and the second on the sky.
5 The figure of speech is *śleṣa*, "polysemy," based on the use of several words in two meanings: *guṇa:* bowstring, qualification, virtues, worth; *guru:* hefty, noble; *sthira:* firm, reliable; *sāra:* substance, capability; *anuśīlana:* use, acquaintance.
6 Mallinatha says that the crescent moon, one of the objects adorning Shiva's head, was invisible because the god was disguised as a hunter. We may think of the golden light as simply obscuring the light of the moon.
7 Prakashavarsha notes the comparison with the torrential descent of the river Ganga from the sky world onto Shiva's matted hair.
8 Shiva's throat turned blue-black when he drank the poison emitted by the snake Vasuki when the gods and demons churned the cosmic ocean for treasure.

17. The Loss of Arjuna's Weapons

1   Bharavi begins this chapter with a description of Arjuna in a sequence of six grammatically connected verses, the first five of which focuses on an aspect of the hero's state of mind as he continues his single-handed combat with Shiva and his troops.

2   When the Ganga descended from the celestial region to aid King Bhagiratha, who had performed austerities to bring her down to purify the ashes of his ancestors, Shiva softened the impact of the river's descent by catching the torrent in his matted hair.

3   The figure of speech is *śleṣa,* "polysemy." Several words are used in two meanings to enable the comparison between arrows and counselors: *saṃskāravattva:* "having ancient associations" and "being polished or honed"; *prayoga:* "grammatical usage," "application"; and *śikṣā:* "stylistic virtues," "practice."

4   A pun on *hasta* (hand, an elephant's trunk) enriches the comparison. Kama, the god of love, was burned to ashes by fire from Shiva's forehead eye.

5   The figure of speech is *mālopamā,* "garland of similes."

6   The figure of speech is *kāraṇamālā* "garland of causes." A "scent elephant" (*gandhahastin*) is a particularly esteemed type of elephant, born in the spring season, whose very scent (and not just the smell of ichor) subdues or agitates other elephants (*Mātaṅgalīlā* 1.40).

7   "The single moon appears double": a stock simile adduced in various systems of Indian philosophy to explain perceptions of multiplicity (false cognition).

8   The simile of the reflected sun is used in the monist Vedanta philosophy to explain the relationship between the essential real and the world appearance. See *Kir.* 14.41.

9   The figure of speech is *arthāntaranyāsa,* "corroboration."

10   An elaborate instance of the figure of speech *śleṣa,* pivoting on the double meanings of several words and phrases: *ṛju:* "unerring" and "possessing moral integrity"; *aparvan:* "without joints" and "the wrong time"; and *bhaṅga:* "breakage" and "downfall."

11   The phrase *avāṅmukhībhūtaphala-* yields two meanings: "whose heads face downward" and "who have failed in their mission."

12   The figure of speech is *mālopamā,* "garland of similes," stretching over two verses.

13   The figure of speech is *nidarśanā,* "demonstration, teaching a lesson," in which an action teaches a lesson.

14 Angered when the river Ganga (see *Kir.* 17.5) flooded his hermitage, the sage Jahnu drank up her waters, but released them at Bhagiratha's request.

15 *Pitiable in his deeds: "vikārmukaḥ karmasu śocanīyaḥ"*: Bharavi draws a fanciful etymological connection, based on similarity in sound, between *kārmuka* (a bow) and *karma* (deed).

18. Wrestling Match, Theophany, and Boon

1 *Udagra:* a type of mountain elephant whose head is higher than its withers, considered to be the best fighting elephant (*Mātaṅgalīlā* 50–51, n20.).

2 Arjuna grabs Shiva's feet in a wrestler's maneuver, intending to throw his opponent. However, "grasping the feet" (*caraṇagrahaṇa*) can also be interpreted as the devotee's gesture of taking refuge in the deity. Shiva is pleased with Arjuna's heroism as well as what might be interpreted as his devotion (bhakti).

3 The reference is most likely to the sound of celestial drums, generated spontaneously to mark Arjuna's miraculous restoration and Shiva's grace. The concept of unstruck sound (*anāhatanāda*) as a mystical center of power in the human body was developed in post-Bharavi Tantra and Yoga (e.g., *haṭhayoga*) philosophical thought.

4 Arjuna's hymn in praise of Shiva is a fine example of Sanskrit *kāvya*-style poems of praise and glorification (*stotra*), usually addressed to gods. Bharavi achieves a tour de force by framing the verses in a variety of meters.

5 "Instrumental cause" *nimittaśakti:* in many schools of Shaiva theology, Shiva's power unfolds as activity in the universes, but Shiva is never the *material* cause of action. Bharavi's point is the detachment of Shiva's will from the unfolding of action as karma. In this verse, and in vv. 27–30, 35 and vv. 37–42, Bharavi draws on metaphysical concepts and technical terms from sectarian traditions focused on Shiva, especially the Shaiva *āgama* scriptures and ritual treatises and Shaiva Siddhanta theological texts.

6 Bharavi plays on the word *dakṣiṇa* (gracious, pleasing, facing south). Shiva's embodiment as Dakshinamurti (*dakṣiṇāmūrti*), the god facing south, who meditated, seated beneath a banyan tree, and instructed sages in the knowledge of the Vedas and *āgamas*. This form of Shiva was popular in south Indian Shaiva religion and iconography from the Pallava era onward. See Rao 1985a: 273–292.

7 The concept of karma as fetters (*pāśa*) is central to Shaiva Siddhanta theology. "Divine sport" is *līlā*. Shiva paradoxically exists beyond the material universe (maya), yet manifests himself in wondrous (maya) forms.

8 Shiva is the originator of the subtle causes, or atoms, of all things.

9 In vv. 37–40 Arjuna praises Shiva in his manifestations as wind, fire, water, and ether (space). These are four of a set of eight manifestations.

10 The theology and literature of south Indian, especially Tamil, bhakti abounds in narratives of devotees who resisted or opposed Shiva and were blessed with his grace. A prominent example is the Tamil Shaiva poet saint Sundaramurti Nayanar. See Peterson 1989: 302–322.

11 Bharavi's description of the Pashupata weapon, also known as the "Pashupata weapon of Rudra" in v. 45 below, is very close to the iconic representation of the weapon provided in the *Aṃśumadbhedāgama*, section 71 (Rao 1985c: 59). For a detailed discussion see Rao 1985b: 125.

12 Bharavi describes the embodied deity of the mantra Shiva has bestowed on Arjuna as *triguṇaparivārapraharaṇa*, "carrying a weapon that embodies the ensemble of the three attributes of material nature (lucidity, passion, and quiescence)." The *Kāmikāgama* identifies Shiva's trident (*triśūla*) as the weapon that embodies these attributes (Rao 1985a: 293).

GLOSSARY

āgama Medieval liturgical and sectarian texts related to the worship of Hindu gods such as Shiva

AIRAVATA (*airāvata*) A mythic white elephant, mount of the god Indra

ANDHAKA "Blind one," a demon slain by Shiva

APSARAS A celestial nymph, a dancer in the court of Indra, king of paradise

artha Success, one of the four aims of life

ASHVASENA (*aśvasena*) Name of a *nāga* snake

asura A type of demon; *asuras* are the enemies of the gods

BADARI (*badarī*) Name of a hermitage in which Arjuna and Krishna performed austerities in their identities as the sages Nara and Narayana

BHAGIRATHA (*bhagīratha*) A king of the solar dynasty, who propitiated Shiva with extreme austerities and won the boon of bringing the river Ganga down from heaven to the netherworld to purify the ashes of his ancestors

BHAVANI (*bhavānī*) "Wife of Bhava (Shiva)," a name of the goddess Parvati

BHIMA (*bhīma*) Second oldest of the five Pandava brothers

BHISHMA (*bhīṣma*) "The terrible warrior," celibate great-uncle of the Kuru princes, and also a marshal in the Mahabharata war

BRAHMA (*brahmā*) The creator god in the Hindu triad

brahma In some Indian philosophical systems, the essential real underlying all phenomena

BRAHMAN (*brāhmaṇa*) The highest of the four social classes. "Twice-born" (*dvija*), because the initiation ritual is seen as a second birth

BRIHASPATI (*bṛhaspati*) Preceptor of the gods, regent of the planet Jupiter, god of eloquence and speech

dānava A kind of demon, offspring of Danu

DHANAMJAYA (*dhanaṃjaya*) "Winner of wealth," an epithet of Arjuna

DHARMA (*dharma*) Also Yama, or Yamadharmaraja, god of justice and death, divine progenitor of Yudhishthira

DHRITARASHTRA (*dhṛtarāṣṭra*) Blind king of the Kurus, Pandu's elder brother and father of Duryodhana and his brothers, the Kauravas

DRAUPADI (*draupadī*) Daughter of

Drupada, king of Panchala, wife of the five Pandava brothers and queen-consort of Yudhishthira. *See also* Krishna Draupadi

DRONA (*droṇa*) The Brahman preceptor of the Kuru princes in the science of arms, and also a marshal in the Mahabharata war

DRUPADA King of Panchala and father of Draupadi

DUHSHASANA (*duḥśāsana*) A son of the Kaurava King Dhritarashtra and younger brother of Duryodhana

DURYODHANA Kaurava prince, eldest of the ninety-nine sons of king Dhritarashtra; Duryodhana ruled the Kuru kingdom after exiling the Pandavas

gaṇa A member of Shiva's host of spirit attendants

GANDHARVA Demigod, celestial musician, companion of apsaras women

GANDIVA (*gāṇḍīva* or *gāṇḍiva*) A bow gifted to Arjuna by the god Varuna, along with two inexhaustible quivers

GANGA (*gaṅgā*) The sacred river Ganga (Ganges). The Ganga is called "River with three paths," with courses in the sky, on earth, and in the netherworld

GARUDA (*garuḍa*) Golden eagle and mount of the god Vishnu

GAURI "The fair," a name of Parvati, consort of Shiva

guhyaka Mountain spirit living in the Himalayas, a servant of Kubera, god of wealth, and guardian of his treasures. *See* yaksha

guṇa Innate attribute, specifically, the three attributes inherent in material nature (*prakṛti*)

HARA "The seizer," an epithet of Shiva

INDRA (*indra*) King of the gods and divine progenitor of Arjuna

indragopa Velvety red rain mite. Rain mites swarm on the ground in the rainy season, carpeting it

INDRAKILA (*indrakīla*) "Indra's pike or staff," a mountain named after the god; place of Arjuna's austerities

JAHNU (*jahnu*) Angered when the river Ganga flooded his hermitage, the sage Jahnu drank up her waters, but released them at the request of King Bhagiratha

JAMADAGNI (*jamadagni*) A sage, father of Parashurama

JISHNU (*jiṣṇu*) "Conqueror" or "Victor," an epithet of Arjuna

kāma Love, one of the four aims of life

KAMA (*kāma*) The love god

KARNA (*karṇa*) Premarital son of Kunti. Honored by Duryodhana when the Pandavas mocked him for his low birth, Karna fought on the Kaurava side in the Mahabharata war

KAURAVAS Paternal kin to the Pandavas, and their enemies in the Mahabharata war

kāvya Stylized literature in

Sanskrit and allied languages

KHANDAVA (*khāṇḍava*) Name of a forest featuring in an episode in the *Mahābhārata*; Arjuna and Krishna cleared the Khandava forest with the help of Agni, the fire god

kirāta A mountain tribal hunter

KRISHNA DRAUPADI (*kṛṣṇā draupadī*) Krishna, "Dark lady," a name of Queen Draupadi

KRISHNA DVAIPAYANA *See* Vyasa

KRISHNA (*kṛṣṇa*) Incarnation of Vishnu, brought up among the Vrishni (Yadava) cowherds. Benefactor of the Pandavas. Closely associated with Arjuna in the Mahabharata war

KSHATRIYA (*kṣatriya*) A member of the warrior class, ranked next to the Brahman among the four classes of the Hindu social system

KUBERA God of wealth

KUNTI (*kuntī*) Also known as Pritha. Wife of Pandu, mother of three of the five Pandava brothers

KURU (*kuru*) Name of a kingdom, and of the family of the Pandavas and Kauravas

kuśa A kind of grass used in Hindu ritual

MANASA (*mānasa*) A sacred lake in the Himalayas

MANDARA (*mandara*) Name of a cosmic mountain. The gods and demons used Mandara as a stick when they churned the ocean of milk to obtain ambrosia and other treasures

MERU *See* Sumeru

mṛdaṅga A two-headed drum

MUKA (*mūka*) The name of the demon who turned himself into a boar and attacked Arjuna

NAKULA One of the Pandava twins. Nakula and Sahadeva, sons of Madri, are the youngest of the five Pandava brothers

NARA Literally, "man"; a persona of Arjuna as an ancient sage who performed asceticism in the Badari hermitage for thousands of years with Narayana (Krishna)

NARAYANA (*nārāyaṇa*) The form of Vishnu lying in the primeval cosmic waters

PANDAVA (*pāṇḍava*) Son of Pandu

PANDU (*pāṇḍu*) Kuru prince, elder brother of Dhritarashtra and father of the five Pandava brothers

PARASHARA (*parāśara*) Name of a sage, father of Vyasa

PARASHURAMA (*paraśurāma*) "Rama of the ax." A Brahman warrior, son of the sage Jamadagni

PARTHA (*pārtha*) "Son of Pritha," a name of Arjuna and of the two other sons of Pandu and Pritha (Kunti)

PARVATI (*pārvatī*) "Daughter of the Mountain (Himalaya)," the goddess-consort of Shiva

PASHUPATA (*pāśupata*) Name of a divine weapon bestowed on

413

Arjuna by the great god Shiva as a response to the hero's devoted asceticism and martial prowess

PINAKA (*pināka*) The name of Shiva's bow

PRITHA (*pṛthā*) *See* Kunti

PURUSHA. (*puruṣa*) Supreme Person. Vishnu in his primordial form as the unitary cosmic person

RADHA (*rādhā*) A charioteer's wife, adoptive mother of the warrior Karna

rajas "Passion," one of the three innate attributes of material nature

rākṣasa A type of demon

RAMA (*rāma*) King of Kosala, hero of the *Rāmāyaṇa* epic

rasa Aesthetic emotion evoked in and by a literary work; originally conceived as a set of eight; a ninth rasa, *śānta* (the calm), was added in the ninth century

RUDRA "Roarer," a name of Shiva

SAHADEVA (*sahadeva*) Twin brother of the Pandava Nakula

SARASVATI (*sarasvatī*) Goddess of speech, learning, and the arts

sattva "Lucidity," the highest of the three innate attributes of material nature

SAVYASACHIN (*savyasācin*) "Ambidextrous archer," an epithet of Arjuna

SHAMBHU (*śambhu*) "Bestower of blessings," a name of Shiva

SHESHA (*śeṣa*) The cosmic serpent that serves as the god Vishnu's couch when he sleeps in the ocean of milk

stotra Hymn of praise of a deity

SUMERU (also *meru*) A golden mountain situated at the center of Jambudvipa, the earth continent

SUYODHANA A name of the Kaurava prince Duryodhana

TAKSHAKA (*takṣaka*) King of the snakes

tamas "Quiescence" or "Darkness," lowest of the three innate attributes of material nature

TVASHTA (*tvaṣṭā* or *tvaṣṭṛ*) Blacksmith of the gods

VARAHA (*varāha*) The third incarnation of Vishnu, in the form of a boar who rescued the earth sphere from a demon

VARUNA (*varuṇa*) God of the waters, guardian of the western direction

VASUKI (*vāsuki*) Name of a snake

VINA (*vīṇā*) A lute-like stringed instrument. Not only the gandharvas, but the Goddess Sarasvati, the sage Narada, and the demon Ravana also play the vina

VISHNU (*viṣṇu*) The preserver god, one of the three gods of the Hindu triad

VRISHNI (*vṛṣṇi*) A pastoral clan, also known as Yadava; kinsmen of the Pandavas. Krishna belongs to the Vrishni clan

VRITRA (*vṛtra*) In the *Rig Veda,*

a serpent dragon who challenged
the god-hero Indra and was slain
by the god

VYASA (*vyāsa*) The sage Krishna
Dvaipayana (*kṛṣṇa dvaipāyana*),
son of Parashara and Satyavati.
Father of Pandu, Dhritarashtra,
and Vidura. Author of the
Mahābhārata epic

YAJNASENA (*yajñasena*) A name of
Drupada, king of Panchala and
father of Draupadi

YAKSHA (*yakṣa*) A class of
demigods living in the
Himalayas; servants of Kubera,
god of wealth

YUDHISHTHIRA (*yudhiṣṭhira*)
Eldest of the five Pandava
brothers, born to Kunti as the gift
of the god Dharma (hence called
"son of Dharma")

BIBLIOGRAPHY

Editions and Translations

Kirātārjunīya of Bhāravi, with the Commentary *Ghaṇṭāpatha* of Mallinātha. 1814. Edited by Vidyakara Mishra and Babu Rama. Kidderpore: Sanskrit Press.

Kirātārjunīya of Bhāravi, with the Commentary *Ghaṇṭāpatha* of Mallinātha. 1885. Edited with various readings by Narayan Balakrishna Godabole and Kashinath Pandurang Parab. Bombay: Nirnaya Sagar Press.

Kirātārjunīya of Bhāravi, with the Commentary *Ghaṇṭāpatha* of Mallinātha and various readings. 1889. Edited by Pandit Durgaprasad and Kashinath Pandurang Parab. Bombay: Nirnaya Sagar Press.

Kirātārjunīyam by Bhāravi, with the Commentary of Mallinātha and an Introduction in English. By Mahamahopadhyaya Satish Chandra Vidyabhushan. 1913. Edited, etc., by Pandit Ashubodha Vidyabhushan and Pandit Nityabodha Vidyaratna. 7th ed. Calcutta: Gobardhan Press.

Kirātārjunīya. With the commentary *Śabdārthadīpikā* of Citrabhānu. 1918. Edited by T. Ganapati Sastri. Trivandrum Sanskrit Series 63. Sargas 1-3. Trivandrum: Government Press.

Kirātārjunīya of Bhāravi, with the Commentary *Ghaṇṭāpatha* of Mallinātha and various readings. 1933. Edited by Pandit Durgaprasad and Kashinath Pandurang Parab. 12th ed. Bombay: Nirnaya Sagar Press.

Kirātārjunīya. Canto I, with the Commentaries of Devarājayajvan and Vidyāmādhava. 1934. Edited by Kshitis Chandra Chatterji. *Calcutta Oriental Journal* 1, 8: (May): 1-39.

Kirātārjunīya of Bhāravi. n.d. (1) Text with the *Laghuṭīkā* commentary of Prakāśavarṣa, Devanāgarī manuscript. Bayerische Staatsbibliothek (München) Cod. sanscr. 463. http://bildsuche.digitale-sammlungen.de/index.html?c=viewer&bandnummer=bsb00075063&pimage=1&v=100&nav=&l=de.

Kirātārjunīya of Bhāravi. n.d. (2) GRETIL http://fiindolo.sub.uni-goettingen.de/gretil/1_sanskr/5_poetry/2_kavya/bhakirpu.htm. [Göttingen digitized text of the *Kirātārjunīya* of Bharavi in roman script.]

Kirātārjunīyam, Sargas 1–3. 2008. Text, with the commentaries of Nṛsiṃha, Prakāśavarṣa, and Jonarāja. Edited by Viroopaksha V. Jaddipal. Vol. 1. Delhi: Amara Grantha Publications.

Bahadur, K. C. Kaisher. 1972. *The Kirātārjunīye of Bhāravi.* Kathmandu: Ratna Pustak Bhandar. Sargas 1–6.

Bahadur, K. C. Kaisher. 1974. *The Kirātārjunīye of Bhāravi.* Kathmandu: Ratna Pustak Bhandar. Sargas 7–12.

Cappeller, Carl. 1912. *Bhāravi's Poem Kirātārjunīya or Arjuna's Combat with the Kirāta.* Harvard Oriental Series 15. Cambridge, Mass.: Harvard University Press (German).

Dutt, Romesh Chunder. 1894. "The Hunter and the Hero." In *Lays of Ancient India.* London: Kegan Paul, Trench and Trübner, pp. 119–224.

Pangarker, Lakshman Ramchandra. 1902. *Kirātārjunīyam of Bhāravi.* With English Translation (Cantos I–X). Bombay.

Other Sources

Abhyankar, Kashinath Vasudev. 1961. *A Dictionary of Sanskrit Grammar.* Gaekwar's Oriental Series No. 134. Baroda: Oriental Institute.

Arjunawiwāha: The Marriage of Arjuna of Mpu Kaṇwa. 2008. Edited and Translated by Stuart Robson. Bibliotheca Indonesica 34. Leiden: Koninglijk Instituut voor Taal-Land-en Volkenkunde.

Arthaśāstra of Kauṭilya. 2013. *King, Governance, and Law in Ancient India: Kauṭilya's Arthaśāstra.* A new annotated translation by Patrick Olivelle. New York: Oxford University Press.

Benjamin, Walter. 1968. "The Task of the Translator." In *Illuminations.* Translated by Harry Zohn. Edited and with a foreword by Hannah Arendt. New York: Harcourt Brace Jovanovich, pp. 69–82.

Bhagavadgītā. 1986. *The Bhagavad-Gita: Krishna's Counsel in Time of War.* Translated by Barbara Stoler Miller. New York: Bantam Books.

Doniger, Wendy. 1973. *Śiva: The Erotic Ascetic.* New York: Oxford University Press.

Fantasia. 1940. Animated film. Directed by Norm Ferguson et al. Walt Disney Productions.

Gerow, Edwin. 1971. *A Glossary of Indian Figures of Speech.* The Hague: Mouton.

Ingalls, D. H. H. 1962. "Words for Beauty in Classical Sanskrit Poetry." In *Indological Studies in Honor of W. Norman Brown*, ed. Ernest Bender. American Oriental Series 47. New Haven, Conn.: American Oriental Society, pp. 87–107.

———. 1968. *Sanskrit Poetry from Vidyākara's Treasury.* Translated by Daniel H. H. Ingalls. Cambridge, Mass.: Harvard University Press.

Kāmasūtra of Vātsyāyana Mallanāga. 2002. *Kāmasūtra: A New, Complete English Translation of the Sanskrit Text.* Edited by Wendy Doniger and Sudhir Kakar. New York: Oxford University Press.

Kāvyādarśa of Daṇḍin. 1970. First Edition, edited with an original commentary by Rangacharya Raddi Shastri. Second edition, K. R. Potdar. Poona: Bhandarkar Oriental Research Institute.

Kāvyālaṃkāra of Bhāmaha. 1928. *The Kāvyālaṃkāra of Bhāmaha.* Edited with introduction by Batuk Nath Sharma and Baldeva Upadhyaya. Kashi Sanskrit Series 61. Varanasi: Chowkhamba Sanskrit Series Office.

Katz, Ruth Cecily. 1989. *Arjuna in the Mahābhārata: Where Krishna Is, There Is Victory.* Columbia: University of South Carolina Press.

Kielhorn, F. 1900. "Aihole Inscription of Pulikesin II. Saka-Samvat 556." *Epigraphia Indica* 6, 1 (January): 1-12.

Kumārasaṃbhava (The Birth of Kumāra) of Kalidasa. 1985. *The Origin of the Young God: The Kumārasaṃbhava of Kālidāsa.* Translated, with annotation and an introduction, by Hank Heifetz. Berkeley: University of California Press.

Lienhard, Siegfried. 1984. *A History of Classical Poetry: Sanskrit, Pali-Prakrit.* History of Indian Literature vol. 3, fasc. 1, ed. J. Gonda. Wiesbaden: Otto Harrassowitz.

Madhurāvijaya of Gaṅgādevī. *Madhurā Vijaya or Vīrakamparāyacarita. An Historical Kāvya by Gaṅgā Devi.* Edited by G. Harihara Sastri. Trivandrum: Sridhara Power Press, 1924.

Mahābhārata. Critically edited in 19 volumes. 1933-59. General editor, Vishnu Sitaram Sukthankar. Vol. 3 (in two). *Vana.* Poona: Bhandarkar Oriental Research Institute.

Manusmṛti. 2004. *The Law Code of Manu.* A new translation based on the critical edition by Patrick Olivelle. New York: Oxford University Press.

Mātaṅgalīlā. 1931. *The Elephant-lore of the Hindus: The Elephant-sport (Matanga-lila) of Nilakantha.* Translated from the original Sanskrit with introduction, notes, and glossary by Franklin Edgerton. New Haven, Conn.: Yale University Press.

Nathan, Leonard. 1976. *The Transport of Love: The Meghadūta of Kālidāsa.* Translation and introduction by Leonard Nathan. Berkeley: University of California Press.

Nāṭyaśāstra of Bharata. 2007. *The Nāṭyaśāstra: English Translation with Critical Notes*. By Adya Rangacharya. Delhi: Munshiram Manoharlal.

Peterson, Indira V. 2003. *Design and Rhetoric in a Sanskrit Court Epic: The Kirātārjunīya of Bhāravi*. Albany: State University of New York Press.

———.1989. *Poems to Śiva: The Hymns of the Tamil Saints*. Princeton Library of Asian Translations. Princeton: Princeton University Press.

Pollock, Sheldon I. 2006. *Language of the Gods in the World of Men: Sanskrit, Culture, and Power in Premodern India*. Berkeley: University of California Press.

Rabe, Michael D. 1997. "The Mamallapuram *Praśasti*: A Panegyric in Figures." *Artibus Asiae* 57, 3-4: 189-241.

Raghavan, V. 1968. *New Catalogus Catalogorum*. Vol. 4. Madras: University of Madras.

Rao, M. S. Nagaraja. 1979. *Kiratarjunīyam in Indian Art. With Special Reference to Karnataka*. Delhi: Agam Kala.

Rao, T. A. Gopinatha. 1985a. *Elements of Hindu Iconography*. Vol. 1, pt. 1. 2nd ed. Delhi: Motilal Banarsidass. Original edition, 1914.

———. 1985b. *Elements of Hindu Iconography*. Vol. 2, pt. 1. 2nd ed. Delhi: Motilal Banarsidass. Original edition, 1914.

———. 1985c. *Elements of Hindu Iconography*. Vol. 2, pt. 2. 2nd ed. Delhi: Motilal Banarsidass. Original edition, 1914.

Roodbergen, J. A. F. 1984. *Mallinātha's Ghaṇṭāpatha on the Kirātārjunīya*, I-VI. Part One: Introduction, Translation, and Notes. Leiden: E.J. Brill.

Sāhityadarpaṇa of Viśvanātha. 1965. *The Sāhityadarpaṇa (Paricchedas 1, 2 10 Arthālaṅkāras) with Exhaustive Notes*. By P. V. Kane. 5th ed. Delhi: Motilal Banarsidass.

Sāṃkhyakārikā of Īśvarakṛṣṇa. 1995. With the *Tattvakaumudī* of Śrī Vācaspati Miśra. Translated by Swami Virupakshananda. Madras: Sri Ramakrishna Math.

Śiśupālavadha. 1905. *The Śiśupālavadha of Māgha* with the commentary *Sarvaṅkaṣā* of Mallinātha. Edited by Pandit Durgaprasad and Pandit Sivadatta. Revised by W. L. Shastri Fansikar. Bombay: Nirnayasagar.

Smith, David. 1985. *Ratnākara's Haravijaya: An Introduction to the Sanskrit Court Epic*. Delhi: Oxford University Press.

Steiner, George. 1978. "On Difficulty." In George Steiner, *On Difficulty and Other Essays*. New York: Oxford University Press, pp. 18-47.

Warder, A. K. 1977. *Indian Kāvya Literature*. Volume 3: *The Early Medieval Period: Śūdraka to Viśākhadatta*. Delhi: Motilal Banarsidass.

Yogasūtra of Patañjali. 1979. *The Yoga of Patañjali.* With an Introduction, Sanskrit Text of the Yogasūtras, English Translation and Notes. By M. R. Yardi. Bhandarkar Oriental Series 12. Poona: Bhandarkar Oriental Research Institute.

INDEX

423

ABOUT THE BOOK

Murty Classical Library of India volumes are designed by Rathna Ramanathan and Guglielmo Rossi. Informed by the history of the Indic book and drawing inspiration from polyphonic classical music, the series design is based on the idea of "unity in diversity," celebrating the individuality of each language while bringing them together within a cohesive visual identity.

The Sanskrit text of this book is set in the Murty Sanskrit typeface, commissioned by Harvard University Press and designed by John Hudson and Fiona Ross. The proportions and styling of the characters are in keeping with the typographic tradition established by the renowned Nirnaya Sagar Press, with a deliberate reduction of the typically high degree of stroke modulation. The result is a robust, modern typeface that includes Sanskrit-specific type forms and conjuncts.

The English text is set in Antwerp, designed by Henrik Kubel from A2-TYPE and chosen for its versatility and balance with the Indic typography. The design is a free-spirited amalgamation and interpretation of the archives of type at the Museum Plantin-Moretus in Antwerp.

All the fonts commissioned for the Murty Classical Library of India will be made available, free of charge, for non-commercial use. For more information about the typography and design of the series, please visit *http://www.hup.harvard.edu/mcli.*

Printed on acid-free paper by Maple Press, York, Pennsylvania.